GUIDE TO THE
CREW OF
TITANIC

Cross-section of *Olympic* by W.B. Robinson, created in 1909. The allocation was done in most cases as shown, except that the gymnasium was finally built on the boat deck instead of F-deck. In addition, on *Titanic*, the promenade on B-deck was replaced by additional passenger cabins. (Author's collection)

GUIDE TO THE CREW OF TITANIC

THE STRUCTURE OF WORKING ABOARD THE LEGENDARY LINER

GÜNTER BÄBLER

Cover illustrations
Front, clockwise from top: Group photograph of some of *Titanic*'s female crew survivors, taken at their return in Plymouth; *Titanic*'s captain, Edward John Smith; Firemen and trimmers at work in a boiler room on board *Aquitania. Back, from top*: Death certificate for first-class Bathroom Steward Thomas Frederick Cohén Pennal; *Titanic* leaving Southampton on 10 April 1912. (All author's collection)

First published 2017
This paperback edition published in 2019

The History Press
97 St George's Place, Cheltenham
Gloucestershire, GL50 3QB
www.thehistorypress.co.uk

© Günter Bäbler, 2017, 2019

Edited by Geoffrey Brooks

The right of Günter Bäbler to be identified as the Author
of this work has been asserted in accordance with the
Copyright, Designs and Patents Act 1988.

British Library Cataloguing in Publication Data.
A catalogue record for this book is available from the British Library.

ISBN 978 0 7509 9233 6

Typesetting and origination by The History Press
Printed and bound in Great Britain by TJ Books Limited

CONTENTS

FOREWORD

More than one hundred years have passed since the passenger liner *Titanic* sank on 15 April 1912 on her maiden voyage after colliding with an iceberg. Much has been written about this memorable event since then. The tragedy, which claimed 1,496 lives, has never been forgotten. Only 712 of the 2,208 people on board the ship that night survived, to be brought to New York by the steamer *Carpathia*.

A large passenger ship of 46,328 gross register tons, as *Titanic* was, required a correspondingly large complement to man its engines and navigate it, while the passengers had to be looked after solicitously during the voyage.

Author Günter Bäbler has investigated the working structure of the 887 hired hands, eight musicians and five postal officers. He has gone about the task with scientific precision, and the result is astonishingly accurate. Shipboard life on the *Titanic* was the same as on the many large passenger liners of that epoch: looked at as a whole, such an operation with many employees was equivalent to a small town.

The book throws light on the complement of the *Titanic* and through many small details shows life aboard. All members of the crew are mentioned by name, thus providing remembrance for every man and woman of the crew aboard on that voyage.

Hermann Söldner
Author, *RMS Titanic, Passenger and Crew List*
Oberau, 4 September 2013

INTRODUCTION

How would a ship such as the *Titanic* have looked without her crew? At best a floating miracle of technology gently rising and falling at anchor somewhere. Upon boarding the steamer one might have had the unpleasant feeling of having no business being in this strange place. An eerie quiet would have reigned in which one could not be certain that a nasty surprise was not lurking at every corner. The kitchens lay silent and no guide was available to show the visitor around.

Yet the *Titanic* had a crew. The crew it was who first brought the ship to life. The crew took the luggage aboard, stored the provisions and prepared the meals. It was thanks to the crew that the ship got under way and headed for her destination. Obviously, a crew is indispensable for even a small ship and must have a clearly organised roster before sailing. Just because until now almost nothing has been known as to how the *Titanic* crew was organised does not mean that no organisation existed, for the finest points of the working plan had been thought out to ensure that a solution was on hand for all imaginable occurrences and needs.

For years there has been no work in the *Titanic* literature on the shipboard organisation. If one thinks of the *Titanic* as a firm, and one of the most legendary employers in the world, with 899 people on the payroll, then 100 years forward there must be some people who would be interested to know how this firm worked, yet the management structure of the *Titanic* does not seem to have interested anybody so far. Hitherto no book has mentioned the apparent gap in the source material. I knew that that would change one day, and I suspected that it would fall to me to fill that gap in the research since nobody else seemed to want to do it, or had failed to recognise the need for it.

No book exists whose author attempted to portray the *Titanic* organisation, if only in an appendix. The shipboard meals are an example: various books print out *Titanic* recipes (although these are undocumented and therefore inventions), yet no attempt is ever forthcoming to throw light on the kitchen staff. All that interested parties can infer on the basis of the available information is that the captain had the best job aboard and the trimmers probably the worst – little else can be learned from the literature.

On 27 May 2010 I received an email from Janina Schulte from Düsseldorf: 'I am a student and would like to write my thesis on the legendary ship *Titanic*. In the main I want to concentrate on the teamwork/crewing of the ship. What was the relationship between them, and did they work together as a team? What was the order of ranks aboard ship? What jobs did the various crew members have? For the time being I have a few bits of information about the officers, but there doesn't seem to be much about the rest. It would be fabulous if you could help me out. Perhaps you even have a good tip or link to suggest to me?'

From my enthusiastic reply, Schulte could not have anticipated how intensive the project would turn out to be. I warned her several times about the size of the task, but if she really, really wanted to do the thing properly then I would drop everything to help her. I had a vague presentiment on how much effort was going to be required, but neither of us could have made a reasonable estimate as to what this first email would unleash. Her work in the Communication Design field had been submitted long before, approved by her course tutors, but the organisational diagram was not yet completed: it contained the professions but no names. Much of the result was guesswork. Many questions remained open. After the scholastic side had long been satisfied, I took on the greater work, and my research occupied me for three years.

During my further research I often spoke with the *Titanic* researcher Susanne Störmer and requested her assessment. I reported my results with enthusiasm. In telephone calls I made the observation more than once how incredible it was that to date nobody had ever got to grips with the subject matter. Her dry response, 'Well, now at least you know why,' resounded in my ears for months afterwards, for what she said – that it was simply too big of a subject matter for most people to contemplate undertaking – came as both a burden and a promissory note. By now I found myself in completely unknown territory. I had come so far and could be forgiven if I faltered. What if I overlooked something and left open those gaps that another researcher had no problem in filling? I saw that the end result could not be 100 per cent, for the sources had too many gaps, but more about that later. When I was about 90 per cent finished I was almost manic for the missing 10 per cent, but the situation regarding the data often showed me the limits. Around 95 per cent was all I could manage, beyond that still lies virgin territory. Probably other totally dedicated *Titanic* researchers might get to 97 per cent, but presumably 100 per cent is unattainable. When I remember how many special cases I came across purely by chance, then at least as much information must be lost for ever. The witnesses have all passed on, and the generations of researchers of former eras missed their opportunity, now irretrievable.

Along with the organisational diagram a gigantic mass of documentation was assembled that was not necessary for the end result. Much of the knowledge derived from the research was surprising, and this present book read in conjunction with the organisational diagram can provide further results that would not be perceived from studying the organisational diagram alone.

The most surprising thing about this work is that, despite the dry nature of the historical material, the *Titanic* comes to life. Everywhere aboard there were crew members carrying out their duties. By examining historic construction plans and photos, one will 'meet' these people in the future.

Once the book had appeared in the German language, the subject would not let me go. In order to better understand the crew's way of life, in October 2014 in order to simulate an Atlantic crossing I spent a week living the routine of rest and watch which the fourth officer of the *Titanic* would have followed, inclusive of time lags. Naturally I rose during my rest period to 'report for duty' punctually. Despite my weariness I was unable to drop off to sleep at the word 'go' and so I slept on average 4 hours 58 minutes per calendar day and only once for a total of 3 hours 40 minutes corresponding to the theoretically longest period of sleep enjoyed by the crew. During my 'period on watch' I was frequently standing. I sat rarely, lifts and escalators were forbidden. By tests of concentration and dexterity I examined my reactions. The loss of my efficiency in the course of a 'crossing' was noticeable. Friends confirmed slackness in my responses and a deterioration in my ability to speak a foreign language. In my daily routine, I made numerous mistakes that forced me to give up certain tasks due to tiredness. Finally on the seventh day my alarm clock lost the duel: I slept in and awoke after 7 hours and 20 minutes. Accordingly, in future the theme of 'fatigue' will influence more prominently my assessment of the events which occurred on the maiden voyage of the *Titanic*.

More than two years have passed since the publication of the book in German in December 2013. The German-language readership has come across very few errors or gaps – or at least only a handful has been reported to me. In preparing the manuscript for the translation into English I have been able to insert information received subsequently. The process of having the manuscript translated into English forced me to take another very close look at many details, and yet again I discovered mistakes that I made years ago, some gaps that could be filled and parts where more explanation was needed to understand my guesswork. As occurs so often, time enables an author to identify weaknesses and remedy them. It is now my hope that the English-language readership may perhaps be able to fill a gap here or there in order to help complete the story of the *Titanic* crew.

July 2016
Günter Bäbler

ACKNOWLEDGEMENTS

I used Hermann Söldner's list of the *Titanic* crew as the basis for this project – without his precise listing at the beginning of this work this final result would not have been possible. I thank Hermann Söldner and Peter Engberg-Klarström for numerous corrections of names – thanks to them many names are published correctly in this book for the first time.

My greatest thanks goes to Susanne Störmer: I was in constant touch with her and she often gave me inspiration when I became bogged down in work.

Mark Chirnside was of great help in several matters, but especially in helping to bring the manuscript into shape for this English language edition.

In individual matters of detail I was given advice by Corina Amrein, Christian Amrhein, René Bergeron, Bruce Beveridge, Claudio Bossi, Edwin Davison, Stephanie Elmer, Franck Gavard-Perret, Ioannis Georgiou, Michael Hughes, Arthur Jones, Daniel Klistorner, Mandy Le Boutillier, Ken Marschall, Senan Molony, Rebecca Newton, David Olivera, Jens Ostrowski, Amy Rigg, Brigitte Saar, Bill Sauder, Viktoria Schmidt, Janina Schulte, Steven Schwankert, Oliver Schwarz, Parks Stephenson, Brian Ticehurst, Andrew Williams and Armin Zeyher – my warmest thanks go to all these people.

I must also not forget the many persons having an interest in the *Titanic* theme who provided useful information in the discussion forum www.encyclopedia-titanica.org.

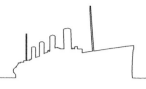

THE AIM

The original aim was simple: a poster on which the name of every crew member was noted. The representation would show the position and work station of each. In all, more than seventy organisational diagrams and partial diagrams were sketched, each version improving in precision over its predecessor.

Of course, one could include a biography of each crew member, perhaps a photo or at least the date of birth and death, but at the risk of everything getting out of hand. The whole thing had to be so purged that the name provided no more than the identity of the person. The wage earned gave an indication of a crew member's social status and relationship to his or her superiors or subordinates in rank, and was therefore retained. All other information not required for an understanding of the command structure was discarded. It is not unlikely that a person with an interest in the *Titanic* will be able to obtain information about every crew member from books and the Internet. It is to be remembered that behind every name lies a story.

PROCEDURES AND EXPLANATIONS

The underlying basis for the work was the crew list published by Hermann Söldner more than fifteen years ago. This current book has allowed for additional forenames or alternative spellings that may have come to light subsequently in official documents. The list compiled in the year 2000 was complete, no names were deleted or new names added. The only doubt involved Lazar Sartori, an assistant glass washer from the à-la-carte restaurant. He was shown as 'failed to join' in the crew list, although in August 1915 the White Star Line informed the British Board of Trade that Sartori had drowned aboard *Titanic*. How the shipping company came by this knowledge cannot be determined.

A real challenge for any photographer was to gather the crew of a ship in one place; therefore, very few attempts were made. In this photograph, about 300 of the 500 crew members of the *Kaiser Wilhelm der Grosse* are assembled at the stern. (Author's collection)

Cast off! At noon on 10 April 1912 the *Titanic* left for her maiden voyage to New York; at this time exactly 900 crew members were on board. (Author's collection)

The moment of the collision was chosen for the organisational diagram. The *Titanic* would almost certainly have disappeared from the collective consciousness had she not sunk. It is only because she went down that we remember today the people who were aboard. Hermann Söldner lists 892 crew members, these being 887 from the muster lists and five post office clerks. Noteworthy is the fireman John Coffey; he came from Queenstown, Ireland, and deserted there on the intermediate stop made on 11 April 1912. The eight musicians were given a second-class ticket by the White Star Line. Since they travelled free, earned money and worked aboard the ship they must be counted as crew members, as are the post office clerks.

Taking into account the post office clerks and musicians, and excluding the deserter, Fireman Coffey, at the time of the sinking there were 899 crew members aboard.

Coffey was not alone in failing to make the transatlantic crossing. Originally several other persons were to have joined the crew, but for various reasons did not show. They were on the list of hirings, but their names were transferred later to another list as absentees or dischargees with a note stating why they failed to join the *Titanic*.

The following list shows that substitutes were found for the men missing from the boiler rooms, and even an additional trimmer was taken on.

Even the vacancy for a sauce cook, a key position in the kitchen, was filled, though he was mustered in haste as an assistant cook: his trade and wage were only corrected after the sinking. A number of stewards and kitchen hands mustered for the voyage but then cancelled were not replaced. Compared to the original crew complement, the *Titanic* sailed with seven fewer crew members. The names and reasons for absence appear in Appendix F.

Absentees	Number of Replacement Staff
1 junior assistant fourth engineer	1
7 firemen	7
4 trimmers	5
1 sauce cook/saucier	1 (mustered as assistant cook)

2 assistant cooks	–
1 plate washer second class	–
3 saloon stewards first class	–
1 saloon steward second class	–
1 steward third class	–
1 assistant waiter, restaurant	–
	1 scullion

Left out of the accounting in this work were the seafarers of other shipping companies using the *Titanic* as a transport for passage in order to get home or reach their next signing-on point. Those of the American Line belonged to the International Mercantile Marine concern and their tickets were arranged internally. The other shipping companies had to buy their staff tickets from White Star Line unless they were travelling privately as a break from their work contracts. There were at least twenty-four seafarers travelling third class aboard *Titanic*. That list is perhaps incomplete. According to eyewitness accounts, some of these seafarer-passengers might have assisted the *Titanic* crew at the evacuation of the ship. For that reason they are listed below by name, nationality and the last or next ship, employer and trade (where known):

Albert Kaurin Andersen	Norway	Coastwise Transportation Company, *Edda*, engineer
Hans Martin Birkeland	Norway	Harloff & Bøe, *Norheim*, seaman
Alfred John Carver	Norway	American Line, seaman
Chip Chang	Hong Kong	Donald Steam Ship Company, *Annetta*, fireman
Foo Cheong	Hong Kong	Donald Steam Ship Company, *Annetta*, fireman
Lang Fang	Hong Kong	Donald Steam Ship Company, *Annetta*, fireman
John Holm	Sweden	Ulmer Park Yacht Club, Bath Beach (New York) captain
Johan Martin Holthen	Norway	Coastwise Transportation Company, *Edda*, second officer
August Johnson	England	American Line, seaman
William C. Jr. Johnson	England	American Line, *Philadelphia*, quartermaster
(Ah) Lam	Hong Kong	Donald Steam Ship Company, *Annetta*, fireman
Len Lam	Hong Kong	Donald Steam Ship Company, *Annetta*, fireman
Bing Lee	Hong Kong	Donald Steam Ship Company, *Annetta*, fireman
Ling Lee	Hong Kong	Donald Steam Ship Company, *Annetta*, fireman
Hee Ling	Hong Kong	Donald Steam Ship Company, *Annetta*, fireman
Fridtjof Arne Madsen	Norway	Norwegian steamer, second officer
Albert Johan Moss	Norway	Harloff & Bøe, *Norheim*, first officer
Samuel Niklasson	Sweden	seaman

Henry Margido Olsen	Norway	Coastwise Transportation Company, *Edda*, engineer
Oscar Wilhelm Olsson	Sweden	*Bulgaria* (Lake Michigan) seaman
Knud Rommetvedt	Norway	Harloff & Bøe, *Norheim*, second officer
Andrew John Shannon (Lionel Leonard)	England	American Line, *St. Paul*, purser
Thomas Storey	England	American Line, *St. Paul*
William Henry Törnquist	Sweden	American Line, *New York*

Four of the American Line seafarers (A. Johnson, W.C. Johnson, Shannon and Törnquist) appeared after the sinking on the Senate Report listings for both crew and third-class passengers, the remainder were correctly categorised as third class. Chang, Cheong, Fang, (Ah) Lam, Bing Lee, Ling, Madsen, Moss, Olsson and Törnquist survived the disaster. The survival rate of these special passengers was 41.6 per cent, while of the other men in third class only 11.7 per cent survived.

The nine-man 'guarantee group' from the builder Harland & Wolff of Belfast were not counted as crew, but were lodged in first and second class. These men were not part of the standard crew and were only aboard to deal with any teething troubles that might crop up on the new ship with a crew unfamiliar with the vessel. Therefore this group is only included for the sake of completeness because on the night of the disaster they mostly stood aside from the crew. All lost their lives:

Thomas Andrews	shipbuilder	first class
William Henry Campbell	apprentice carpenter	second class
Roderick Robert Crispin Chisholm	draughtsman	first class
Alfred Fleming Cunningham	fitter	second class
Anthony Wood Frost	fitter	second class
Robert J. Knight	fitter	second class
Francis Parkes	plumber	second class
William Henry Marsh Parr	electrician	first class
Ennis Hastings Watson	apprentice electrician	second class

Furthermore, several dozen staff travelled with their employers in first and second class. On board they paid attention to the needs of their masters, but it would be illogical to count them as crew since they were not necessary for the running of the *Titanic* and were treated as passengers with few limitations.

Also not taken into account is the so-called 'shore department', those workers who were responsible in port for ordering provisions and storing all articles of consumption.

A list of shipboard trades was drawn up from the crew list. It was easier to sort out the trades than 899 names, especially with the personnel-intensive trade groups. For example, the list of 159 firemen was reduced simply to 'Firemen'.

This leads to the question, how many different jobs were there on board? This cannot be answered exactly, since some crew members did the same work but were classified differently under another job title (e.g. amongst the engineers or also in the kitchens). Despite their different instruments, it is legitimate to classify the musicians as musicians, in the same sense that the chief butcher and his assistants were all classified as butchers, while every steward would have had no problem in performing the duties of a cleaner, lift steward or pantryman.

There were storekeepers both for the Engine and the Victualling Departments respectively, one caring for tools and instruments, the other for provisions – different tasks but identical job titles.

On the other hand there were crew members who performed a different task altogether from that which the improbable entries in the muster give cause to believe. For example, a number of night watchmen were hired as saloon stewards. If one overlooks these special functions, then there were at least forty different trades represented aboard *Titanic*.

Once the framework of the trades had been set up, the names were included as appropriate. What was easy with key positions or straightforward trades was much more difficult with the large trade groups. To what extent could these be broken down? The firemen could be divided into three shifts, for example, but not between individual boiler rooms.

This illustration was created to show the amount of crew members working on board the Cunarder *Mauretania*. In the foreground is the Deck Department, behind them is the Engine Department and in the back is the Victualling Department. The musicians, cooks, stewardesses and other specialists are shown separately. (Author's collection)

For the fine dividing lines there was no option but to study the thousands of questions and answers traded at the US Senate Inquiry and the Wreck Commissioner's Inquiry of the British Board of Trade in the hope that a witness might make it clear who was on watch and when, or if somebody was doing some other job than the muster list led one to believe. Possibly a name might crop up in an answer proving that such-and-such a person was working alongside the witness. Auction catalogues were searched for unpublished letters – perhaps a seaman might have provided a clue in one. Newspaper articles were another source to recourse for information. Other *Titanic* researchers were consulted about individual crew members in the hope of adding fresh information to the organisational diagram.

While doing the research a majority of the sources checked proved to be 'blind alleys' and did not lead to any new insights. How depressing it was to spend all day going over sources and to come away empty-handed, yet it was also a kind of success to research a blind alley thoroughly and recognise finally that it had nothing to yield.

After studying the sources intensively for several months, some connections became clear and often offered only one plausible solution. Many sources can be interpreted in different ways. In that case the interpretation has been accepted that seemed the most logical on the basis of factual substantiation. Nevertheless, several crew groupings are based on an 'educated guess'.

It is interesting that such an organisational chart might not have been possible to construct for another ship for lack of detail, but because of the *Titanic*, conclusions can be drawn about other ships.

The division of work aboard *Titanic* now seems clearer, but questions remain regarding the actual work involved and numerous details. What tasks were implied by the name of a certain trade? For example, it is obvious that a plate washer washed plates, but is that all he did? He would certainly have been required to perform other cleaning work in the kitchen area.

In many cases, discrepancies came to light by coincidence in comparing different statements or documents. Therefore it cannot be ruled out that the discovery of previously unknown sources will in future supplement the picture formed so far or amend it. If on the basis of this book a discussion arises that enables our knowledge to approach closer to the 100 per cent mark, it will be an important contribution to the historical documentation of the *Titanic*.

Where possible, suitable representative material was chosen for illustration purposes, often of other ships, and also photographs from the sister ship *Olympic*, some from later years.

Some small organisational charts in this book demonstrate how the crew was organised. If the surname was not sufficient for identification purposes, the initials of the forenames were added – the full names appear in the crew list (Appendix E). The chain of command is shown in these charts. Crew members in a common box did not have authority to issue instructions to each other but performed the same tasks or were responsible for a particular area in common. Within a box, as a rule, the names fall in alphabetical order. In exceptional circumstances, in the absence of a foreman, a crew member might have been authorised to issue instructions to a crew member of higher status. In individual cases the function of a foreman is only to be understood symbolically, subordinates would often do the same job but in another watch.

Regarding the payment of wages: The British currency became decimalised in 1971. Until then it had consisted of pounds (£), shillings (s) and pence (d). There were 20 shillings to a pound and 12 pence to the shilling, therefore 240 pence to a pound. Most crew members were hired at a monthly rate but were paid at the end of the round trip pro-rata for the number of days worked. The sinking of the *Titanic* terminated the work contract, White Star Line paid wages up to and including 15 April 1912. On top of this, the company paid for food and lodging.

Shipboard time was changed daily and based on the ship's midday position (solar noon). This resulted in a change in the length of the watches daily; heading west, it would lengthen the day by up to 1 hour. On the grounds of complexity, this factor was not considered in the text.

General information respecting regulations, duties and watch arrangements of individual crew members appear in Appendices B and C.

Avers   5 Shilling   Revers
                Englisch

Avers   1 Shilling   Revers   Avers   1 £ Sterling   Revers
          Englisch   Englisch

Until 1971 the British currency was not decimal. Shown here are three coins with the face of Queen Victoria (1819–1901), as they were still in circulation in 1912. The £1 coin (bottom right) correlated to 20s (left 1s, top 5s). (Author's collection)

PAY AND SALARIES, TIPS AND BONUSES

Crew members' remuneration is an important factor for determining the hierarchy. There were no increases in pay for time served. Everybody who did the same job would normally receive the same pay for it. If an employee had greater experience he could seek a higher paid job. In this way he would work his way upwards in the hierarchy and improve his income. Accordingly, a foreman or senior worker would receive more pay than his subordinates (though there were exceptions). This principle was frequently the most valuable indication of the personnel structure and helped unravel entire trade groupings, for example those of the engineers.

In many cases the pay set down in the ship's articles did not correspond to what the individual expected to receive. The pay was what the shipping company paid, but crew members who came into direct contact with passengers, especially those of the first and second class, would receive tips. These were not only an acceptable addition, but in most cases made up the greater part of a crew member's income. At least outwardly, the White Star Line shut its eyes to the tradition, and travellers were advised that tips were voluntary.

Even today many shipping companies offer employees miserable financial terms. Especially in positions that come into contact with passengers, shipping companies are interested in a highly motivated work force. With a good or very good basic pay, even unmotivated employees would receive remuneration enabling them to live comfortably. If some of the pay was left for passengers to meet, then only reliable and attentive employees, able to read a passenger's desires from the proverbial look in the eye in exchange for a good tip, would apply for the job. That was also the case a century ago. As a side effect the companies reduced their operating risk – poor booking of a passage reduced the operating losses because the employees bore some of the risk. Additionally, the tariff advertised for a voyage was more economical, at least at first glance.

The three barbers aboard *Titanic* received no remuneration. The lowest-paid crew member was the page-boy in the restaurant with £1 10s. Together with a few other exceptions the majority of the low-wage earners received £3 15s. It is noticeable that

Tipping in gastronomy on board a vessel was as important as on land – a waiter could earn up to four times more in tips than the official wage. The image shows a waiter in a noble London restaurant around 1912. (Author's collection)

most of these 'low wage earners' were in direct contact with the passengers and thus had a good opportunity of increasing their wage with tips.

Tips have been a problem for travellers for generations. Many are unaware of the customs of other countries and want to avoid over-tipping or under-tipping. Most want to find the happy medium, but what was it in 1912? Albert A. Hopkins in his 1911 book *The Scientific American Handbook of Travel* provided a guide for North Americans visiting Europe. In collaboration with a retired purser he compiled a list with information about what tips were expected and fair.

Tips for saloon stewards, bedroom stewards and bath stewards were more or less obligatory. Tips per passenger in second class were less than first class, but the number of second-class passengers serviced was higher, which equalled things out. Tipping in third class was poor, and so it was worth making the effort to be noticed for the quality of one's service in the hope of being recommended to a higher class on future voyages. The tips extracted below from *The Scientific American Handbook of Travel* have been converted from US dollars into British currency and are to be understood as guidelines only. The lowest first-class fare on *Titanic* in April 1912 was £27 per passenger, when sharing a three-berth stateroom. Unless stated to the contrary these were the tips to be paid per passenger for the entire passage:

Bedroom Steward	10s ticket value between £20 and £25
	12s ticket value £50
	14s ticket value £70
	16s ticket value £80
	£1 ticket value £100
	4s bonus with private bath
Stewardess	only if required, two-thirds of bedroom steward
Saloon Steward	10s
Bath Steward	4s for several baths per voyage
	1s for one bath
Cleaning Stewards	2s 6d (lump sum)
Deck Steward	4s only if required, or if assisting a lady
Smoke Room Steward	2s if saloon used frequently
Restaurant	c. 1d–2d per shilling on the bill
Smoking Room, Lounge etc.	c. 1d per shilling on the bill
Gymnasium Steward	2s only if required
Musicians	A collection, generally towards the end of the voyage, organised amongst the passengers
Second Class	About half the above

The list of tips supplies valuable information as to which jobs aboard were more worthwhile to take up even though the wage was identical on paper. The list also shows that with a heavy booking for a voyage, most stewards could more than double their monthly wage in tips on a single crossing. Both bedroom and saloon stewards would more than double their wage if they just served four passengers with the cheapest tickets on the out and inbound trip. Naturally there was no guarantee, and in the winter income would be closer to the basic wage.

Hopkins recommended passengers not to pay tips until the end of the voyage, since the stewards tended to forget earlier payments and would make a fresh request. Under no circumstances should passengers attempt to under-tip or the stewards would then exert pressure to recover the shortfall. It seems to have been a custom of the time for certain passengers to tip the chief steward upon boarding in order to receive preferential service. This custom was not recommended by Hopkins, because it would not influence the quality of service received.

Basically, the worst paid jobs (with little prospect of tips) were performed by the scullions, pantrymen, storekeepers, plate washers, the glory-hole stewards, the third-class stewards, the telephonist and matron, who all earned less than £4.

Another important indicator of incomes was the offertory for the *Titanic* victims inaugurated by the Lord Mayor of the City of London (a dignitary subject to yearly election but not on a political basis). Relatives domiciled outside Great Britain mostly received a single lump sum from the foundation. Many relatives of crew members with a British address were given a pension paid monthly independent of income and degree of relationship. Those involved were classified into seven groups, A to G, in descending order of income level. Many crew members turn up in a surprising group. The contracted rate of hire apparently played a minor role in how this grouping was worked out. Undoubtedly it was taken into account that the tips received in many cases far exceeded the basic pay, which would have resulted in estimates being made of the income. The exact criteria are not known but according to statute regard was had 'to the yearly earnings of such member of the Crew and to the other circumstances of the case'.

Some employees such as engineers, seamen and firemen had no prospect of tips. For the rest one can work out from the indemnification (or pension) what the income including tips must have been. The following survey does not include victims without relatives in Britain and a number of cases that could not be classified due to doubts:

Class A
Monthly income including tips: *c.* between £16 and £46.
chief officer, first officer, highest ranking engineers, both pursers, chief first class steward, restaurant manager, restaurant chef, restaurant head waiter.

Class B
Monthly income including tips: *c.* between £11 and £17.
(e.g.) ship's surgeon, engineers, boilermaker, chief electrician, first class chef, chief cleaning steward, first class bedroom stewards, senior Turkish bath attendant, racquet steward, gastronomical stewards with special functions, restaurant assistant head waiter, restaurant trancheur.

Class C
Monthly income including tips: *c.* between £9 and £11.
(e.g.) lower ranking engineers, gastronomical stewards with special functions, bath stewards, baggage steward, Turkish bath attendant, first saloon steward, second class bedroom stewards, chief butcher, chief storekeeper, cooks, post office clerks.

Class D
Monthly income including tips: *c.* between £6 and £9.
(e.g.) assistant electrician, engineer's secretary, saloon stewards first class and second class, printer stewards, chief steward third class, captain's steward, cleaning stewards, glory-hole stewards, clothes presser steward, storekeeper.

Class E
Monthly income including tips: *c.* between £5 10s and £8.
(e.g.) storekeeper, stewardesses, cooks, second pantryman.

Class F

Monthly income including tips: *c.* between £3 15*s* and £7.

(e.g.) greasers, leading firemen, mess stewards, assistant storekeepers, bakers, clerks, storekeeper, third class stewards.

Class G

Monthly income including tips: *c.* between £3 15*s* and £6.

(e.g.) seamen, firemen, trimmers, assistant pantrymen, scullions, plate washers.

These pay groups appear well documented and the higher classes are clearly defined. It is probable, however, that the last remuneration paid before signing on for the *Titanic* was taken into account, and possibly this would have been lower. That would explain why crew members in the identical position and the same contract of pay were separated into different classes. Thus the chef hired for first class at a rate of £20 went into Class B but should be listed in Class A.

One assumes that the stewards aboard ship had the moral duty to pay over a proportion of their tips to the cooks, pantrymen and other crew members upon whom they had a certain dependence. This would in some cases explain the overlapping of the income classes.

The surviving stewards, who were required to hold themselves at readiness for the British Board of Trade inquiry, received an indemnity that included an assessment of tips. This is a further indication that tipping was considered a firm component of fixed earnings and not a bonus.

The White Star Line paid to some crew members a higher wage than was agreed on the ship's articles (for example, the quartermasters). The supplements, though not fixed in writing, were nevertheless binding in some trade groups. Bonuses of this type are mentioned ahead in the corresponding chapter where they have been confirmed by the research.

In order to place pay and tips into a relationship, one has to look at the cost of living in the Great Britain of 1912. Around 10 per cent of the population lived below the minimum subsistence level, another 15 per cent in poverty. The average monthly income was below £6, a skilled tradesman earned around £8, unskilled workers about half that. A small house could be rented for about £1 5*s* per month.

The average earnings of the *Titanic* crew were around £5 10*s* (about 30 per cent of the crew received substantial tips on top of this). Work terms aboard ship included free food and lodging, an important additional component to income. The crew members' receipts were enough to get by on, provided they could depend on employment all the year round, but family circumstances condemned many employees to live under very straitened circumstances.

THE CREW DIVISIONS

The organisational structure of a ship developed over the centuries. Much is understandable, but not everything. Traditional trades and the tasks they involved were not elaborated upon when a crew member was hired for the *Titanic*. Whoever went to sea soon understood the hierarchical structure, knew his job and who was in authority above him. Hardly anybody aboard needed to know anything else. For this reason there was no organisational diagram for ships of that time: it was of no interest to anyone. Those responsible for keeping an eye on affairs had been in the game long enough to know the connections. A steamer's crew was divided into three groups:

Deck Department: No doubt this senior department was similar in organisation to that of the sailing ships of the explorers and also the Navy. Its members were responsible for the nautical procedures. According to the ship's articles they numbered aboard *Titanic* sixty-six men, around 7.4 per cent of the crew. Their survival rate was high at 65 per cent because many manned the lifeboats. Twenty-three lost their lives.

Engine Department: The youngest department had only existed since the introduction of artificial propulsion for ships (steam, from about 1838). The group was responsible for the generation of energy for the ship's engines and electrical power. The department had 325 men, 36.6 per cent of the *Titanic* crew. 253 of them lost their lives, the survival rate was 21.9 per cent.

Victualling Department: The transport of passengers to foreign parts was a relatively recent activity. Following the introduction of ships built primarily for passenger transport (from about 1818), the department was under continuous development. It was responsible for all gastronomic requirements and shipboard hotel life. 495 men and women, 55.8 per cent of the crew, worked in this department. 398 lost their lives and the survivors amounted to 19.6 per cent of the department.

The statistics on page 24 are based on the *Titanic* ship's articles, less deserter fireman John Coffey who was not aboard at sailing from Queenstown and cannot be counted as a survivor. Other statistical details appear on page 155.

Each of these three departments had a responsible head, and an appointed deputy or representative beneath him. Captain Edward John Smith was the overall superior, but primarily had responsibility for the Deck Department. His aide was Chief Officer Henry Tingle Wilde, responsible for discipline and order aboard ship. As ships grew in size, some of the captain's burden devolved upon the chief officer who, as staff captain, remains even today the number two aboard competent to oversee the crew. Meanwhile the captain had more management tasks and representative duties to fulfil.

Chief Engineer Joseph Bell headed the Engine Department with Senior Second Engineer William Edward Farquharson as his representative. Purser Hugh Walter McElroy led the Victualling Department of the *Titanic*. Assisted by Purser Reginald Lomond Barker, his other important aides were Chief Steward Andrew L. Latimer and Chef Charles Proctor.

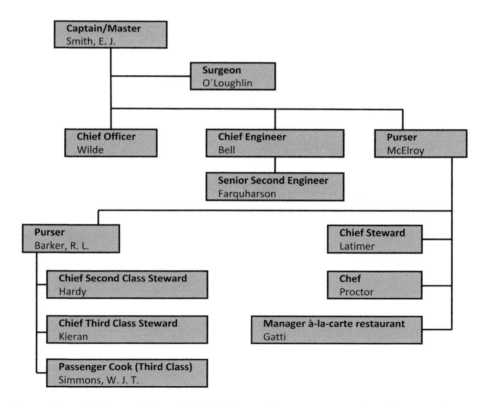

An overview of the key positions within *Titanic's* crew. For most crew members these were the highest-ranking superiors they were in direct contact with. (Diagram by author/Dominik Tezyk)

Strictly speaking, the crew was not hired by the White Star Line but by the captain. The contract in the ship's articles was an agreement between captain and crew member, signed as a witness by a representative of the shipping company. The captain assessed the performance of every crew member after the voyage by an entry in the seaman's book. Provided the crew member had not come to notice adversely, he or she received a 'Very Good' stamp in the book and the work contract thus terminated: there was nothing to prevent a re-hiring. Before leaving the ship, crew members could sign on for the next voyage, enabling the purser to know how many places he had to fill.

All crew members (except postal workers and musicians) of the *Titanic* were entered on one or other of nine muster lists covering the three departmental groups:

Deck Department
Engine Department – Engineers/Miscellaneous
Engine Department – Book 1
Engine Department – Book 2
Engine Department – Book 3
Victualling Department – First Class
Victualling Department – Second Class
Victualling Department – Third Class/Galley
Victualling Department – À-la-carte Restaurant

There were also two correction lists, one containing the names of persons who had not reported for duty, the other with the names of those hired immediately before sailing. The crew was mustered at least an hour before sailing and missing crew members were replaced.

As a result, for this book the three departments have been analysed in detail and, as far as the sources allow, modified to accommodate all the branching. Most complex was the Victualling Department, not only the largest staff group aboard but the one that had the most sub-divisions to cover the various activities of around 500 crew members.

THE DECK DEPARTMENT

The Deck Department embraced the nautical branch from the captain down to the nautical officers and seamen. Its organisational structure had developed over the centuries and contained few surprises, apart from whims of the shipping company. Aboard *Titanic* it consisted of sixty-six men divided into the following trades or professions:

Master	Captain
Nautical Officers by rank:	Chief Officer
	First Officer
	Second Officer
	Third Officer
	Fourth Officer
	Fifth Officer
	Sixth Officer
Sailors by function:	Boatswain
	Boatswain's Mate
	Able-bodied Seaman (AB) (29)
	Seaman (2)
	Quartermaster (7)
	Lookout (6)
	Master-at-Arms (2)
	Lamp Trimmer
	Storekeeper
Others:	Surgeon (2)
	Carpenter
	Joiner
	Mess Steward/Crew Cook (2)
	Window Cleaner (2)

The following four must be counted as Deck Department crew, although they do not appear as such in the muster lists:

John George Phillips	£1 15s/week and £4 5s★	Senior Radio Operator
Harold Sydney Bride	£1/week and £2 2s 6d★	Junior Radio Operator
James Arthur Paintin	£3 15s	Captain's Steward
William Dunford	£4 10s	Hospital Steward

(★ Marconi weekly wage, White Star Line monthly hire)

The wireless operators actually appear on the muster lists of the Victualling Department First Class as 'Telegraphists'. There were telegraphists ashore who had far less technical knowledge. Marconi Wireless Telegraph Company employed them both and called their telegraphists 'Radio Operators', the prefixes 'Senior' and 'Junior' indicating the respective experience and pay grade. Junior Radio Operator Harold Sydney Bride used various descriptions for himself and Phillips. He stated that Marconi paid him £4 monthly plus board and lodging, effectively £1 per week. This 'board and lodging' would refer not to regular duties aboard a ship but rather to voyages as passengers en route to a new work point. It is not clear how White Star Line paid its share of the remuneration; according to its agreement with Marconi the shipping company would only pay out 10s each Saturday to the radio operators as an advance from Marconi, but the muster lists show that John George Phillips was due £4 5s monthly and Bride half of that, £2 2s 6d. Bride actually said at the British inquiry (answers 16654 and 16655) that he was still waiting for about £2 5s from White Star Line but had received nothing, this being confirmed by the sign-off list.

The wireless operators John George Phillips and Harold Sidney Bride were employees of the Marconi Wireless Telegraph Company, but were also on the crew list of *Titanic*'s Victualling Department. Phillips is seen in his Marconi uniform. (Author's collection)

The only known photograph of *Titanic's* wireless cabin was taken on the morning of 11 April 1912 by Francis Mary Hegarty Browne, later known as Father Browne. It shows wireless operator Harold Sidney Bride at his desk. On the right the pneumatic tubes can be seen, connecting the Marconi room with the purser's office. The original photograph was a double exposure, shown here is a restored version. (The Irish Picture Library/Father F.M. Browne SJ Collection, restauration Ken Marschall)

Aboard *Titanic* the radio operators managed a Marconi profit-centre financed by the sending of telegrams. Passengers did not pay the wireless operators for the service: all financial transactions aboard were carried out exclusively by the purser's office. If a passenger wanted to send a telegram, he handed over the form at the enquiry office and paid there and then, the form with the text would then be sent by pneumatic tube to the Marconi Room. The purser's office was therefore the competent authority for the control of the radio operators, which was why they appear on the Victualling Department and not the Deck Department muster lists. The radio operators worked out their hours of duty between themselves so as to ensure that the radio room was manned around the clock. During the day, they relieved each other without a particular timetable. At night, Phillips was usually on duty from 20:00 to 02:00 hours and released by Bride from 02:00–08:00 hours, except for the night of the sinking when Bride intended to take over around midnight.

The radio operators also had the job of transmitting and passing service messages for the officers, a service that under the Marconi White Star Line contract had priority over passenger traffic. Under this arrangement the radio room was placed at the disposition of the Marconi Company free of charge. The 'Report of the Sub-Committee on Wireless Telegraphy' issued by the Merchant Shipping Advisory Committee stated that: '... in our opinion, it should be impressed upon all concerned that the operator should be under the captain's control, and that every message transmitted and received by the operator (other than private messages ...) should be transmitted and received under the control of the Captain.' Harold Thomas Cottam, radio operator of the rescue ship *Carpathia*, said after the tragedy that he had been directly answerable to his captain. The Marconi Company had so-called 'Travelling Supervisors' who made voyages. Since all stations communicated on the same frequency, all wireless operators could be monitored from afar. The Marconi supervisor in the North Atlantic was Gilbert W. Balfour, who was sailing aboard the *Baltic* and heard live the *Titanic's* distress messages and the subsequent radio traffic of the ships intervening to assist.

Although his duty was as Captain's Steward, James Arthur Paintin received the same rate as almost all Stewards: £3 15s. As such he received the orders of the duty officers but was also the captain's domestic help, and could accept and send telegrams on his behalf. Although Paintin saw exclusively to the captain's requirements and probably those of the officers, he came under the jurisdiction of the purser. His dormitory was probably the two-bed steward's cabin on the boat deck, and it is likely that he shared it with a bedroom steward who saw to the six passenger cabins on that deck and perhaps the officers' quarters too.

Hospital Steward William Dunford also had a special position. On the *Titanic* muster lists he served in third class, but since by the nature of his employment he was subordinated to the two ship's surgeons, according to the rules of the White Star Line he was treated as Deck Department while classified organisationally with all other stewards under the purser.

In all, seventy men made up the Deck Department (sixty-six on the muster list plus four who *de facto* belonged to it).

The Captain and the Nautical Officers

The nautical officer corps of the *Titanic* consisted of eight officers including the captain. The White Star Line did not use the term 'officers' but 'mates' in the muster lists. In the tradition of sail these men 'took the helm' in the sense of supervising one of the three watches. In other publications the White Star Line refered to them as 'officers' for ease of understanding and the same convention will be used here. The captain appeared on the muster listing as 'Master' and was the only member of the Deck Department to draw an annual salary:

Edward John Smith	£1,250 per year	Master (£200 bonus if free of accidents)
Senior Officers:		
Henry Tingle Wilde	£25	Chief Officer
William McMaster Murdoch	£17 10s	First Officer
Charles Herbert Lightoller	£14	Second Officer

Junior Officers:

Herbert John Pitman	£9 10s	Third Officer
Joseph Groves Boxhall	£9	Fourth Officer
Harold Godfrey Lowe	£8 10s	Fifth Officer
James Paul Moody	£8 10s	Sixth Officer

This table makes it clear that the way in which salaries were calculated was dependent on the degree of responsibility. Wilde's remuneration reflects his representative function of the captain; on the other hand, the four junior officers never had responsibility over the ship. It is also noteworthy that the senior officers of the sister-ships *Olympic* and *Titanic* both had pay grades higher than their colleagues of other White Star Line ships. For example, the first officer of the *Titanic* earned as much as the chief officer of another ship. Presumably this was the financial recognition for the higher complexity of the work on such a large ship.

The captain exercised the power of command bestowed upon him by the shipping company over everyone aboard his ship. Thus all crew members and all passengers were

The bridge of *Titanic*'s sister, *Olympic* – the bridge was the nautical officers' workplace. (Author's collection)

under the obligation to obey his orders. His catalogue of jobs was comprehensive and he was not attached to any particular watch. He was 'on duty' and responsible for his ship around the clock. The captain's remuneration was never revealed in the muster lists, but was negotiated presumably with the shipping company and without the involvement of trade unions. Captain Smith was one of the best-paid seafarers of his time.

Chief Officer Henry Tingle Wilde was Captain Smith's representative. According to the White Star Line work guidelines he was to draw the attention of the captain respectfully but firmly to errors in navigation or other deficiencies. Besides this control function for the captain he was responsible for the loading of the freight and also stood his watch in turns with the first and second officers. This trio of the so-called 'senior officers' alternated on the bridge. If the captain was not present, the watch officer had jurisdiction according to the captain's instructions laid down previously. On 9 April 1912 David Blair, second officer, left the ship at Southampton, to be replaced by Wilde. In the reshuffle, Murdoch was relegated from chief officer to first officer and Lightoller from first officer to second officer. The three senior officers worked the following roster daily:

Captain Edward John Smith and his three senior officers: Henry Tingle Wilde, William McMaster Murdoch and Charles Herbert Lightoller. (Author's collection)

Chief Officer Henry Tingle Wilde	02:00–06:00 and 14:00–18:00hrs
First Officer William McMaster Murdoch	10:00–14:00 and 22:00–02:00hrs (relieving Lightoller for his evening meal)
Second Officer Charles Herbert Lightoller	06:00–10:00 and 18:00–22:00hrs (relieving Murdoch for his midday meal)

The meal breaks were both of 30 minutes' duration, normally from 12:30–13:00hrs, and from 19:00–19:30hrs. Besides their bridge watch, the officers had other tasks to perform including inspections, tours of the ship and the synchronisation of all clocks aboard.

By tradition the seamen were divided into starboard and port watches (more on these terms on page 37). The four junior officers were paired off to each watch. The term 'watch' also meant the time period. In order to avoid anybody having to stand the unloved middle watch after midnight, there were two short 'dog watches' (from 16:00–18:00 and from 18:00–20:00hrs) for the daily changeover. One result of this arrangement was that the junior officers worked 10 hours one day and 14 hours the next. At sea they could never rest for more than about 3 hours 40 minutes. The roster was planned in a way that (apart from 18:00hrs) the watch changeover of the junior and senior officers was staggered to enable regular changes of face.

Fifth Officer Lowe hinted to Senator William Alden Smith of the US inquiry (page 388) how overtired the officers were: '… You must remember that we do not have any too much sleep and therefore when we sleep we die.' The White Star Line held to this system rigidly, which had originated from the days of sail. The junior officers worked the following hours:

Port Watch:
Third Officer Herbert John Pitman and
Fifth Officer Harold Godfrey Lowe

Even dates in April 1912	04:00–08:00, 12:00–16:00 and 18:00–20:00hrs
Odd dates in April 1912	00:00–04:00, 08:00–12:00, 16:00–18:00 and 20:00–24:00hrs

Starboard Watch:
Fourth Officer Joseph Groves Boxhall and
Sixth Officer James Paul Moody

Even dates in April 1912	00:00–04:00, 08:00–12:00, 16:00–18:00 and 20:00–24:00hrs
Odd dates in April 1912	04:00–08:00, 12:00–16:00 and 18:00–20:00hrs

Titanic's four junior officers: Herbert John Pitman, Joseph Groves Boxhall, Harold Godfrey Lowe and James Paul Moody. (Author's collection)

Below: The captain's room on board the *Oceanic.* The spacious suite was a privilege of the captain; on *Titanic* there was, in addition to the bedroom and a private bath, a large living room with a seating area and work desk. (Ioannis Georgiou collection)

The nautical officers were accommodated on the boat deck abaft the bridge. Every officer had his own cabin but shared a bathroom with the other officers. The captain occupied a suite with a living room and a bathroom near the bedroom. The officers had their own smoking room, and a section of the boat deck was cordoned off as the officers' promenade, preventing the passengers having access to the bridge. Farther astern was the officers' mess near the third smoke stack. A dumb waiter from the first- and second-class kitchen supplied the meals directly into the officers' mess pantry. Presumably the captain's steward was responsible for the officers' meals.

The Quartermasters

Seven veteran seamen were employed as helmsmen. All such quartermasters were hired at the monthly rate of £5 5s:

Arthur John Bright
Robert Hichens
Sidney James Humphreys
Alfred John Olliver
Walter John Perkis
George Thomas Rowe
William Wynn

According to the muster lists the quartermasters received £5, as did other seamen. Second Officer Lightoller informed the US inquiry (page 428), however, that the quartermasters received a monthly supplement of 5s each. This payment is confirmed in the sign-off list where it is recorded that for the unfinished voyage each quartermaster received 1s more than the other seamen. Six of the seamen mustered as quartermasters were divided into the two watches where they followed the same rhythm as the junior officers:

Port Watch:
Arthur John Bright, Walter John Perkis, William Wynn

Even dates in April 1912	04:00–08:00, 12:00–16:00 and 18:00–20:00hrs
Odd dates in April 1912	00:00–04:00, 08:00–12:00, 16:00–18:00 and 20:00–24:00hrs

Starboard Watch:
Robert Hichens, Alfred John Olliver, George Thomas Rowe

Even dates in April 1912	00:00–04:00, 08:00–12:00, 16:00–18:00 and 20:00–24:00hrs
Odd dates in April 1912	04:00–08:00, 12:00–16:00 and 18:00–20:00hrs

Two of the quartermasters had their station on the bridge. One stood 2 hours at the wheel holding the ship to her course, the other stood by to run messages. Then they changed positions for the remaining 2 hours. It was considered impossible to concentrate for more than 2 hours on the dancing compass needle. The third quartermaster stood alone on the docking bridge, and at the time of the collision this was George Thomas Rowe. Presumably the lack of a rest period during the watch was the reason for the quartermasters' 5s supplement.

For the first time, in 1911 the White Star Line hired seaman with the rank of quartermasters for the *Olympic*. On other ships the helmsmen continued to be regular able-bodied seamen. The basic hire for seamen and quartermasters was the same, the latter being seamen hired for a special task.

On her maiden voyage, *Olympic* had only four quartermasters, from the second voyage there were six. From 20 September 1911 (and apart from 4 February 1912), *Olympic* always sailed with a 'supernumerary' seventh man. Whenever seven quartermasters were aboard,

Most steamers had an able seaman at the wheel. *Olympic* and *Titanic* selected quartermasters for this duty. On the bridge two quartermasters split their 4-hour watch in the wheel house. One stood for 2 hours at the telemotor, while the other was on standby for errands or to take over the rudder at any time; after 2 hours they would swap their duty. This photograph was taken on board the *Kronprinzessin Cecilie* in 1912. (Author's collection)

One quartermaster had a 4-hour watch on the aft navigation bridge. (Author's collection)

Sidney James Humphreys was always one of them. He changed over to the *Titanic* in April 1912. His duties there are described later. The six quartermasters and the supernumerary Humphreys all survived, forming the largest trade group aboard not to lose a member when the ship went down.

The Boatswain, the Boatswain's Mate and the Seamen

Twenty-nine able-bodied seamen and two seamen (with lesser experience) were hired aboard *Titanic*. Traditionally they were also divided up, as were the junior officers and quartermasters, into permanent port and starboard watches and were responsible for maintenance work on their respective side of the ship. As required in poor visibility, some would do duty as additional lookouts. Every watch had a 'shift leader', this was Boatswain Alfred W.S. Nichols for the port watch and Boatswain's Mate Albert Haines for the starboard watch. Nichols also sold serge trousers, jackets, shipping company pullovers, caps and cap tallies to the seamen:

Olympic's boatswain or boatswain's mate on the starboard bridge wing with a megaphone, 1911. (Ioannis Georgiou collection)

| Alfred W.S. Nichols | £8 10s | Boatswain |
| Albert Haines | £6 10s | Boatswain's Mate |

The wage for Able-bodied Seamen and (ordinary) Seamen alike was £5:

Able-bodied Seamen:

J. Anderson
Ernest Edward Archer
Thomas Henry Bradley
Walter Thomas Brice
Edward John Buley
Frederick Charles Clench
George James Clench
Frank Couch
Stephen James Davis
Frank Olliver Evans
James Forward
Harry Holman
Robert John Hopkins
Albert Edward James Horswill
Thomas William Jones
William Arthur Lucas

William Henry Lyons
David Matherson
William McCarthy
George Francis McGough
George Alfred Moore
Frank Osman
Charles Henry Pascoe
William Chapman Peters
John Thomas Poingdestre
Joseph George Scarrott
Charles Willam F. Taylor
Philip Francis Vigot
William Clifford Weller

Seamen:
William Smith
Bertram Terrell

It is not a simple matter to understand the organisation of the seamen. The US inquiry commission noticed this too. Senator Theodore Elijah Burton asked A.B. Seaman Frank Osman about how the Deck Department was organised (page 540):

Burton:	How many seamen were there?
Osman:	Forty-four, altogether.
Burton:	You did not have all the boat's crew there, then; there are more than 44 in the crew, are there not? You mean by that able seamen, do you not?
Osman:	Yes, sir.
Burton:	You do not mean quartermasters, and such as that?
Osman:	No; I do not count quartermasters with the seamen.
Burton:	Do you count lookout men with the able seamen?
Osman:	Yes. They all live in the same place. But the quartermaster is in a different place, on the other side.
Burton:	You do not mean that those were all of the crew, even excluding the quartermasters, do you?
Osman:	That is all there is in the crew, sir.
Burton:	Just count those again?

During the passage of the *Titanic* from Southampton to Cherbourg, passenger Francis Browne took this photograph under the bridge, showing a sailor looking forward. (The Irish Picture Library/Father F.M. Browne SJ Collection)

Osman: There was 25 altogether in both watches, 13 in one watch and 12 in the other; then there was 2 deckmen, the cook of the forecastle, 2 window cleaners, 6 lookout men, and 2 masters-at-arms counted with the seamen.

Burton: You are just counting the men in your mess?

Osman: Yes, sir.

Burton: How many quartermasters?

Osman: Six quartermasters. One boatswain, boatswain's mate, carpenter and joiner.

When working this out it is obvious that Osman became confused and contradicted himself. Meanwhile, Senator Francis Griffith Newlands was interrogating A.B. Seaman George Alfred Moore (pages 559, 560):

Newlands: What did that mean, that the entire crew was to go up on the boat deck?

Moore: All the able seamen.

Newlands: Would that include firemen?

Moore: It had nothing to do with firemen; only the two watches, the port and starboard watches.

Newlands:	How many were there of them, about 40?
Moore:	No; 13 in one watch and 12 in the other. Then there was a man who used to work in the alleyway, and there were promenade daymen, saloon daymen and second-class daymen.
Newlands:	How many in all?
Moore:	How many able seamen?
Newlands:	Yes.
Moore:	There were 6 quartermasters, 6 lookout men, 13 in the port watch, 12 in the starboard watch and 7 day hands.

The seamen were therefore not only divided into the two watches, but also into the so-called 'day hands'. Moore spoke of a man in the alleyway and also of a number of day hands, therefore three teams of two. These men scrubbed or dried the decks during the day, depending on the weather, polished the brasswork and lashed down the deck chairs. According to the shipping company guidelines smart, able-bodied seamen had to be selected for this task, and an impeccable uniform was expected. The day hands worked from 06:00–17:00hrs under the chief officer, who relinquished his bridge watch to the second officer at 06:00hrs and could then give the day hands the orders for the day. One can infer that the seamen and the day hands were employed almost exclusively on the outside areas of the ship, and the day hands may have been divided up as follows:

1 day hand alleyway	probably means well decks/outside areas, third class.
2 day hands promenade	first class, A-deck, outside promenade.
2 day hands saloon	probably boat deck, first class.
2 day hands second class	second-class promenade on boat deck, B- and C-deck.

The distribution of the day hands is based on Moore's statement. Normally the 'saloon deck' signified D-deck, but this was a fully enclosed deck running the length of the ship. However, some shipping lines called first class 'saloon'. The White Star Line did this before 1904, so presumably Moore meant the first-class section of the sun or boat deck. The day hands were not alone responsible for these sections, but were released only for this purpose and other seamen helped out as required.

The thirty-one hired able-bodied seamen and ordinary seamen were composed of thirteen port, twelve starboard and seven day hands: 13+12+7=32, and so there was one supernumerary, and this was Sidney James Humphreys. Both Osman and Moore spoke correctly of there being six quartermasters, for they numbered him with the seamen. He brought the total to thirty-two.

A.B. Seaman Walter T. Brice, interrogated by Senator Jonathan Bourne (page 652), replied:

2 dayhands saloon deck (first class, photograph *Olympic*, April 1912)

2 dayhands promenade (first class)

2 dayhands (second class)

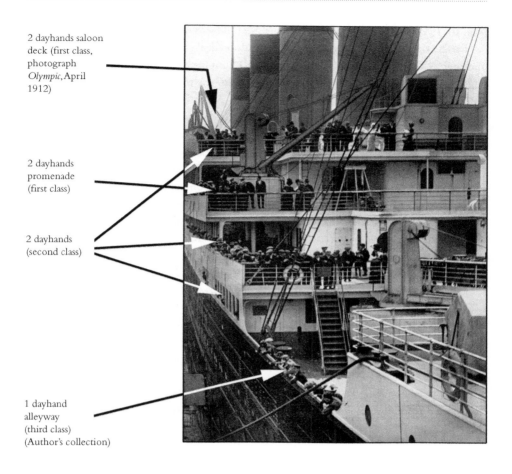

1 dayhand alleyway (third class) (Author's collection)

Bourne: Who had charge of the boat?
Brice: Mr. Humphreys.
Bourne: What was his position?
Brice: He was an able seaman.
Bourne: Who designated him to take charge of the boat, the officer?
Brice: No, sir.
Bourne: He took charge?
Brice: He took charge himself.
Bourne: Why did he take charge in preference to you? Did he rank you?
Brice: No, sir.
Bourne: You were equal in rank?
Brice: The only difference was that he was on the saloon deck.
Bourne: He took charge?
Brice: He took charge.

Now the information can be pieced together. According to A.B. Seaman Moore, of the seven day hands two worked on the promenade and saloon deck, two in second class and one was in charge of the well decks. According to Brice, Humphreys was one of the two day hands on the saloon deck. As such he was numbered with the thirty-two seamen. At the same time, he must have been the leader of the day hands. Why the White Star Line hired him as a quartermaster is not known, but presumably they did so as a foreman and paid him 5s per month extra for the responsibility.

Ten of the thirty-two seamen did not survive the sinking, and many of the twenty-two survivors were questioned at the inquiries. It might be thought that the seamen could be easily divided amongst the three groups, but it became one of the hardest nuts to crack of the entire exercise. From the sources available the complete quotas were not possible to compile. Only a few statements were so unequivocal as to allow exactitude.

The sequence on the muster lists turned out to be a blind alley. The list of seamen begins with twelve able-bodied men and Seaman Bertram Terrell at the tail. Then come eleven able-bodied seamen followed by Seaman William Smith, and finally six more able-bodied seamen. It might have been tempting to understand this sequence as thirteen men port side, twelve starboard side and six day hands, but as such it would not correspond even closely with the statements made by the survivors. It seems as though the reports of the size of the groups served only to arrive at a desired number of crew. One assumes that splitting them into watches followed a tradition that the crew formed the watches themselves, once on board.

It seemed reasonable to assume that in an emergency the men of the port watch would be assigned to the portside lifeboats and the same would apply to the starboard watch. But here again it soon transpired that the boat lists for an emergency do not correspond

Surviving seamen from the *Titanic* at the Seamen's Friend Society in New York. Many wear their White Star Line Guernsey they were rescued in. (Author's collection)

with the watches during routine sailing. Also, the ships aboard that the seafarers had served previously also provided no reliable indication of the watch to which an individual seaman was assigned.

Making identification of who was in which group of the three was made more difficult by the change of watch due just after the collision, for whoever was awake could belong to any of the three groups, while those still asleep could be day hands or port watch remaining in their bunks to the last possible minute. The survivors were only questioned about their activity shortly before the collision on the night in question. Because it was a Sunday night, plans for other jobs had been drawn up so that where a man happened to be on that night provided no clear indication as to his watch group. On other days of the week the seaman would have been occupied with cleaning jobs. Therefore, using the crew mess at the time of the collision is not a convincing indication of which men were off watch. It is frustrating that even with this small group containing so many survivors, the arrangement of men into the three groups was not possible – every variation had strong arguments for and against and a final accepted division seems not possible from the sources available. Here is the most likely (still incomplete) arrangement, however:

Port Watch, 13 Seamen:
J. Anderson
Ernest Edward Archer
Albert Edward James Horswill (or day hand)
Thomas William Jones (or starboard watch)
George Alfred Moore

Starboard Watch, 12 Seamen:
Walter Thomas Brice
Edward John Buley
Frank Olliver Evans
William Arthur Lucas
George Francis McGough
Frank Osman
William Chapman Peters
John Thomas Poingdestre
Joseph George Scarrott

Day Hands, 7 Seamen:
Sidney James Humphreys (saloon deck)
Frederick Charles Clench (alleyway)
George James Clench (uncertain)

Titanic's second-class section of the boat deck during the stop at Queenstown. This was one of the workplaces of the seamen, who spent most of their watches doing cleaning and maintenance work. (Author's collection)

The notation in parentheses above results from statements made by or about the individual, which are not unequivocal. Possibly personal acquaintances played a role in where a person was. For example, very probably the Clench brothers worked together; George James Clench was therefore probably also a day hand even though there is nothing else to support the assumption.

The two ordinary seamen William Smith and Bertram Terrell were probably assigned one each to a main watch, but who to which is not known. The following able-bodied seamen went into one of the preceding three groups:

Thomas Henry Bradley
Frank Couch
Stephen James Davis
James Forward
Harry Holman
Robert John Hopkins
William Henry Lyons
David Matherson
William McCarthy
Charles Henry Pascoe
Charles Willam F. Taylor
Philip Francis Vigot
William Clifford Weller

The hours of work of the seamen in the two main watches corresponded to those of the junior officers:

Port Watch:

Even dates in April 1912	04:00–08:00, 12:00–16:00 and 18:00–20:00hrs
Odd dates in April 1912	00:00–04:00, 08:00–12:00, 16:00–18:00 and 20:00–24:00hrs

Starboard Watch:

Even dates in April 1912	00:00–04:00, 08:00–12:00, 16:00–18:00 and 20:00–24:00hrs
Odd dates in April 1912	04:00–08:00, 12:00–16:00 and 18:00–20:00hrs

Day Hands:

Daily	06:00–17:00hrs

If the port and starboard watches worked alternating shifts as did the seamen – the 'watch on, watch off' system – the question arises as to why the two main watches were of different sizes. Why did the port watch have an additional man? The leader of the port watch, Boatswain Alfred W.S. Nichols, was often called away because of the size of the ship to involve himself in control activities. It would then be justifiable to count him amongst the idlers, those crew members not assigned to a fixed watch. This would also support suggestions that A.B. Seaman J. Anderson was in the position of an 'assisting boatswain' and therefore acted as leader of the port watch. Possibly he was training for the rank of boatswain's mate, which would explain why he was not paid extra for the supplementary duty.

The seamen slept in a room with forty-four bunks on E-deck in the bow. The men of the major watches never had more than 4 hours' rest during the whole voyage. Further interruptions were caused by the change of the lookout watches every 2 hours, and to make things worse this room was directly beneath the third-class lounge. The surroundings

Crew quarters in the forecastle of a large German liner in 1912. The seamen of the *Titanic* all slept in one room with forty-four berths. (Ioannis Georgiou collection)

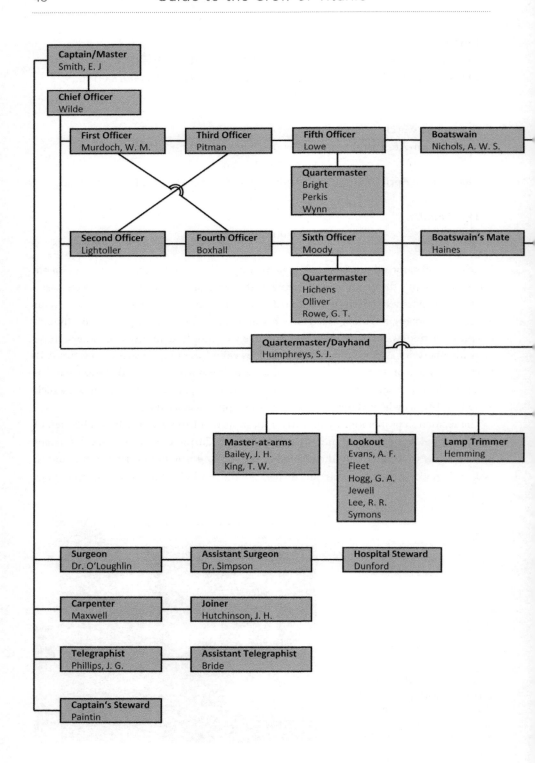

Captain/Master
Smith, E. J

Chief Officer
Wilde

First Officer
Murdoch, W. M.

Third Officer
Pitman

Fifth Officer
Lowe

Boatswain
Nichols, A. W. S.

Quartermaster
Bright
Perkis
Wynn

Second Officer
Lightoller

Fourth Officer
Boxhall

Sixth Officer
Moody

Boatswain's Mate
Haines

Quartermaster
Hichens
Olliver
Rowe, G. T.

Quartermaster/Dayhand
Humphreys, S. J.

Master-at-arms
Bailey, J. H.
King, T. W.

Lookout
Evans, A. F.
Fleet
Hogg, G. A.
Jewell
Lee, R. R.
Symons

Lamp Trimmer
Hemming

Surgeon
Dr. O'Loughlin

Assistant Surgeon
Dr. Simpson

Hospital Steward
Dunford

Carpenter
Maxwell

Joiner
Hutchinson, J. H.

Telegraphist
Phillips, J. G.

Assistant Telegraphist
Bride

Captain's Steward
Paintin

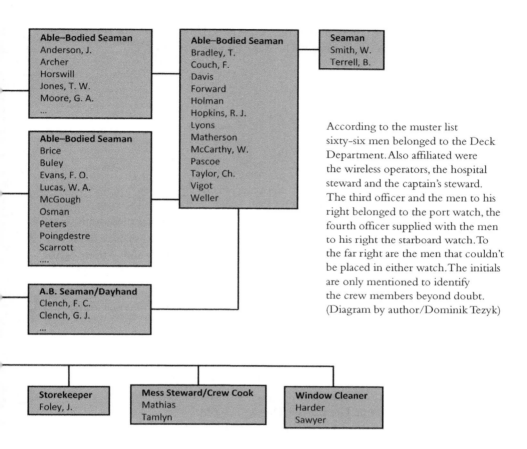

According to the muster list sixty-six men belonged to the Deck Department. Also affiliated were the wireless operators, the hospital steward and the captain's steward. The third officer and the men to his right belonged to the port watch, the fourth officer supplied with the men to his right the starboard watch. To the far right are the men that couldn't be placed in either watch. The initials are only mentioned to identify the crew members beyond doubt. (Diagram by author/Dominik Tezyk)

were therefore anything but conducive to a good sleep. The strict rhythm of work, on the other hand, probably guaranteed that a man fell into a deep sleep minutes after his watch ended.

There are records of an incident with an exhausted sailor on *Oceanic* in November 1911. Several attempts by different shipmates to wake him up were not successful. He was lifted out of his bunk but he crawled back. Finally he was pulled out of the bunk and fell between the stanchion and a table. He was brought into the ship's hospital with a broken collarbone.

The Lookouts

As was clear from the interrogation of A.B. Seaman Alfred Moore, even the arrangement of the lookouts added to the confusion. The wage for lookouts was £5:

Alfred Frank Evans
Frederick Fleet
George Alfred Hogg
Archie Jewell
Reginald Robinson Lee
George Thomas MacDonald Symons

These men were able-bodied seamen who kept watch in the so-called crow's nest for obstructions in the direction of travel. The White Star Line supplied them with warm jackets since their work location was exposed to the headwind. As did the nautical officers, lookouts had to undergo a sight test. They were examined as to their ability to recognise shapes, but the main interest of the official oculist was to detect any kind of colour blindness. It is interesting that, despite the regularity of lookout duty during the hours of darkness, night vision was not tested. For this function, the lookouts were not assigned to an alternating two-watch system, but worked on another schedule:

Alfred Frank Evans and George Alfred Hogg
00:00–02:00, 06:00–08:00, 12:00–14:00 and 18:00–20:00hrs

Archie Jewell and George Thomas MacDonald Symons
02:00–04:00, 08:00–10:00, 14:00–16:00 and 20:00–22:00hrs

Frederick Fleet and Reginald Robinson Lee
04:00–06:00, 10:00–12:00, 16:00–18:00 and 22:00–24:00hrs

The lookouts were the only group who never worked more than 2 hours in a single shift. This was necessary, given the responsible and tiring nature of the work. Even though, like the seamen of the port and starboard watches, they never had more than 4 hours' rest, they were probably better rested than the latter. Second Officer Lightoller and Lookout Frederick Fleet deposed to Senator William Alden Smith of the US inquiry (pages 428 and 325) that the men in the crow's nest received a bonus of 5s per round trip, not per month. This was not recorded in the muster lists and the extra payment does not feature in the sign-off list. Presumably they did not get the extra payment because the full round trip had not been made. The lookouts formed the second-largest trade group after the quartermasters to survive the sinking without loss to their number. In August 1913, Reginald Robinson Lee became possibly the first crew member of the *Titanic* to die after the sinking.

Olympic's foremast with the crow's nest, the workplace for the lookout men, and the bridge on the boat deck in the background. Some crew members enjoy the mild spring day in New York. The photograph was taken three weeks after the sinking of the *Titanic*. (Author's collection)

The Specialists

There were some crew members of the Deck Department who by reason of their special function were not included in larger groupings:

Dr William Francis Norman O'Loughlin	£10	Surgeon
Dr John Edward Simpson	£8 10s	Assistant Surgeon
William Dunford	£4 10s	Hospital Steward
John Maxwell	£9 10s	Carpenter
John Hall Hutchinson	£6	Joiner
Samuel Ernest Hemming	£5 5s	Lamp Trimmer
John Foley	£5 5s	Storekeeper
Job Henry Bailey	£5 10s	Master-at-Arms
Thomas Walter King	£5 10s	Master-at-Arms
Bill Harder	£4	Window Cleaner
Robert James Sawyer	£4	Window Cleaner
Montague Vincent Mathias	£4	Mess Steward/Crew Cook
Frederick Tamlyn	£4	Mess Steward/Crew Cook

The surgeons Dr William Francis Norman O'Loughlin and Dr John Edward Simpson were not nautical officers but were given officers' rank to reinforce their authority. In the muster list they were both described as 'surgeon', in the passenger list Dr Simpson was annotated as 'assistant surgeon', and during the voyage was mainly responsible for second and third class. A surgeon had hardly any prospect of promotion. Once his salary was fixed it would hardly change over decades. Despite his comparably modest salary, Dr O'Loughlin was given a two-room cabin on C-deck, Dr Simpson had a smaller cabin nearby. The surgeons were always on call and were directly subordinate to the captain or his representative on the bridge. Medically trained personnel could be called upon unexpectedly at any time, and so the surgeons were always on call and on duty if needed.

The surgeon was enormously important for crew morale and could use his authority to settle a dispute. He was the only person aboard who in certain matters had more authority than the captain. If he wrote up a crew member as sick, the captain could not countermand it, and he needed to furnish no information as to the reason for his diagnosis. Should the captain persist in questioning the surgeon's decision, he could expect consequences from the shipping company and the maritime authorities. The surgeons had to report a sick crew member to the chief officer, second engineer or the purser, according to the department involved. The crew sick bay was on C-deck near the bow. All special medical occurrences had to be entered into the ship's log and countersigned by the surgeon. In the event of passenger deaths, coffins were carried aboard and the surgeon could embalm the body at the request of family members for a fee of up to £20. The surgeons also paid attention to the hygienic conditions (particularly in the kitchens) and to adequate ventilation, particularly in third class. Dr O'Loughlin was aged 62 years and was the oldest crew member of *Titanic*. He had been a servant of the shipping line since May 1872. The second oldest was Captain Smith, also 62, but three months younger than the surgeon.

Passengers who fell ill aboard were treated without charge. Existing illnesses (as well as toothache) of first- and second-class passengers were treated for a fee that helped supplement the relatively meagre income of the surgeons. The surgery for first class was on the starboard side of C-deck, directly below it was the hospital with four rooms for patients and even a padded room. By law first and second class aboard ship had to be combined as 'cabin class' and treated separately from third class. Nevertheless, second- and third-class passengers astern shared a surgery with the waiting room on D-deck and were treated there by Dr Simpson. At the port of departure, third-class passengers were required to undergo a health examination. Ill passengers were refused leave to travel. This was to avoid being refused entry at the port of disembarkation and because they would not be able to afford the medical fees shipboard. If they fell ill during the voyage, then they would be given treatment without charge, as were the passengers of the higher classes. Second- and third-class passengers falling sick were treated in their own cabins, there being no hospital rooms as such. The surgeons had additional representative duties on board in all dining rooms: in first class they hosted at the surgeons' table.

Hospital Steward William Dunford signed-on in third class but was mainly responsible for the care of the first and second class. His sleeping quarters lay between the hospital station on D-deck so that he was on hand at night to respond to a patient's bell.

A carpenter would be aboard ship by tradition. In the days of sail, there would have been a sailmaker too. These skilled, well-qualified men were needed for maintenance work and repairs. They were traditionally known as the 'idlers' and were on call to do a repair around the clock. Carpenter John Maxwell worked not only with wood, one of his duties was to check over the hull. He had to measure the water level in the double bottom regularly and look after the fresh water. He was also responsible for the instruments in the wheelhouse and on the bridge, the oiling of the wheel chain, cleanliness of the winches, the hatches and the tarpaulins. Next to the seamen's mess were the carpenter's shop and store. Because of the size of *Titanic*, he had John Hutchinson, a joiner, to assist, to whom he could delegate work.

By reason of the sheer size of ships of the Olympic class, numerous new positions were created. These were not for traditional idlers, but seamen with supplementary duties who were therefore not subordinated directly to the captain but to the officer of the watch. Work that could be done by one or other of the crew on smaller ships justified a specialist on *Titanic*. During the US Senate Inquiry (page 663), A.B. Seaman Samuel Hemming, hired as a lamp trimmer, was asked about his duties. He stated in evidence that he was responsible for the upkeep of all oil lamps aboard and for the mixture of colours. At dusk at sea an oil lamp had to be exhibited on a mast (usually a forward mast) in addition to the electrical navigation lights. Numerous reserve lamps had to be kept ready and the navigation lights of the emergency boat lit. The lamps for all other lifeboats were always to be kept ready for use in the wheelhouse. A red lamp had to be hung at nightfall at the foot of every external stairway and in all passenger areas on deck. Red light does not affect night vision, and the deck crew could move around without having to continually accustom their eyes to changing light conditions.

John Foley worked as a storekeeper on a newly created idler post. He looked after certain materials and handed them out to the crew as required. According to the muster lists, Hemming and Foley earned £5 per month; when paid off like the quartermasters they received pro rata 1*s* extra for their supplementary work, and so their monthly pay was therefore £5 5*s*. Hemming did both jobs between Belfast and Southampton while Foley travelled as quartermaster. They shared a cabin on C-deck.

Every ship carried at least one so-called 'Master-at-Arms' aboard, responsible for maintaining order amongst the passengers and crew as well as observing the opening times of the public rooms. Job Henry Bailey and Thomas Walter King probably worked out their work hours between themselves, but unless called by someone they usually slept at night. They shared a cabin on E-deck in the bow and were only a short distance away from the most likely trouble centres: the crew quarters and the lodgings of the emigrants.

The two window cleaners Bill Harder and Robert James Sawyer naturally did their work mainly during the day. Their hours of work presumably coincided with that of the day hands.

Olympic's wheelhouse with the oil lamps, compasses, hatchets and provisions for half the lifeboats; there was a similar shelf on the port side. The lamps were maintained by the lamp trimmer. (Author's collection)

As a result of the constant changeovers of the deck crew's watches, there were hungry seamen to be found all day. Good food is one of the most important pleasures of a sea voyage, and this is more important for the crew than the passengers. The law provided that a seaman should have meat daily and the ship must carry 4.5 litres per man of water for drinking, cooking and washing. The ingredients for the specified well-balanced meals were prescribed precisely. It was the job of Mess Stewards Montague Vincent Mathias and Frederick Tamlyn to ensure that the letter of the law was followed and also look after the bodily well-being of the seafarers aboard. The description 'Mess Steward' in the hiring lists is misleading. Mathias and Tamlyn were not stewards in the crew dining rooms, but crew cooks. Both ran the seamen's mess on the portside of C-deck in the bow and shared the galley with the cooks of the firemen's mess.

6

THE ENGINE DEPARTMENT

The *Titanic* was driven by two steam piston engines and a low-pressure turbine. Three hundred and twenty-six men had been mustered for a single purpose: in their various functions to ensure that the *Titanic* had the desired engine efficiency and electrical power. As already mentioned, Fireman John Coffey deserted at Queenstown leaving 325 men. Most of these worked in boiler rooms 2 to 6; boiler room 1 was not in operation during the first days of the maiden voyage.

Unravelling the organisation of the Engine Department presented itself initially as a major challenge. Since no one had made a serious attempt to do so previously, a careful analysis of the available data was necessary. An additional impediment was that even the crew was confused by the complicated job titles, and many crew members when facing the questions during the inquiries were unable to agree about with whom they had had dealings aboard.

Also, for this department the jobs were sorted corresponding to the wage paid. Four jobs made up the lion's share of the engine room staff: on *Titanic* there were fifteen leading firemen, 159 firemen, seventy-three trimmers and thirty-three greasers; their names were all entered on three separate hiring lists. These lists will be looked at further on. Taking away these 280 men from the initial complement of 325 leaves us with forty-five men who are to be found on their own hiring list, that of the Engine Department operations staff.

The importance that the shipping company attached to the engine room is clear from a glance at the hiring list. Besides Captain Smith (who drew an agreed annual salary), there were about fifty men aboard *Titanic* who earned £10 or more monthly, twenty-two of them in the Engine Department. Another indication of the importance of the engineers: besides their own mess they had a separate smoking room on the boat deck and for their own promenade a section of the boat deck situated between the third and fourth funnels that separated the first class from second class.

The technicians had their accommodation on F-deck near the steam machinery. Chief Engineer Bell had the largest cabin with bedroom and living quarters. He was the only member of the crew besides the captain to have his own bath – the other engineers had two baths between them. The higher ranking engineers down to the junior third engineer had a single cabin with portholes; the rest shared a two- or three-person cabin, most of these being without daylight.

The chief engineer of the *Titanic*, Joseph Bell, and his assistant, William Edward Farquharson, were among the most important men on board, which is reflected by their salaries of £35 and £22 respectively. (Author's collection)

To show forty-five men in an organisational diagram seemed easy. However, very few of them had the same job description. Nothing was passed down or preserved in writing regarding how the *Titanic* engineers were organised. That Joseph Bell was the chief engineer and Senior Second Engineer William Edward Farquharson was his representative, and that both were at the apex of the pyramid, was obvious from their income of £35 and £22 monthly respectively. Bell was in charge of the entire Engine Department and Farquharson was responsible for the engine-room men analogous to the jurisdiction of the chief officer in the Deck Department.

Yet how can one assess the job of the junior assistant third engineer? What weight should be placed on each prefix 'junior', 'assistant' and 'third'? Is a fourth engineer better placed if he does not have the prefix 'junior'? No logic was recognised behind all this for some time. Arranging things based on a man's pay did not provide a system behind the prefixes. It was made all the more difficult because none of the engineers survived the disaster, and so no first-hand statements as to their work exist. The following reconstruction is therefore based on circumstantial evidence.

The Second, Third and Fourth Engineers

To begin with an observation: Thomas Hulman Kemp, hired as an extra assistant fourth engineer, had a special function mentioned in a later chapter.

After the loss of the *Titanic*, the monthly journal *The Marine Engineer and Naval Architect* published short biographies of the ship's engineers, setting out their careers. These descriptions were only useful to a limited extent because, depending on the size and routes sailed by a ship, a 'demotion' to a lower position on a better ship might actually be a promotion.

Group photograph of the *Olympic* engineers, taken in 1911. The full dress uniform, as seen here, was only obligatory for chief and senior engineers, but it seems as though all had purchased this prestigious uniform. White trousers were officially not foreseen with full dress. Among them are fourteen engineers who did not survive the *Titanic*'s sinking. Even when some were promoted after the photograph was taken, it had no influence on their visible rank insignia: 1) William Dickson Mackie, junior fifth engineer, 2) Frank Alfred Parsons, senior fifth engineer, 3) Peter Porter Sloan, chief electrician, 4) Boykett Herbert Jupe, assistant electrician, 5) Francis Ernest George Coy, junior assistant third engineer, 6) Bertie Wilson, senior assistant second engineer, 7) Leonard Hodgkinson, senior fourth engineer, 8) Arthur Ward, junior assistant fourth engineer, 9) Jonathan Shepherd, junior assistant second engineer, 10) Herbert Gifford Harvey, junior assistant second engineer, 11) Henry Ryland Dyer, senior assistant fourth engineer, 12) Robert Millar, extra fifth engineer, 13) John Henry Hesketh, second engineer, 14) George Fox Hosking, senior third engineer. (Author's collection)

Once again, the British inquiry minutes were able to throw light on the matter. Leading Fireman Frederick W. Barrett stated in Britain (answers 1853 and 1855) that at the time of the collision Shepherd and Hesketh were on watch. A little later he was in boiler room 5 where he met Harvey and Wilson (answer 1957). These four engineers can be arranged according to their rank and pay:

John Henry Hesketh	£18	Second Engineer
Bertie Wilson	£13	Senior Assistant Second Engineer
Herbert Gifford Harvey	£12 10s	Junior Assistant Second Engineer
Jonathan Shepherd	£12 10s	Junior Assistant Second Engineer

From this, one may infer something. From his pay grade it is to be ascertained that the senior assistant second engineer ranked higher than the two junior assistant second engineers, and that the word 'assistant' must have a deeper significance. The four engineers make a good subject for comparison, since they all have the prefix 'second'. On the *Titanic*

The second engineers of the *Titanic* were in the engine and boiler rooms when the liner collided with an iceberg: John Henry Hesketh, Norman John Harrison, Bertie Wilson, Herbert Gifford Harvey and Jonathan Shepherd. (Author's collection)

there was a fifth 'second', Norman John Harrison. If the four 'seconds' were on watch at the time of the collision, it is very probable that Harrison was also attached to this watch. Indeed, surviving Trimmer George Henry Cavell stated at the British inquiry that Harrison was in charge of his section (answer 4434).

Three shifts were worked in the boiler rooms (4 hours on, 8 hours off). If the engineers also worked these shifts, then all five 'seconds' formed one shift. Accordingly, the third and fourth engineers formed the other shifts. This fits the pattern if the engineers were grouped as follows:

John Henry Hesketh	£18	Second Engineer
Norman John Harrison	£18	Junior Second Engineer
Bertie Wilson	£13	Senior Assistant Second Engineer
Herbert Gifford Harvey	£12 10s	Junior Assistant Second Engineer
Jonathan Shepherd	£12 10s	Junior Assistant Second Engineer
George Fox Hosking	£16 10s	Senior Third Engineer
Edward Charles Dodd	£15 10s	Junior Third Engineer
Charley Hodge	£12	Senior Assistant Third Engineer
Francis Ernest George Coy	£11 10s	Junior Assistant Third Engineer
James Cameron Fraser	£11 10s	Junior Assistant Third Engineer
Leonard Hodgkinson	£14	Senior Fourth Engineer
James Muil Smith	£13 10s	Junior Fourth Engineer
Henry Ryland Dyer	£11	Senior Assistant Fourth Engineer
Henry Watson Dodds	£10 10s	Junior Assistant Fourth Engineer
Arthur Ward	£10 10s	Junior Assistant Fourth Engineer

This arrangement makes it clear that an engineer could advance his career either within a group or by switching to another watch. The disparity in pay between the three shifts, man for man, even though they did the same work, shows the hierarchical structure. The prefix 'senior' is absent from the title of Second Engineer Hesketh, presumably to avoid confusion with Senior Second Engineer Farquharson of the upper-command circle.

At the time of the collision then the second engineers were working the watch from 20:00–24:00hrs, and then again from 08:00–12:00hrs. How the 'third' and 'fourth' watches were arranged cannot be determined from survivors' statements. It seems likely that the unloved middle watch from 00:00–04:00hrs would have fallen on the fourth watch, to provide the probable watch scheme as follows:

Second Engineers	08:00–12:00 and 20:00–24:00hrs
Third Engineers	04:00–08:00 and 16:00–20:00hrs
Fourth Engineers	00:00–04:00 and 12:00–16:00hrs

It seems logical that one of the three assistants would always have had charge of two boiler rooms. Frederick Barrett, Leading Fireman from boiler room 6, stated that Junior Assistant Second Engineer Jonathan Shepherd was his superior officer. At the moment when the collision occurred, Barrett was in conversation with shift leader Hesketh, from which it may be inferred that Norman John Harrison must have been in the engine rooms. The other two watches, led by the third and fourth engineers respectively, had two shift leaders each, a senior and a junior engineer. There are two plausible scenarios: either one supervised the boiler rooms and the other the engine rooms, or they were responsible one each for the port and starboard engine.

A conclusion on the division of work could be drawn from the official inquiry into the collision between the sister ship *Olympic* and HMS *Hawke* in September 1911. The higher-ranking second engineer was on the portside, the junior second engineer on starboard. This would have also been the split on *Titanic*. Hesketh was responsible for the port engine, Harrison for the starboard one, and the corollary was that the senior third and fourth engineers were on the port engine and the corresponding junior engineers on the starboard one. Hesketh was in conversation with Barrett in boiler room 6 during the collision, although his responsibility was the port engine. Possibly he was being represented there by the chief engineer or the senior second engineer.

This watch system combines fifteen engineers with confusing rank titles into a logical scheme. Naturally the question arises how such a complicated arrangement came into being. The probable explanation lies in the size of *Titanic*. When smaller steamers crossed the oceans, none had six boiler rooms. Fewer engineers were involved per watch. With the increasing size of ships, the engineers required assistants, and the terms 'senior' and 'junior' were introduced in the attempt to bring some logic into the system. This left over a few specialists such as the fifth and sixth engineers, whose jobs are described below.

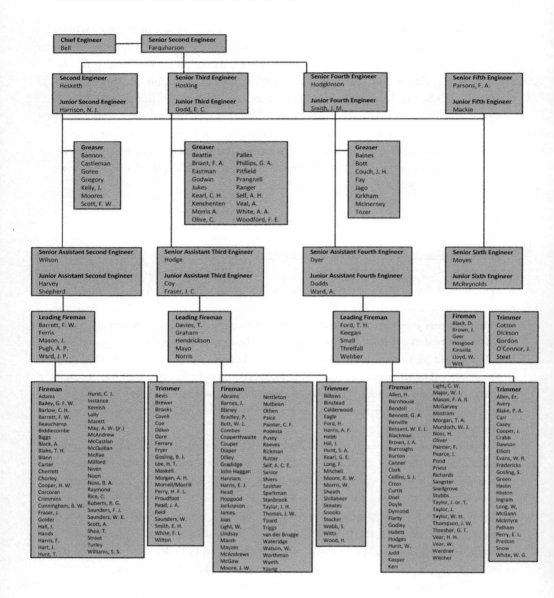

Chief Engineer
Bell

Senior Second Engineer
Farquharson

Second Engineer
Hesketh

Junior Second Engineer
Harrison, N. J.

Senior Third Engineer
Hosking

Junior Third Engineer
Dodd, E. C.

Senior Fourth Engineer
Hodgkinson

Junior Fourth Engineer
Smith, J. M.

Senior Fifth Engineer
Parsons, F. A.

Junior Fifth Engineer
Mackie

Greaser
Bannon
Castleman
Goree
Gregory
Kelly, J,
Moores
Scott, F. W.

Greaser
Beattie   Palles
Briant, F. A.   Phillips, G. A.
Eastman   Pitfield
Godwin   Prangnell
Jukes   Ranger
Kearl, C. H.   Self, A. H.
Kenchenten   Veal, A.
Morris A.   White, A. A.
Olive, C.   Woodford, F. E.

Greaser
Baines
Bott
Couch, J. H.
Fay
Jago
Kirkham
McInerney
Tozer

Senior Assistant Second Engineer
Wilson

Junior Assistant Second Engineer
Harvey
Shepherd

Senior Assistant Third Engineer
Hodge

Junior Assistant Third Engineer
Coy
Fraser, J. C.

Senior Assistant Fourth Engineer
Dyer

Junior Assistant Fourth Engineer
Dodds
Ward, A.

Senior Sixth Engineer
Moyes

Junior Sixth Engineer
McReynolds

Leading Fireman
Barrett, F. W.
Ferris
Mason, J.
Pugh, A. P.
Ward, J. P.

Leading Fireman
Davies, T.
Graham
Hendrickson
Mayo
Norris

Leading Fireman
Ford, T. H.
Keegan
Small
Threlfall
Webber

Fireman
Black, D.
Brown, J.
Geer
Hosgood
Kinsella
Lloyd, W.
Witt

Trimmer
Cotton
Dickson
Gordon
O'Connor, J.
Steel

Fireman
Adams   Hurst, C. J.
Bailey, G. F. W.   Instance
Barlow, C. H.   Kemish
Barrett, F. W.   Lally
Beauchamp   Marett
Biddlecombe   May, A. W. (jr.)
Biggs   McAndrew
Black, A.   McCastlan
Blake, T. H.   McQuillan
Blann   McRae
Carter   Milford
Cherrett   Niven
Chorley   Noon
Cooper, H. W.   Noss, B. A.
Corcoran   Raymond
Crimmins   Rice, C.
Cunningham, B. W.   Roberts, R. G.
Fraser, J.   Saunders, F. J.
Golder   Saunders, W. E.
Hall, J.   Scott, A.
Hands   Shea, T.
Harris, J.   Street
Hart, J.   Turley
Hunt, T.   Williams, S. S.

Trimmer
Bevis
Brewer
Brooks
Caveli
Coe
Dillon
Dore
Ferrary
Fryer
Gosling, B. J.
Lee, H. T.
Maskell
Morgan, A. H.
Morrell/Morrill
Perry, H. F. L.
Proudfoot
Read, J. A.
Reid
Saunders, W.
Smith, E. H.
White, F. L.
Wilton

Fireman
Abrams   Nettleton
Barnes, J.   Nutbean
Blaney   Othen
Bradley, P.   Paice
Butt, W. J.   Painter, C. F.
Combes   Podesta
Copperthwaite   Pusey
Couper   Reeves
Diaper   Rickman
Dilley   Rutter
Gradidge   Self, A. C. E.
John Haggan   Senior
Hannam   Shiers
Harris, E. J.   Smither
Head   Sparkman
Hopgood   Stanbrook
Jackopson   Taylor, J. H.
James   Thomas, J. W.
Joas   Tizard
Light, W.   Triggs
Lindsay   van der Brugge
Marsh   Wateridge
Mayzes   Watson, W.
McAndrews   Worthman
McGaw   Wyeth
Moore, J. W.   Young

Trimmer
Billows
Binstead
Calderwood
Eagle
Ford, H.
Harris, A. F.
Hebb
Hill, J.
Hunt, S. A.
Kearl, G. E.
Long, F.
Mitchell
Moore, R. W.
Morris, W.
Sheath
Shillabeer
Skeates
Snooks
Stocker
Webb, S.
Witts
Wood, H.

Fireman
Allen, H.   Light, C. W.
Barnhouse   Major, W. J.
Bendell   Mason, F. A. R.
Bennett, G. A.   McGarvey
Benville   Mintram
Bessant, W. E. L.   Morgan, T. A.
Blackman   Murdoch, W. J.
Brown, J. A.   Noss, H.
Burroughs   Oliver
Burton   Painter, F.
Canner   Pearce, J.
Clark   Pond
Collins, S. J.   Priest
Cross   Richards
Curtis   Sangster
Doel   Snellgrove
Doyle   Stubbs
Dymond   Taylor, J. or. T.
Flarty   Taylor, J.
Godley   Taylor, W. H.
Hallett   Thompson, J. W,
Hodges   Thresher, G. T.
Hurst, W.   Vear, H. H.
Judd   Vear, W.
Kasper   Wardner
Kerr   Witcher

Trimmer
Allen, Er.
Avery
Blake, P. A.
Carr
Casey
Cooper, J.
Crabb
Dawson
Elliott
Evans, W. R.
Fredericks
Gosling, S.
Green
Haslin
Hinton
Ingram
Long, W,
McGann
McIntyre
Pelham
Perry, E. L.
Preston
Snow
White, W. G.

To ensure continuous propulsion and electrical power around the clock most men of the Engine Department worked in a three-watch system, which usually meant 4 hours on, 8 hours off. The men in the first column worked from 8–12 and 20–24 hours, the men in the second column most probably from 4–8 and 16–20 hours, and those in the third most probably from 0–4 and 12–16 hours. The fifth and sixth engineers worked in a two-watch system in the engine and turbine rooms. (Diagram by author/Dominik Tezyk)

The Fifth and Sixth Engineers

For the distribution of the fifth and sixth engineers we have very little to go on. These are the officers involved:

Frank Alfred Parsons	£10	Senior Fifth Engineer
William Dickson Mackie	£9 10s	Junior Fifth Engineer
Robert Millar	£9 10s	Extra Fifth Engineer
William Young Moyes	£9	Senior Sixth Engineer
William McReynolds	£8 10s	Junior Sixth Engineer

The theme of the 'extra fifth engineer' will be taken up in the next chapter. The regular fifth and sixth engineers each had a senior and junior. Since none of the engineers survived, recourse must be had to the greasers, who worked together with the engineers. Four of the thirty-three greasers survived. Tom Ranger and Frederick William Scott were required to testify before the British inquiry. At the time of the collision, Ranger was with Chief Electrician Peter Porter Sloan repairing ventilator fans on E-deck, and his statement contains nothing useful regarding the organisation of the engineers.

Scott, the other greaser interrogated, was on watch in the turbine room from 20:00–24:00hrs at the time of the collision. Here follows an extract from the record of the interrogation by Adair Roche, counsel on behalf of the Marine Engineers Association at the British inquiry:

Roche (5725):	Who was in charge of your section, the turbine room?
Scott:	One of the juniors I think it was, about the sixth.
Roche (5726):	What is his name; do you know?
Scott:	No.
...	
Roche (5729):	And were the other engineers you saw on deck those belonging to your section, the turbine room?
Scott:	They were doing six-hour watches then; some had come on at 8 to 2.

There seems to be an error of transcription in the last question and answer because the reply does not fit at all. However, the answer is useful. The following information can be inferred from the exchange:

a) Scott was not certain which engineers were with him in the turbine room.
b) He believed that it was a junior, 'about the 6th'.
c) The adverb 'then' shows that the watches kept by these engineers were not always of 6 hours, and by using the plural 'they were doing', it can be determined that more than one engineer kept this watch.

An engineer at the engine room's telegraph, unknown steamer. (Author's collection)

A 6-hour shift is a circumstantial indication that 'watch on, watch off' was the rhythm in force. As an alternative to the dog-watches (of the Deck Department), the longer watches brought with them a daily change in rhythm. The longer a watch lasted, the longer the off-watch personnel could sleep. It was sensible to have two watches each covering parts of the night, therefore from 20:00–02:00hrs and from 02:00–08:00hrs. This alternative system of watches is called the 'Swedish Watch System'. If the engineers were working 6-hour shifts but the greasers 4-hour shifts that could explain why Scott did not know the engineers with whom he was working on the evening of 14 April 1912. From what he says, one guesses that it was the fifth and sixth engineers in this rhythm.

What were these engineers doing? They were apparently working in the area of the engines and turbine, and not in the boiler rooms. Apart from Mackie the men were young and inexperienced: it was McReynolds first voyage on any ship. Since earlier White Star Liners (without a turbine) also had fifth and sixth engineers on board, they were not in charge of the turbine.

Seven months before *Titanic* went down, her sister-ship *Olympic* had collided with the cruiser HMS *Hawke*, resulting in damage to both ships. An official inquiry was held in November 1911. Four minutes before that collision the turbine and the central propeller had been started up, which means that at the time of the collision, the engineers had taken over their regular watches, were at their assigned post and were therefore at the same positions as aboard the *Titanic* when her own collision occurred.

From the depositions it can be taken that the junior fifth engineer was at the starboard engine, and the junior sixth engineer at the port engine. The respective senior engineers were not interrogated, which allows one to assume that they were off-watch at the time. If this arrangement was also followed by the *Titanic*, and the juniors were on watch during the collision, then the engineers were working as follows:

Senior Fifth Engineer Frank Alfred Parsons (starboard engine) and
Senior Sixth Engineer William Young Moyes (port engine)

Even dates in April 1912	08:00–12:00 and 16:00–20:00hrs
Odd dates in April 1912	02:00–08:00, 12:00–16:00 and 20:00–02:00hrs

Junior Fifth Engineer William Dickson Mackie (starboard engine) and
Junior Sixth Engineer William McReynolds (port engine)

Even dates in April 1912   02:00–08:00, 12:00–16:00 and 20:00–02:00hrs
Odd dates in April 1912   08:00–12:00 and 16:00–20:00hrs

The above scheme is the best possible approximation. The watch scheme does not coincide
exactly with Scott's statement that the turbine room was in the charge of 'about the 6th
engineer'. Confusion about places in the relevant rooms during the interrogation of Scott
might be the reason. And still, it is possible that the fifth and sixth engineer were on top
of their engine room duty also in charge of the turbine room, as will be explained in the
next chapter.

The engineers supervised engine revolutions and temperatures. They also had disciplinary
powers over some of the greasers. At sea there were practically no orders from the bridge
to carry out. It must have been a rather humdrum life, for the decisions were taken by the
shift leaders. The jobs were made for young men to win their spurs. The heat was less than
in the boiler rooms; therefore the men could work two instead of three watches.

This watch scheme indicates a similarity to that of the deck officers. The senior officers
had the three-watch system (as did the shift leaders of the Engine Department) and
the junior officers worked the two-watch
system (corresponding to the fifth and sixth
engineers). It is very likely that the engineers
relieved each other for meals as the senior deck
officers did.

A further point to make in this analysis of
the second to sixth engineers is that, contrary
to the portrayal in films, they were not to be
found in large numbers in the engine room: of
the nineteen men, a maximum of four were
present there and only three at the time of the
collision. Second Engineer Hesketh was absent
from his work station at the port engine, and
was in conversation in boiler room 6.

The aft end of the starboard engine (in the
foreground one of the two low-pressure cylinders)
of the *Olympic* at Harland & Wolff in Belfast.
(Author's collection)

The starting platform in *Aquitania*'s engine room gives an idea of the respective area on *Titanic*. At sea only very few engineers and greasers were on duty. (Author's collection)

The Specialised Technicians and Lone Workers

Specialist functions in the Engine Department were carried out by the following staff:

George Alexander Chisnall	£12	Boilermaker
Hugh Joseph Fitzpatrick	£11	Junior Boilermaker
Arthur John Rous	£9	Plumber
Alfred George Foster	£7	Storekeeper
August Kenzler	£7	Storekeeper
Charles Thomas N. Newman	£6	Assistant Storekeeper
Henry Rudd	£6	Assistant Storekeeper
Thomas Hulman Kemp	£10 10s	Extra Assistant Fourth Engineer (Refrigeration)
Robert Millar	£9 10s	Extra Fifth Engineer
Henry Philip Creese	£10 10s	Deck Engineer
Thomas Millar	£9 10s	Assistant Deck Engineer
Peter Porter Sloan	£12	Chief Electrician
Alfred Samuel Allsopp	£11	Second Electrician
Albert George Ervine	£8	Assistant Electrician
Boykett Herbert Jupe	£8	Assistant Electrician

William P. Kelly	£8	Assistant Electrician
Alfred Pirrie Middleton	£8	Assistant Electrician
William Luke Duffy	£6	Writer/Engineers' Secretary
Thomas Knowles	£6	Fireman Messman/Crew Cook
Arthur William May (Sr)	£6	Fireman Messman/Crew Cook
John Coleman	£6	Mess Steward/Crew Cook
Stanley Blake	£5	Mess Steward/Crew Cook
Cecil William Fitzpatrick	£3 15s	Mess Steward
George Gumery	£3 15s	Mess Steward

In keeping with the tradition of 'idlers' in sail, steamships had a boilermaker and a plumber. These men belonged to the maintenance and repair team. On the *Titanic* they were boilermaker George Alexander Chisnall, his assistant Hugh Joseph Fitzpatrick and the plumber Arthur John Rous. Like other 'idlers' they were required to hold themselves ready around the clock for all eventualities.

They worked closely with the storemen, of whom there were four in the Engine Department: Alfred George Foster, August Kenzler, Charles Thomas N. Newman and Henry Rudd. The first two worked for £7 per month, the other two for a pound less. Thus it is probable that they also worked watch on, watch off, one storekeeper and an assistant storekeeper together. Probably they not only handed out tools but also did repairs in the workshops. As to their watches, no information has become available. They had to always be at hand; how they worked it out between themselves was secondary, and it is not known if they worked the longer shifts or the dog watches to reduce their exposure to the unfavoured watches.

Another 'idler' was the extra assistant fourth engineer, a specialist responsible for the refrigeration system. Aboard *Titanic* this was Thomas Hulman Kemp. Provisions had to be refrigerated during the almost one-week long voyage. This included perishable freight as well as goods for consumption aboard, some of the latter being held for the return voyage. Kemp had to enter the temperature of the cold rooms into a logbook every 4 hours. The refrigerating machinery was located in the engine room near the port engine. Kemp made his apprenticeship at Harland & Wolff so he was familiar with the inbuilt refrigerating system. The post was not on the career ladder; aboard *Olympic* the same man did the job for years. On smaller ships, greasers were hired for the purpose – possibly Kemp had several greasers to assist him.

The duties of Extra Fifth Engineer Robert Millar have not been recorded. In the muster lists of the *Megantic* and *Laurentic*, however, there are some pointers. Both ships were almost similar in structure but *Laurentic* had a turbine in addition to the two steam-driven engines. Like the ships of the Olympic class, the *Laurentic* also had an extra fifth engineer, whereas

One of two refrigerating engines before its installation on the port side of the engine room. (Author's collection)

The electric deck cranes and steam winches were maintained by the deck engineers. Shown here is the aft deck of the *Olympic* in 1921. (Author's collection)

the *Megantic*, with no turbine, did not. From that it can be deduced that Robert Millar was probably responsible for the *Titanic* turbine. Like the refrigeration system, when running it did not require constant attention around the clock. A single engineer could note the revolutions and temperature regularly and give instructions to the greasers. Therefore Robert Millar was most probably an idler; when absent the fifth and sixth engineers could take over his duties. With this in mind, the testimony of Greaser Frederick William Scott about those engineers in charge makes absolute sense.

Deck Engineer Henry Philip Creese and Assistant Thomas Millar had been trained at Harland & Wolff and were familiar principally with many mechanical installations aboard. They were responsible for the steering engines and gear, but also the hoists and lifts, deck cranes and the gymnasium equipment. How they worked their hours is not known. Presumably they worked watch on, watch off so that one or other of them was always on hand for repairs.

Chief Electrician Peter Porter Sloan was assisted by Second Electrician Alfred Samuel Allsopp and the four Assistant Electricians Albert George Ervine, Boykett Herbert Jupe,

William P. Kelly and Alfred Pirrie Middleton. They were competent for all electrical installations aboard *Titanic*. More than 320km of cable ran through the ship, supplying power to countless electrical appliances such as the 10,000 light bulbs. They were also responsible for lifts and dumb waiters, heaters and fuses. Ervine wrote from Queenstown in a letter to his mother that he worked the 08:00–12:00 and 20:00–24:00hr turns. That would mean that the electricians worked three shifts, as did the engineers and firemen. The chief electrician would also stand his watch, of which there were three, each with two men.

The evidence given by Greaser Tom Ranger mentioned earlier indicates that up to the moment of impact Chief Electrician Sloan was in the electrical store on E-deck where they were both repairing ventilators. Ranger began his shift at 18:00hrs but there is nothing to say that the electricians did not have a shift change at 20:00hrs, as Ervine wrote. Thus Sloan and Ervine had the most pleasant shift, which allowed them to sleep from midnight to 08:00 hrs. Ervine also told his mother that when leaving Southampton he and his friend Middleton were watching the near-collision with the steamer *New York* from the top of the fourth funnel (which is an indication that the electricians had identical watches both when leaving port and at sea). Middleton was therefore also off watch, and since the 08:00–12:00hr watch is already completed, he must have been in the 04:00–08:00 and 16:00–20:00hr watch because in the third watch he would not have been able to watch from the fourth funnel. After the disaster, Boykett Herbert Jupe's father wrote a letter in which he described his son as 'Electrical Engineer No 3'. In fact, the oldest of the assistants would inscribe himself first in the hiring lists, bringing his experience from the *Olympic*. Presumably he was leader of the third watch and did not work together with Second Electrician Allsopp, who led his own watch. This leaves us with William P. Kelly, who was not a shift leader and was thus in the 12:00–16:00hr shift, and enables us to erect the following watch scheme for the electricians (in two variations):

Peter Porter Sloan and Albert George Ervine
08:00–12:00 and 20:00–24:00hrs

A. S. Allsopp or B. H. Jupe and Alfred Pirrie Middleton
04:00–08:00 and 16:00–20:00hrs

A. S. Allsopp or B. H. Jupe and William P. Kelly
00:00–04:00 and 12:00–16:00hrs

The mess stewards of the Engine Department formed a colony with the hands. The shipping companies knew from experience how important good and nourishing fare was for these men who did such heavy labour. The firemen's mess with eighty-seven seats and the greasers' small mess were located in the bow on C-deck. The word 'mess' is generally used to describe a refectory/lounge for ship's men.

The twenty-five main feeder switchboards before the installation on a gallery in the generator room. (Author's collection)

Additionally, the engineers had their own mess on E-deck. Mess Stewards Cecil William Fitzpatrick and George Gumery earned £3 15s, the same as most *Titanic* stewards. Fitzpatrick stated in a newspaper interview after the accident that he served in the engineers' mess. The food for these officers came from first and second class, being transported by a dumb waiter from the large kitchen one deck down into the pantry by the engineers' mess. Since the engineers worked around the clock, the two stewards might have arranged their shifts so that one of them would always be in the mess. Because serving the engineers was not directly a matter for the chief engineer, the two stewards probably took their instructions from the engineers' secretary responsible for the organisation of the Engine Department.

Of the six men hired for the Engine Department messes, two had the additional classification 'Mess Steward'. John Coleman earned £6, Stanley Blake £5. The steward's pay on the *Titanic* however was £3 15s irrespective of whether the steward served the captain or one of the three ship's classes. This noticeably higher remuneration is a clear indication that both of them were not stewards but cooks, similar to Thomas Knowles and Arthur William May (Sr) who each earned £6 as a 'firemen's messman'. The term 'mess steward' was as misleading for the Engine Department as it was for the Deck Department and actually meant 'crew cooks'. Cooking was done in a crew galley on the port side of C-deck together with the crew cooks of the Deck Department, Mathias and Tamlyn. A total of 280 hungry, heavy labourers arrived here around the clock, more than 300 if one counts in the seamen. It might be a fair guess that some kitchen assistants employed in first and second class also worked here, either directly or doing preparation in the main kitchen. How the watches were divided up is not known. The only indication appears in a letter written by Knowles' daughter, in which she states that her father, who survived the sinking, was not on duty at the time of the collision.

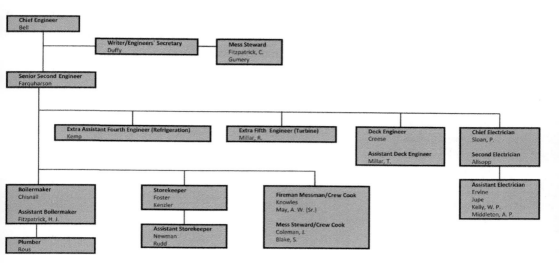

An overview of the crew members in the engine department with a special function. Included are the mess stewards, who served the meals in the engineer's mess, and the crew cooks, who worked together with those from the Deck Department. In the daily routine the extra assistant fourth engineer and the extra fifth engineer were probably led by the respective shift leaders in the engine room. (Diagram by author/Dominik Tezyk)

Near the engineers' mess pantry was the engineers' office, containing a bed where William Luke Duffy, secretary to Chief Engineer Bell, spent most of his time. The chief engineer had to render various reports daily to the captain and calculate the coal consumption. Duffy maintained for Bell numerous log books covering the various engines and aggregates: the temperatures in the engine and boiler rooms were noted several times per day. Additionally, he drew up repair lists for entering port. These requests came not only from the Engine Department, but also the Chief Steward.

Of these forty-five men who were mustered as the operations staff for the engines, only Crew Cook Thomas Knowles and Mess Steward Cecil William Fitzpatrick survived: neither testified later during the inquiries.

The Greasers

The engine installation of a ship was not an easy thing to replace, and therefore it was cared for so that it might give decades of service in impeccable condition. The greasers were hired to carry out the maintenance. All moving parts were cleaned and lubricated to reduce the heat of friction and protect the surfaces against corrosion. Naturally there were many parts that could be lubricated automatically so that only the oil sump needed to be refilled. On the other hand, the lubrication of the propeller shafts in the stern tubes required much attention. One greaser worked in the shaft tunnel and at least two in the engine rooms, where they also served the engine telegraphs. The greasers were also responsible for the maintenance of pumps, generators and the rudder unit. In the muster lists, greasers were divided up into three watches; the wage for greasers was £6 10s:

Watch 1, 8 men, 00:00–04:00 and 12:00–16:00hrs
Richard Baines
William Thomas Bott
Joseph Henry Couch
Thomas Joseph Fay
Joseph Jago
James Kirkham
Thomas Arthur McInerney
James Tozer

Watch 2, 18 men, 04:00–08:00 and 16:00–20:00hrs
Joseph Beattie
Albert Briant (M. Stafford)
Charles Eastman
Frederick Charles Godwin
Henry James Jukes
Charles Henry Kearl
Frederick Charles Kenchenten
A. Morris (Frank Arthur Briant)
Charles Olive
Thomas Henry M. Palles
George Albert Phillips
William James Pitfield
George Alexander Prangnell
Tom Ranger
Alfred Henry Self
Arthur Veal
Alfred Albert White
Frederick Ernest Woodford

Watch 3, 7 men 08:00–12:00 and 20:00–24:00hrs
John Joseph Bannon
Edward Castleman
Frank Goree
David Gregory
James Kelly
Richard Moores
Frederick William Scott

Greasers at work in a propeller shaft tunnel, c. 1908. (Author's collection)

A remark about Albert Briant and Frank Briant: They signed on for *Titanic* as Michael Stafford and Arthur Morris respectively but according to their descendants were brothers. Frank Briant is said to have taken the name of his stepfather. This cannot be confirmed by available historical documents nor ruled out.

The bulk of the greasers filled the second watch. A similar unequal distribution of the greasers to this watch was also the practice aboard *Olympic*. One assumes that the greasers had a supervisor for each shift. According to the deck plans there was a sleeping room for thirty greasers and one for four leading greasers. It would seem more reasonable, despite the divisions in the muster list, that the thirty-three greasers on the *Titanic* were made up of three groups each of one leading greaser and ten ordinary greasers. What then would account for the unequal watches? It is not contradictory that leading greasers were not identified as such and were mustered at the common rate of pay, for certain seamen also received fixed supplementary pay for special functions not set down in the hiring lists.

Greasers Tom Ranger and Frederick William Scott were questioned by the British Wreck Commissioner's Inquiry. Scott belonged to Watch 3 and was on duty at the time of the collision, which coincides with his statement. Ranger was in Watch 2 and was off-watch from 20:00 until 04:00hrs. Instead, he was on watch from 18:00hrs and at the time of the collision repairing ventilators with Chief Electrician Sloan.

On sailing ships it was the seamen who did the maintenance work. With the introduction of steam, specialists were required for the upkeep of the engines. It seems that the greasers were a kind of 'engine seamen' in that sense. Their rate of pay was higher than the firemen, they saw to the upkeep of the engines and carried out cleaning work and also other tasks that at first glance might not seem to be the job of a greaser.

The apparent imbalance of personnel within the three watches, Ranger's work outside the watch system and the knowledge that the greasers were 'the seamen of the engine room' leaves room for the following speculation. The seamen on deck were not only separated into the traditional port and starboard watches; some of them were employed as day hands, although hired as able-bodied seamen. Could this system have had its equivalent in the engine room? The greasers normally work in three shifts of seven or eight men. If one accepts that around ten men of the much larger 04:00–08:00 watch also worked below deck as day hands, this would have been ideal for the engine-room operating staff. Because the greasers in the three shifts saw to the maintenance of the installations, the day hands, amongst whom Ranger belonged, provide the perfect explanation for the various queries surrounding the greasers. The uncertainty about the dormitory for four leading greasers is solved by three watches while the fourth supervised the day hands. The greasers, like the seamen, had their own mess while the firemen and trimmers ate together in a large room.

For the day-hand variation there are only indirect pointers, but undocumented arrangements were nothing unusual on the *Titanic*. Since most crew men in the engine room had fixed jobs it seems sensible that a few men with a technical grasp for jobs outside the routine might have been seconded.

The accommodation for the greasers was on the starboard side in the very tip of the bow on G-deck, exactly where the *Titanic* collided with an iceberg. It is impossible that the greasers would have slept through it. The survival rate amongst the greasers was 12 per cent. Of the 00:00–04:00 watch, who were due to report a few minutes after the collision, nobody survived, and none of the bodies was ever recovered. According to their own statements, two of the four surviving greasers were working, the other two possibly as well, as they belonged to Watch 2 and were possibly day hands. It is very likely that on that night, the greasers' dormitory was the location where the first men lost their lives. Most of the bunks were against the outer hull wall. A slight buckling of the hull at the side by only a few centimetres could have jammed the narrow dormitory door and only exit, trapping the greasers who survived the collision. The portholes had a diameter of only 23cm, insufficient for a man to pass through. If the door had jammed, the greasers had only a few minutes until their accommodation filled with sea water. Help was hardly to be expected in that situation. This would explain the low survival rate of the greasers: of the thirty-three, only Prangnell, Ranger, Scott and White came though the sinking alive.

The Leading Firemen

The career ladder for unskilled workers in the Engine Department ended with the greasers and leading firemen. There was practically no possibility of promotion to engineer as at the outset of the steam age.

The leading firemen and the underlings led by them in the boiler rooms never came into contact with the first- and second-class passengers. The sleeping rooms, messes and workplaces were so arranged that such a meeting would be scarcely possible, and so the White Star Line issued no code of dress for these large groups. The climate in the boiler rooms made such regulations superfluous: the workers protected their bodies against burns and scalds by the use of long clothing.

Each boiler room had a leading fireman governing the firemen and trimmers, and two leading fireman would have one assistant engineer above them. Boiler room 1 was probably not in use during the maiden voyage of the *Titanic*. The boilers in rooms 2 to 6 were fired during the crossing, although in boiler room 2 the boilers were fired one after the other during the trip. The three-watch system was in operation in the boiler rooms: like most engineers, the firemen worked 4 hours on, 8 hours off.

Leading firemen, firemen and trimmers were allotted to a watch directly at hiring, the muster lists indicating whether this was the 00:00–04:00, 04:00–08:00 and 08:00–12:00hr shift. Five boiler rooms for three watches required fifteen leading firemen, but the lists had only thirteen. Who were the other two? The lists for the 00:00–04:00 and 08:00–12:00hr watches have five each, but there are only three in the 04:00–08:00hr watch. In all shifts the greasers signed up first, then leading firemen, firemen and finally the trimmers. In the second shift the greasers are followed by Leading Firemen Hendrickson, Mayo and Davies, then Firemen Norris and Graham. The name of each fireman was stamped 'Fireman', and 'Ldg' added in handwriting for leading firemen. The pay in the latter case was £6 10s, 10s more than an ordinary fireman. For Norris and Graham, however, the additional prefix was struck out and replaced by something illegible.

In the list transcripts it was thought that these men were ordinary firemen. Since no correction appeared in any other entry in the firemen's muster rolls and without Graham and Norris the 04:00–08:00hr shift would be two leading firemen short, it seems likely that, despite the crossing-out of 'Ldg', both completed as leading firemen. A further indication is that Graham, who survived the sinking, should have signed the paying-off list, as did all crew survivors, but the signature is missing from his line, as is the outstanding pay, showing that it was necessary to clarify what his shipboard function actually had been. The 08:00–12:00hr watch lists were also corrected: initially six leading firemen had been listed, Thomas Henry Blake was then revised down to ordinary fireman.

Leading firemen all received a wage of £6 10s. They worked as follows:

Watch 1, 00:00–04:00 and 12:00–16:00hrs
Thomas Henry Ford
James Keegan
William Small
Thomas Threlfall
Francis Albert Webber

Watch 2, 04:00–08:00 and 16:00–20:00hrs
Thomas Davies
Thomas G. Graham
Charles Oscar Hendrickson
William Peter Mayo
James Edward Norris

Watch 3, 08:00–12:00 and 20:00–24:00hrs
Frederick W. Barrett
William Ferris
J. Mason
Arthur Percy Pugh
James William Ward

How the leading fireman were divided up between the boiler rooms is not recorded. All that is known is that Frederick Barrett was working in boiler room 6 at the time of the collision, William Ferris in boiler room 2. Besides Barrett, Graham, Hendrickson and Threlfall survived the collision.

The Firemen

The largest trade group on *Titanic*, and who actually did the same job constantly, was the firemen, who numbered 159 (if Leading Firemen Graham and Norris are not counted with them). The pay, £6, seems relatively good for a worker in those days. Only with this financial inducement would it have been possible to find people to do this strenuous work. The work consisted of shovelling coal into the boiler furnaces under the instructions of engineers and leading firemen, and with an eye to the automatic indicators.

The twenty-nine boilers of *Titanic* had 159 furnaces, apparently one per each fireman (but plus John Coffey, who signed on and then deserted at Queenstown), and therefore the numerical agreement is coincidence. Since the firemen worked in three shifts, each man must have been responsible for three fire holes, which was one side of a double-ended boiler. As boiler room 1 was not in use, however, the precise distribution does not have a simple arithmetical solution. Like the leading firemen, the ordinary firemen were mustered into three watches. As some firemen did not report aboard *Titanic* in time, they were replaced at short notice by the following seven men; to which watches these were assigned can no longer be established:

David Black
Joseph Brown
Alfred Ernest Geer
Richard William Hosgood
Louis Kinsella
William Lloyd
Henry Dennis Witt

The other 152 firemen were spread over three watches at signing on, presumably most of the foregoing seven substitutes went to the Watch 3 with the lowest complement.

Boiler room on board *Aquitania* with a fireman on the left and a trimmer with his barrow on the right. There are no known photographs of such rooms taken on board an *Olympic*-class steamer. (Author's collection)

Each watch had a large dormitory in the bow. The 00:00–04:00hr watch slept on F–deck, the 04:00–08:00hr watch on D–deck starboard side and the 08:00–12:00hr watch on the portside:

Watch 1, 52 men, 00:00–04:00 and 12:00–16:00hrs

Henry Allen	William John Hodges
Robert Barnhouse (Charles Barnes)	Walter Hurst
Frank Bendell	Charles Edward Judd
George Alfred Bennett	Fredrik Kasper
Edward Benville	Thomas Kerr
William Edward L. Bessant	Christopher William Light
Albert Edward Blackman	William James Major
John Alfred Brown	Frank Archibald Robert Mason
Arthur Peel Burroughs	William Mintram
Edward John Burton	Thomas A. Morgan
John Canner	William John Murdoch
William Clark	Henry Noss
Samuel J. Collins	Harry Oliver
William Alfred Cross	Frank Painter
Arthur Curtis	John Pearce
Frederick Olive Doel	George Pond
Laurence Doyle	Arthur John Priest
Frank Dymond	Joseph James Richards
Edward Flarty	Charles Edward Sangster
George Auguste Godley	George Charles Snellgrove
George Alexander Hallett	James Henry Stubbs

J. (or T.) Taylor
James Taylor
William Henry Taylor
John William Thompson
George Terrill Thresher

Henry Harry Vear
William Vear
Fred Albert Wardner
Albert Ernest Witcher

Watch 2, 52 men, 04:00–08:00 and 16:00–20:00hrs

William Thomas Abrams
John Barnes
James Blaney
Patrick Bradley
William John Butt
George Combes
Albert Harry Copperthwaite
Robert Frderick W. Couper
John Henry E. Diaper
John Arthur Christopher Dilley
Ernest Edward Gradidge
John Haggan
George Herbert Hannam
Edward John Harris
Alfred Charles Head
Roland Hopgood
John Henry Jackopson
Thomas James
N. Joas
W. Light
Charles William Lindsay
Frederick Charles Marsh
Thomas Jubilee Mayzes
William Airley McAndrews
Erroll Victor McGaw
John William Moore

George Walter Nettleton
William Nutbean
Charles Alfred Othen
Richard Charles John Paice
Charles Frederick Painter
Alfred John Alexander Podesta
William Robert H. Pusey
Frederick Ernest Reeves
George Albert D. Rickman
Sidney Frank Rutter
Albert Charles Edward Self
Harry Senior
Alfred Charles Shiers
Harry James Smither
Henry William Sparkman
Augustus George Stanbrook
John Henry Taylor
Joseph Waitfield Thomas
Ernest Arthur Tizard
Robert William Triggs
Wessel Adrianus van der Brugge
Edward Lewis Wateridge
William Watson
William Henry Worthman (Jarvis)
James Robert Wyeth
Francis James Young

Watch 3, 48 men, 08:00–12:00 and 20:00–24:00hrs

Robert John Adams
George Frank W. Bailey
Charles Henry Barlow
Frederick William Barrett
George William Beauchamp
Reginald Arthur Charles
   Biddlecombe
Edward Charles Biggs

Alexander Black
Thomas Henry Blake
Eustace Horatius Blann
James Carter
William Victor Cherrett
John Henry Chorley
Henry William Cooper
Denis Corcoran

A stoker at work under the watchful eye of an engineer on board an unknown steamer, around 1912. (Author's collection)

James Crimmins
Bernard William Cunningham
J. Fraser
William Lewis Golder
J. Hall
Bernard Hands
Frederick Harris
James Hart
Thomas Hunt
Charles John Hurst
Thomas Instance
George Kemish
Thomas Louis Lally
George John Marett
Arthur William May (Jr)
Thomas Patrick McAndrew
W. McCastlan

William McQuillan
William Alexander McRae
George Milford
John Brown Niven (McGregor)
John Thomas Noon
Bertram Arthur Noss
Philip Raymond (S. Sullivan)
Charles Rice
Robert George Roberts
Frank Joseph Saunders
Walter Ernest Saunders
Archibald Scott
Thomas Shea
Thomas Albert Street
Richard Turley
Samuel Solomon Williams

Surviving stokers from the *Titanic* at the Seamen's Friend Society in New York. (Ioannis Georgiou collection)

Fireman William Henry Worthman adopted the surname of his stepfather following his mother's remarriage, and therefore he appears in the lists as Jarvis. Often James Hart is considered to be Thomas Hart, but Thomas Hart, who was not aboard, only used the sinking of the *Titanic* as a means of explaining the loss of his seaman's book. It is not known why John Brown Niven signed on using the alias J. McGregor. S. Sullivan's mother was Janetta Raymond; presumably he was born as Philip Raymond, but the reason he used the name Sullivan cannot be ascertained.

Forty-three of the 159 firemen survived, therefore about 27 per cent. Of the men who were on watch at the time of the collision, only six survived (12.5 per cent).

The Trimmers

Low down in the hierarchy were the trimmers who, for a wage of £5 10s monthly, fetched from the bunkers the large blocks of pit-coal weighing up to 40kg, broke them down into manageable lumps and carted them to the firemen. Though it sounds simple, the work was hard and dangerous in temperatures of up to 50°C (122°F). Just to get at the blocks of coal in the suffocating, dusty air was a challenge. The coal was stacked metres high in the bunkers. Careless removal of one block could set off a landslide.

The trimmers were also assigned to one of three shifts on signing-on; there is no information as to the watches of the following five substitutes:

Alfred Cotton
William Dickson
John Dowie Gordon

John O'Connor
Robert Steel

Otherwise, the three watches were staffed as follows:

Watch 1, 24 men, 00:00–04:00 and 12:00–16:00hrs

Ernest Allen
James Albert Avery
Percival Albert Blake
Richard Stephen Carr
Thomas Casey
James Cooper
Henry James Crabb
Joseph Dawson
Everett Edward Elliott
William Robert Evans
Walter Francis Fredericks
Sidney Gosling

George Green
James Haslin
William Stephen Hinton
George Ingram
William Long
James McGann
George William McIntyre
George Pelham
Edgar Lionel Perry
Thomas Charles Alfred Preston
Eustace Philip Snow
William George White

Watch 2, 22 men, 04:00–08:00 and 16:00–20:00hrs

James Billows
Walter William Binstead
Hugh Calderwood
Alfred James Jacob Eagle
H. Ford
Amos Fred Harris
Albert William Hebb
James Hill
Sylvanus Alfred Hunt
George Edward Kearl
Frank Long

Lorenzo Horace Mitchell
Ralph William Moore
William Morris
Frederick Robert Sheath
Charles Frederick Shillabeer
William Frederick Skeates
W. Snooks
Henry Dorey Stocker
S. Webb
William Francis Witts
Henry Wood

Watch 3, 22 men, 08:00–12:00 and 20:00–24:00hrs

Joseph Henry Bevis
Matthew Henry Brewer
Sidney Brooks
George Henry Cavell
Harry Coe
Thomas Patrick Dillon
Albert James Dore

Antonio Ferrary
Albert Ernest Fryer
Bertram James Gosling
Henry Thomas Lee
Leopold Adolphus L. Maskell
Arthur Herbert Morgan
Ronald Samuel Morrell/Morrill

Henry F. L. Perry   W. Saunders
Ricard Royston Proudfoot   Ernest Harry Smith
Joseph Alfred Read   Frank Leonard White
Robert Thomas Reid   William Wilton

After these long lists of names of firemen and trimmers one naturally wonders how these were split down into groups. Forty-four of the 159 firemen and twenty of the seventy-three trimmers survived, but there are too few statements that, apart from individual cases, suggest the arrangement in the various boiler rooms. Also, the lighting of additional boilers during the voyage makes it impossible to analyse the split into the rooms. Per shift there were three assistant engineers, five leading firemen, forty-eight ordinary firemen and twenty trimmers in the boiler rooms. That can be made out from the evidence given to John Simon, solicitor-general at the British Wreck Commissioner's Inquiry, by Leading Fireman Frederick W. Barrett:

Simon (1851):   How many firemen or stokers are there in a watch working with you in No 6?
Barrett: There are eight firemen in No 6 section and four coal trimmers. That is what they call the men who wheel the coal.
Simon (1852):   And yourself as well?
Barrett: Yes, and an engineer.

There were only four boilers in boiler room 6 because that was where the ship's hull began to narrow towards the bow. The four boilers could be coaled from both sides, and were called double-ended boilers. One fireman was responsible for every eight boiler ends, therefore for every three fires. The four trimmers brought coal for the eight firemen.

Boiler rooms 2 to 5 had five boilers each, all of which could be coaled from both sides and so were the workplace for ten firemen each. Together with those from boiler room 6 that makes forty-eight men. The additional boiler in rooms 2 to 5 does not mean there was another trimmer, there were not enough aboard. Trimmer George Henry Cavell confirmed to John Simon at the British inquiry:

Simon (4186):   Were you one of the regular trimmers for No. 4 right through the trip?
Cavell: Yes.
Simon (4187):   How many coal bunkers are there in No. 4 section?
Cavell: There are six doors and four bunkers.
Simon (4188):   Two on the starboard side and two on the port side?
Cavell: Yes.
Simon (4189):   And six doors?
Cavell: Yes.

Simon (4190):	How many trimmers are there to a section?
Cavell:	Four trimmers to a section.
Simon (4191):	So that you would have three mates with you?
Cavell:	Yes.

Five rooms with four men each is twenty trimmers per watch. For the three watches, sixty of the seventy-three trimmers were working and 144 of the 159 firemen. Therefore, fifteen firemen and thirteen trimmers did not fit into the watch scheme.

As various ovens for the shipboard kitchens had to be fired, some men were probably not working in the boiler rooms but in the kitchen area. The bunkers for the first- and second-class kitchen could hold more than 50 tons of coal.

Men without a predetermined workplace in a boiler room had to be ready to fill the gap should a colleague be injured. Every day, up to twenty firemen and trimmers went to the surgeon with burns, sprains or other injuries. At the doctor's consultation in the mornings the surgeon had to be alert and not issue a sick note to too many malingerers. During a round trip it was not unusual to re-distribute the jobs, as, according to requirements and conduct, even at sea there could be promotions and demotions in the boiler rooms.

The question of how many boilers were lit was answered by Leading Fireman Barrett at the British inquiry. According to him (answer 2203), for the first two days there were twenty of the twenty-nine boilers lit, twenty-one on days three and four. On the morning of 14 April another three were lit, but Barrett was uncertain if they were connected to the engines. Fireman Alfred Charles Shiers remembered at the Limitation of Liability Hearings in October 1913 that these boilers were connected at 19:00hrs.

The technically simpler single-ended boilers in boiler room 1 were not lit prior to the collision. They would have been serviced probably without the need for a leading fireman: the dormitory for the leading firemen had only fifteen beds, therefore one each for the leading firemen of five boiler rooms. Boiler room 1 would then have needed fifteen fireman and six trimmers over the three shifts, presumably led by a junior engineer who was responsible for boiler rooms 1 and 2. The crew would have been sufficient for full steam, and there were another seven trimmers without a fixed watch for the kitchens.

It should not be forgotten that during most of the maiden voyage of the *Titanic* the crew was obliged to fight a slow-burning fire in a coal bunker of boiler room 5. According to reports, up to twelve men were involved in attempting to bring this fire under control, to cool the coal and bring it away to the furnaces in various boiler rooms. This had an effect on the crew numbers in several boiler rooms.

The trimmers had a dormitory for each watch in the bow on E-deck, and they shared the mess with the firemen.

Twenty of the trimmers of a total of seventy-three survived (27.4 per cent). Like the firemen, the trimmers who were on watch at the moment of the collision had a much lower survival rate, 18.2 per cent. In contrast to that stands the survival rate of those intended to go on watch, at 41.7 per cent. A survey of the various survival rates can be found on page 155 and 156.

7

THE VICTUALLING DEPARTMENT – FIRST CLASS

With 495 crew members, according to the muster list, the Victualling Department formed the largest group aboard *Titanic*. Attending to the passengers in the three ship's classes and the crew itself meant an enormous expense in time and energy. The *Titanic* could accommodate 3,547 persons: 2,208 were on board for the maiden voyage. With so many people living, working, sleeping and being fed in such a confined space it is clear that the logistic master planning began with the design of the ship. The streams of people were organised aboard with great skill. In the corridor and stairway systems of the various classes and crew, people often lived close to each other without ever coming face to face. A goods lift delivered supplies of provisions from the stock rooms into the kitchen, while smaller lifts forwarded cooked meals from the shipboard kitchens and past the passenger cabins unnoticed into the deck officers' or engineers' mess.

The eight musicians and five post-office clerks must be added to the 495 crew members of the Victualling Department, but not the mess stewards nor crew cooks who were left in their corresponding sections. As mentioned earlier in this book, the hospital steward, captain's steward and the two radio operators were attached to the Deck Department. If one deducts these four and adds the musicians and postal clerks, then the Victualling Department had 504 crew members for assignments.

Ninety-seven of these 504 persons survived, around 19.2 per cent. The boards of inquiry considered them to be of little interest and only a few were interrogated. Therefore it is not surprising that large gaps exist in our knowledge about the department. Some of the following organisational arrangement is based on assumptions but should be understandable. The command structure seems to have been a rather steep one. That means that, apart from personnel-intensive groups such as saloon stewards, a leader had only a relatively small number of workers under his control. An example is the purser's office. Naturally all clerks, bell boy stewards, the telephone steward and the stenographer came under the purser, but in the daily routine there was little point in having the bell boys directly answerable to the purser, and so the clerks were their immediate superiors. The enquiry office was not far from the workplace of the telephone steward; nevertheless, in practice neither did he come under the purser, since the latter's duties took him all over the ship, whereas the clerks were always present.

As the organisation of this majority of the *Titanic* crew stretched across all three classes of the ship and the crew, it is very complex. For this reason each has been given its own chapter and sub-chapters. At the head of the Victualling Department was the purser. On *Titanic* this was Hugh Walter McElroy. He received £20 monthly; only a handful of men aboard earned more. McElroy had an interior cabin a few paces from his office.

All threads led to the purser: every crew member (also from the Deck Department and Engine Department) would hand him his discharge book for his employment to be confirmed. The purser ran the cashier's office and paid the crew their hire. The passengers entrusted him not only with their valuables for safekeeping in the purser's safe, but also with all kinds of personal matters. As did the captain and surgeon, in the dining saloon he represented the White Star Line at his own table, the purser's table. The purser also administered the alcoholic drink aboard: if the bars had to be restocked, all roads led to him – only he had the key for the storerooms containing the alcohol. Without doubt he had the best viewpoint over the crew, passengers and freight, and his report would have been the best possible help for this book, but McElroy did not survive the disaster. In general little information has come down regarding the work of the purser. Charles T. Spedding, a friend of McElroy and purser of the *Caronia* at the time when *Titanic* went down, unfortunately ended his biography with the sentence: 'I have made no attempt to describe life generally on board ship, for whatever I wrote would be of no interest to the old traveller, and the first voyager would find when he got on board that things were quite different to what he expected.'

In addition to the captain, the *Titanic's* passenger list only introduced the two doctors, the pursers and the chief steward to the passengers. Interestingly both pursers were mentioned in the list, even though Reginald Lomond Barker would rarely have been in first class. The reason for this was that the upper half of this page was set for both first and second class, the printers only exchanged 'First' against 'Second'. Therefore, in the second class the wrong chief steward was listed. (Author's collection)

FIRST CLASS PASSENGER LIST

PER

ROYAL AND U.S. MAIL

S.S. "Titanic,"

FROM SOUTHAMPTON AND CHERBOURG
TO NEW YORK
(Via QUEENSTOWN).

Wednesday, 10th April, 1912.

Captain, E. J. Smith, R.D. (Commr. R.N.R.).
Surgeon, W. F. N. O'Loughlin.
Asst. Surgeon, J. E. Simpson.   Pursers { H. W. McElroy
                          { R. L. Barker.
Chief Steward, A. Latimer.

Besides McElroy there was a second purser, Reginald Lomond Barker, who kept McElroy's back free and had responsibility for the second and third class; his work will be explained with the second class. The Chief Steward of first class, Andrew J. Latimer, headed the enormous division of stewards and the Chef Charles Proctor also had a large empire to control. These sections will also be described later.

Although this division was mainly responsible for the service, these crew members also had a responsibility for shipboard security. They were the first people for the passengers to approach on matters of security and supplied information. They enforced no-smoking regulations and ensured that passengers did not leave the areas permitted to them. In case of emergency it was their responsibility to fight against a fire, make sure that passengers appeared on deck wearing lifejackets, that portholes were closed and manually operated bulkhead doors were shut.

All Victualling Department stewards had the same basic uniform (of coarser material for third class) and wore a pin with a number for identification purposes, for example in the case of a complaint. Stewards having a special function had the corresponding insignia sewn to the collar with gold thread. Further information about the variety of uniforms can be found in Appendix A.

The Purser's Office

Together with the captain, a ship's purser probably had the most important position aboard. He had to know the whole ship and its crew and have an answer for every question, or at least know who might be able to provide an answer. He discussed the menu plan daily with the cooks and arranged the list of requirements for the storekeepers. He had representative obligations in the dining saloon – he sought passengers in first class for his table. If the captain was unable to get away, then he held Sunday prayers in first class. For possible emergencies he collaborated with the first officer in drawing up lists for the lifeboats. McElroy could not possibly do all this work alone. He had a whole staff of

co-workers to see to every imaginable passenger need, keep the ledgers of account, pay seamen's hire, make the entries in the seamen's discharge books and prepare the paperwork for the shipping company and the authorities (such as the bills of lading and customs declarations) at the destination. This staff was composed as follows:

Purser Hugh Walter McElroy was one of the most important men on board the *Titanic*. He was responsible for ensuring that all passengers had valid tickets, was in charge of all purchases for a trip, paid the wages to the crew and was the contact point for all kinds of requests. (Author's collection)

Hugh Walter McElroy	£20	Purser
Austin Aloysius Ashcroft	£5	Clerk
Ernest Waldron King	£5	Clerk
John Reginald Rice	£5	Clerk
Abraham Mansoor Mishellany	£6	Printer Steward
Ernest Theodore Corben	£4	Assistant Printer Steward
George Frederick Turner	£4 10s	Stenographer
Lawrence Alexander Perkins	£3 15s	Telephone Steward
Arthur Barratt Jr	£2	Bell Boy Steward
Clifford Henry Harris	£2	Bell Boy Steward
William Albert Watson	£2	Bell Boy Steward

The three clerks were McElroy's representatives in the first-class enquiry office on C-deck and handled all kinds of passenger requests. On sailing day they distributed post and telegrams to the passengers: they hired out deckchairs and woollen blankets, sold railway

The purser's desk was the contact point for all kinds of enquiries, like finding a place on the ship, helping with the immigration formalities, sending telegrams or exchanging money. In the office a secretary can be seen and on the right are two bell boys. This photograph was taken on board *Olympic* around 1925. (Author's collection)

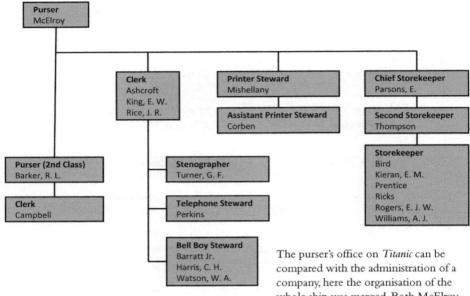

Purser
McElroy

Clerk
Ashcroft
King, E. W.
Rice, J. R.

Printer Steward
Mishellany

Assistant Printer Steward
Corben

Chief Storekeeper
Parsons, E.

Second Storekeeper
Thompson

Purser (2nd Class)
Barker, R. L.

Clerk
Campbell

Stenographer
Turner, G. F.

Telephone Steward
Perkins

Storekeeper
Bird
Kieran, E. M.
Prentice
Ricks
Rogers, E. J. W.
Williams, A. J.

Bell Boy Steward
Barratt Jr.
Harris, C. H.
Watson, W. A.

The purser's office on *Titanic* can be compared with the administration of a company, here the organisation of the whole ship was merged. Both McElroy and Barker were hired as pursers, but Barker with considerably lower pay, because he was only responsible for second and third class. (Diagram by author/Dominik Tezyk)

Olympic's switchboard before its installation on board. With the telephone switchboard, Telephone Steward Lawrence Alexander Perkins could connect fifty telephones on board and seven calls were possible at the same time. (Author's collection)

tickets, postcards with stamps and recorded passengers' complaints. The office also kept passengers' valuables in the safe and acted as a bureau de change, carrying out transactions in US dollars, pounds sterling, French francs and German marks. Invoices for services rendered aboard could be settled in these currencies or with travellers' cheques at the end of the voyage. To avoid having the clerks absent themselves from the office in pursuit of enquiries, the three bell-boy stewards held themselves at readiness to run messages.

Stenographer George Frederick Turner must also have worked mainly in the enquiry office. For a fee, passengers could dictate a letter to him for typing. Presumably, like the telephone steward, he came under the auspices of the clerks. The switchboard worked by Telephone Steward Lawrence Alexander Perkins was located a few metres from the lifts on C-deck. His drop-flap exchange had lines to fifty shipboard telephones. These were installed in the most important centres such as the restaurant, Turkish bath, the smoke room and bakery, but also with the men with key positions such as the surgeon, the senior officers, pursers, chief steward or the chef. Perkins could have up to seven lines connected at a time. Independent of the switchboard, there were numerous fixed connections aboard between one phone and another that did not require the intervention of Perkins. The switchboard was only manned by day. On the night of the disaster this may have had an adverse effect on communications.

Printer Steward Abraham Mansoor Mishellany and his assistant Ernest Theodore Corben carried out printing work for the two pursers' offices, the chief stewards and the chef.

The printing shop on a North German Lloyd steamer, around 1910. In the foreground is the printing machine, and in the background the texts were set. The two printers on *Titanic* produced menus, passenger lists, programmes, tickets, etc. It is uncertain if they also printed a daily newspaper with news received via wireless – on *Olympic* this service was introduced in July 1912. (Author's collection)

Beside the passenger lists for first and second class and menus for all three ship classes, during a voyage there were sometimes competitions or concerts being canvassed. The bedroom stewards would have special passenger lists printed with the cabin numbers. An innovation aboard *Olympic* in the summer of 1912 was a daily edition of the *Ocean Times*, drafted from telegraphed despatches. They were added into the pre-printed magazines. Whether or not the *Titanic* offered this service on her maiden voyage is not recorded. The print room was located near the second-class pantry on D-deck.

There follow the various office holders of the first-class stewards' department. The other classes will be described later.

The Storekeepers

The *Titanic* transported huge quantities of food for consumption and as freight. Eight storekeepers reported to the purser. They were responsible for storing goods at the correct temperature and humidity, and supplied the kitchens and bakeries. The delivery of foodstuffs was carried out using a goods lift, which connected the food stores on the Orlop- and G-deck (as well as the potato store on E-deck) with the main kitchen on D-deck. The third-class kitchen and crew galley were supplied over the E-deck passages and staircase. Frank Winnold Prentice was the only survivor of the following:

Edward Parsons	£6	Chief Storekeeper
Herbert Henry Thompson	£4 5s	Second Storekeeper
Charles Frederick Bird (Morgan)	£3 15s	Storekeeper
Edgar Michael Kieran	£3 15s	Storekeeper
Frank Winnold Prentice	£3 15s	Storekeeper

Storage of tinned food on board a North German Lloyd steamer, around 1910. (Author's collection)

Cyril Gordon Ricks	£3 15s	Storekeeper
Edward James William Rogers	£3 15s	Storekeeper
Arthur John Williams	£3 15s	Storekeeper

The Chief Stewards

The most important man at the side of purser McElroy was Chief Steward Andrew J. Latimer. His pay was £20 and he was responsible for all stewards in first class. Second and third class had their own chief stewards. Latimer's representatives were George Charles Dodd, the chief steward and his two assistants William Thomas Hughes and Joseph Thomas Wheat.

Andrew J. Latimer	£20	Chief Steward
George Charles Dodd	£10	Second Steward
William Thomas Hughes	£8	Assistant Second Steward
Joseph Thomas Wheat	£8	Assistant Second Steward
Edward Bessant	£4	Baggage Steward

The second steward had responsibility for the baggage aboard White Star Liners. Aboard *Titanic* this was George Charles Dodd, assisted by Baggage Steward Edward Bessant, who was slightly better paid than most stewards, with £4. In port he was responsible for loading baggage into the freight room and for unloading – a logistic master performance on such

Fifty-five-year-old First Class Chief Steward Andrew L. Latimer was a victualler and hotel proprietor before he joined the Dominion Line and, later, White Star Line. He was the only steward who had on his cap the White Star Line badge – all other stewards had an enamel white star instead. (Whitfield/Rigby collection)

Towards the end of the voyage and in good weather the baggage of the passengers was prepared on the forward well deck. This photograph was taken on board the *Olympic*, around 1921. (Author's collection)

In bad weather the baggage was prepared on the promenade deck of the *Olympic, c.* 1922. (Author's collection)

a large ship. Dodd and Bessant would also have organised the other stewards to fetch and carry luggage to and from the cabins. Undoubtedly during the voyage passengers would be sure to request a bag or suitcase from the freight room. Additionally, it was possible to have the White Star Line accept luggage for safekeeping ashore.

The table arrangement in the dining saloon was also handled by the second steward and his assistants with regard to passengers' wishes – and also the wishes of the captain, purser and surgeon, who each ate at their own table with invited passengers. The large table at the centre of the dining saloon was the captain's table; the surgeon and purser probably had the two large oval tables port and starboard. The second steward also noted requests for meals outside the set dining hours or to be served in a passenger's cabin. The chief steward and second steward had their own office adjacent to the first-class pantry where they worked on passenger requests and organised the crew.

Of the men listed on page 87, the only survivor was Wheat, who testified before the British Wreck Commissioner's Inquiry. Understandably his main evidence was information about the sinking, and he turned out to be an important witness to the stages as the ship settled and the flooding. One might have hoped for his precise statements as to the organisation of the stewards, but he was not asked.

The chief stewards were in charge of the two large groups of saloon and bedroom stewards and numerous stewards with special tasks. The two large groups will be looked at first.

The Saloon Stewards

First, a short explanation of the word 'steward', which was very all-purpose aboard ships. In general it meant a trained worker in service, a crew member who performed a service function that was more or less precisely defined. Despite being all 'stewards', many accomplished very different tasks.

The dining rooms of the *Olympic* (seen here) and the *Titanic* were the largest-sized rooms of their time at sea. Up to 554 passengers could be served at once. On her maiden voyage 324 passengers travelled on the *Titanic* in first class, they were served by a total of ninety-four saloon stewards. (Author's collection)

In the dining saloon, breakfast was served between 08:00 and 10:00hrs, lunch at 13:00hrs and dinner at 19:00hrs. Lights were turned off at 23:00hrs. The saloon stewards were present in the dining saloon about 1 hour before and after each meal. After the first meal, with rather random seating, the passengers were served from their second meal onward by the same steward, always at the same table. The chief stewards were in attendance at mealtimes to ensure that all passed off smoothly. Outside regular hours three men were competent for preparations and supervision of the saloon stewards:

William Stephen Moss	£6	First Saloon Steward
William Burke	£4 10s	Second Saloon Steward
Alfred James Goshawk	£4	Third Saloon Steward

William Stephen Moss appeared on the muster list just as 'Saloon Steward', the 'First' was added for clarification, since the salary gave away his position. Burke survived the sinking and told the US Senate Inquiry (page 821) that he was responsible for the forward starboard-side section of the dining saloon, where he served Isidor and Ida Strauss exclusively. Presumably these prominent guests became his charge as an experienced waiter, but at the same time he also had to keep an eye on the saloon stewards in his section. Burke's mention of his

The first meal ever served on *Titanic* for regular passengers was captured by Francis Browne in this photograph during the luncheon on 10 April 1912. (The Irish Picture Library/Father FM Browne SJ Collection)

competence for the forward starboard side leads one to think that the dining saloon was divided up into four large areas; the fifth was the central section with the captain's table. From that one may infer that the three leading saloon stewards were each in charge of an area of their own, and the second steward's two assistants covered the other two.

Passengers could have debited to a so-called 'Wine Bill' all drinks that they consumed in the saloon. On the last evening before arrival the steward would then present his passengers with their total account.

According to the muster list, ninety-six stewards were hired to attend to the passengers in first class; to make this duty clear they were called 'saloon stewards'. Five of these did not work in the saloon but acted as night watchmen on the various decks. Of these five, only James Johnston and probably James Adamson Toshack have been identified, possibly Herbert Cave as well. The other two are not known; therefore, two names on the following list of ninety-three stewards belong to the night watchmen. Unfortunately the muster lists do not provide the information as to whether a saloon steward was a waiter or an assistant waiter, but it can be assumed that they worked in pairs.

All saloon stewards were hired at a monthly rate of £3 15s:

Percy Snowden Ahier	George Frederick Crowe
Frank Richard Allsop	Alfred Arnold Deeble
Allen Mardon Baggott	Alfred Henry Derrett
Edward Henry Bagley	Percival Stainer Deslandes
Ernest Thomas Barker	James Richard Dinenage
Arthur William Barringer	William Henry Dyer
William Barrows	George Russell Evans
Edwin Alfred Best	Henry Charles Fairall
Bernard John Boughton	Aragõa Drummond Harrison
John Boyd	Frederick Hartnell
John Henry Boyes	Edward Martin Hendy
Harry Bristow	Leonard James Hoare
Edward Brown	William Robert Henry House
Walter James Brown	Arthur Albert Howell
Ewart Sydenham Burr	Victor Reginald Jones
Robert Henry Butt	Percy Edward Keen
John Butterworth	Harry Ketchley
James Edward Cartwright	William Ford Kingscote
Charles Casswill	Arthur Alfred Kitching
William Frederick Cheverton	George Knight
Albert Edwin Coleman	William Lake
Gilbert William Cook	Albert Edward Lane
Frederick Horace Crafter	Arthur Lawrance
Albert Hector Crisp	Paul Georges Lefebvre

Alexander James Littlejohn
Humphrey Lloyd
William Watson Lucas
Charles Lydiatt
James McGrady
Charles Donald McKay
Arthur McMicken
John Richard McMullin
Arthur Mellor
S. Nicholls
Walter Hayward Orpet
William Henry Osborne
Hubert Prouse Perriton
Charles William Pryce
John Edward Puzey
James Ransom
Frederick Dent Ray
William James Francis Revell
Gilbert Rimmer
James William Robinson
Edgar Maurice Rowe
William Ernest Saunders
John Joseph Shea

Frederick Charles Simmons
Edward Skinner
John Smillie
Reginald George Smith
John Henry Stagg
Harry John Stroud
John Herbert Strugnell
John Crane Symonds
William John Taylor
Albert Charles Thomas
Benjamin James Thomas
Fred Toms
Leopold Olorenshaw Turner
Thomas Henry Edom Veal
William Ward
Tom Warwick
Thomas Herbert Weatherston
Edneser Edward Wheelton
Leonard Lisle Oliver White
Thomas Arthur Whiteley
Henry Frederick C. Wormald
Harry Yearsley

There were in total ninety-one stewards and three leading saloon stewards responsible for the service of 324 passengers in the dining room. As numerous passengers occasionally ate in the à-la-carte restaurant (and were therefore absent from the dining saloon), one may judge how attentive the waiters in first class must have been. Survivor Aragõa Drummond Harrison told a newspaper reporter that he worked in the smoke room on the night of the sinking. Obviously the saloon stewards helped as needed by the other gastronomic stewards. Of the saloon stewards, nineteen survived the sinking.

The Bedroom Stewards

The second large group of stewards in first class were the thirty-five cabin stewards, or bedroom stewards, as they were called in the muster list. The first listed steward on *Olympic* was marked as 'chief', without extra pay. No one was marked as 'chief' on *Titanic*, but if it had been the first, then John Poole Penrose would have been the leader, otherwise they reported to the chief steward and his assistants. Each bedroom steward was arithmetically

The port pantry of first class on the *Olympic* in 1911. Here the saloon stewards picked up the hot meals ordered by the passengers – the bains-marie (water baths) and hotplates kept them warm. The stewards filled hot drinks themselves into the pots hanging from the ceiling. (Author's collection)

responsible for 11.4 cabins and 24.5 passengers if the ship was fully booked, but on the maiden voyage only for 9.3 passengers inhabiting five to six cabins. The stewards literally read the desires of the passengers from the look in their eyes, and were as good as butlers. In addition, they kept an eye on all cabins, day and night, since no keys were given to the passengers.

Titanic's stewards used vacuum cleaners in various sizes to clean the cabins – a novelty in 1912. As part of the service, they also brought hot water to the cabins in the evenings and whenever requested by passengers. Additionally, each section had a small pantry. Cabins and bathrooms were all equipped with a bell to summon a steward: the call would appear on one of two mechanical boards (one for each side of the ship) in every pantry, indicating who had rung. Shoes were cleaned free of charge: the passenger left them outside the cabin door for the steward to collect. If a passenger preferred to take a meal in the cabin instead of the dining saloon, it would be brought by the bedroom steward. It was customary aboard passenger ships for a steward to be assigned to a fixed block of cabins. In contrast to hotels ashore, guests and bedroom stewards had a more personal relationship. It is noticeable how both sides then (and now) would speak of 'my steward' and 'my passengers' respectively. It was a temporary household arrangement founded on mutual interest. On top of the passenger cabins they looked after the cabins of the higher-ranking crew members, including the doctors, purser or restaurant manager.

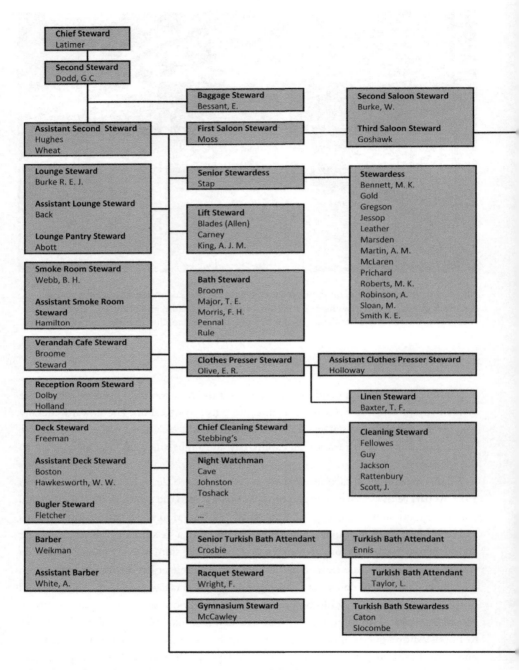

An overview of the first-class steward's department. Of the five night watchmen only three are known by name, two other saloon stewards belonged to them. The hierarchy of the Turkish bath is not determined solely by the job title, but also by the pay. (Diagram by author/Dominik Tezyk)

Saloon Steward

Ahier	Fairall	Puzey
Allsop	Harrison, A. D.	Ransom
Baggott	Hartnell	Ray
Bagley	Hendy	Revell
Barker, E. T.	Hoare	Rimmer
Barringer	House	Robinson, J. W.
Barrows	Howell	Rowe, E. M.
Best	Jones, V. R.	Saunders, W. E.
Boughton	Keen	Shea, J. J.
Boyd	Ketchley	Simmons, F. C.
Boyes	Kingscote	Skinner
Bristow, H.	Kitching	Smillie
Brown E.	Knight, G.	Smith, R. G.
Brown, W. J.	Lake	Stagg
Burr	Lane	Stroud, H. J.
Butt, R. H.	Lawrance	Strugnell
Butterworth	Lefebvre	Symonds
Cartwright	Littlejohn	Taylor, W. J.
Casswill	Lloyd, H.	Thomas, A. C.
Cheverton	Lucas, W. W.	Thomas, B. J.
Coleman, A. E.	Lydiatt	Toms
Cook	McGrady	Turner, L. O.
Crafter	McKay	Veal, T. H. E.
Crisp	McMicken, A.	Ward, W.
Crowe	McMullin	Warwick
Deeble	Mellor	Weatherston
Derrett	Nicholls	Wheelton
Deslandes	Orpet	White, L. L. O.
Dinenage	Osborne	Whiteley
Dyer, W. H.	Perriton	Wormald
Evans, G. R.	Pryce	Yearsley

Bedroom Steward

Allan	Etches	McMurray
Anderson, W. Y.	Faulkner	O'Connor, T. P.
Bishop	Geddes	Penrose
Bond	Gill, J. S.	Roberts, H. H.
Brewster	Hayter	Siebert
Crawford	Hewitt	Stone, E.
Crumplin	Hill, J. C.	Swan
Cullen	Hogg, C. W.	Theissinger
Cunningham, A.O.	Ide	Ward, E.
Davies, G. R.	Janaway	Ward, P. T.
Donoghue	Kirkaldy (Clark)	Wareham
	McCarty, F. J.	Wittmann

Bedroom stewards received a hire of £3 15s monthly:

Robert Spencer Allan
Walter Yuill Anderson
Walter Alexander Bishop
William John Bond
George Henry Brewster
Alfred James Crawford
Charles George C. Crumplin
Charles James Cullen
Andrew O. Cunningham
Gordon Raleigh Davies
Thomas Francis Donoghue
Henry Samuel Etches
William Stephen Faulkner
Richard Charles Geddes
Joseph Stanley Gill
Arthur Hayter
Thomas Hewitt
James Colston Hill
Charles William Hogg
Harry John Ide
William Frank Janaway
Thomas Benjamin Kirkaldy (Clark)
Frederick James McCarty
William McMurray
Thomas Peter O'Connor
John Poole Penrose
Hugh Henry Roberts
Sidney Conrad Siebert
Edmund Stone
William Swan
Franz Alfred Daniel Maximilian Theissinger
Edward Ward
Percy Thomas Ward
Robert Arthur Wareham
Henry Wittman

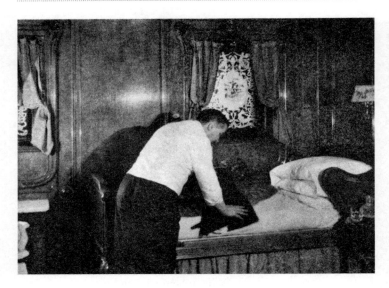

Cabin steward
in a cabin on
B–Deck on
Olympic, c. 1924.
(Author's
collection)

Bedroom stewards worked alternate shifts including nights. Working from the known personal relationships between bedroom stewards and passengers, it was possible from survivors' accounts to assign fourteen stewards to certain cabins or at least sections. As bedroom stewards covered the entire first-class area, this information gives a better idea of the extent of their work domain. Six of the bedroom stewards survived:

Walter Alexander Bishop	B69, B71, B73, B75, B77, B79, B81, and others on B–deck
George Henry Brewster	E–deck
Alfred James Crawford	B3, B5, B49 and others on B–deck, forward, starboard
Charles James Cullen	C51 and others on C–deck, forward, starboard
Andrew O. Cunningham	C85, C87, C89, C91, C93, C123, C125, C127 plus one cabin
Henry Samuel Etches	A36, B84, B86, B88, B90, B92, B94, B96, B98
William Stephen Faulkner	C11 and others on C–deck, forward, starboard
James Colston Hill	D–deck, forward
Thomas Benjamin Kirkaldy (Clark)	B–deck
John Poole Penrose	D20 and others on D–deck, forward, port side
Edmund Stone	E1 to (presumably) E8 and possibly others on E–deck
Franz Alfred Daniel Maximilian Theissinger	E63, E66, E67, E68 and others on E–deck, astern
Robert Arthur Wareham	A11 and others on A–deck, forward, starboard
Henry Wittman	C–deck

The Night Watchmen

According to the muster lists there were no night watchmen aboard *Titanic*. At the British Board of Trade hearings, Counsel Sidney Rowlatt uncovered the fact rather fortuitously that there were fixed night watchmen posts:

Rowlatt (3340):	James Johnson, is that your name?
Johnston:	Yes.
Rowlatt (3341):	You live, I think, in Liverpool?
Johnston:	Yes.
Rowlatt (3342):	Were you on the '*Titanic*' as saloon steward?
Johnston:	In the saloon, not the saloon steward.
Rowlatt (3343):	Which saloon was it?
Johnston:	The first saloon. I was night watchman; I had charge of the night watch. There were five of us went on every night.
Rowlatt (3344):	I want to get the part of the ship first – which was it?
Johnston:	The first saloon.
...	
Rowlatt (3354):	Was it your job to go on every night?
Johnston:	Yes.
Rowlatt (3355):	Did you go on the night of the accident?
Johnston:	I went on at 11 o'clock.
Rowlatt (3356):	You simply had to go into the saloon and wait?
Johnston:	Well, no. Everyone gets a watch and at 12 o'clock when the bedroom stewards turn over we take their watch. There is a bedroom steward and a night watchman on each deck, and all the third class and all the second class reported to me each night when they came on watch.
Rowlatt (3357):	Now what you had to do was simply to stay in that saloon as I understand?
Johnston:	No, I took E - what they call the saloon – the reception room and the pantry, on.

Although Rowlatt had the surname confirmed, the steward's name was Johnston and not Johnson. Another error crept in, either in the response to the question or in the stenographer's notes, where D-deck is obviously meant where the mentioned rooms were located and that deck was known as saloon deck. The witness statement makes it clear, however, that he was only a saloon steward on paper. At night it would appear that five saloon stewards and five bedroom stewards paired up on the five decks of first class with passenger cabins. The bedroom steward, for example, could supply an extra blanket here or there, if requested the saloon steward would organise small snacks and drinks. But who were these ten men? Johnston names another during his testimony:

| Rowlett (3378): | What happened next? |
| Johnston: | … I followed Mr Andrews and went down to E deck to see if Duscheck was there. He was down there on watch on that deck … |

By Duscheck he must have meant James Adamson Toshack, unless 'Duscheck' was the nickname of another colleague. It is also quite possible that Herbert Cave was a night watchman – on his body a passenger list with cabin numbers was found, this would not make much sense if he was a saloon steward. Since he had been hired as such, however, he was probably one of the night watchmen and in that function would have needed the list. The identity of the other two saloon stewards who worked at night is not known. A few saloon stewards reported that they were sleeping when the collision occurred and would therefore not have been night watchmen. Therefore only a few of the circle of potential night watchmen can be eliminated, but the following three seem to be confirmed or highly likely. A night watchman earned £3 15s, like a saloon steward:

Herbert Cave
James Johnston
James Adamson Toshack

Whether the job of night watchman was a coveted one cannot be established. It does not seem likely that the night watchmen were as heavily tipped as the stewards, who had a more regular contact with clients.

For the bedroom stewards the night shift was handled in a different manner, and once again the crew organisation of Titanic consisted of exceptions, as the testimony elicited from Bedroom Steward Andrew Cunningham by Senator William Alden Smith at the US inquiry (page 791) shows:

Smith:	Where were you the Sunday afternoon and evening preceding this accident?
Cunningham:	It was my afternoon off. I was off that Sunday afternoon.
Smith:	You were off that afternoon?
Cunningham:	Yes, sir. It happened to be my turn for the middle watch, or from 12 to 4. So I was excused from duty from 9 until the time I was called to go on the middle watch.
Smith:	Were you on duty when this accident happened?
Cunningham:	I was just called, sir.
Smith:	What did you do when you found that there was an accident?
Cunningham:	I was stationed on D-deck, forward, that night.
Smith:	In charge of what?
Cunningham:	Of the bells; to answer bells – the wants of any passengers.

The night-watchman posts for bedroom stewards were therefore not fixed jobs, they changed every night. Some of the stewards remained awake until midnight, then the middle watch took over. The middle watch were then relieved by other stewards at 04:00hrs so that by 05:30hrs all the remaining bedroom stewards were back (except those of the middle watch, who were on duty again at 07:30hrs). The men for the middle watch had a watch-free afternoon and evening after 21:00hrs beforehand, which made the middle watch attractive. Other stewards took over their assigned cabins for them during the afternoon and evening.

Andrew Cunningham had night watch alongside Henry Samuel Etches on the night of the sinking. The identities of the other three bedroom stewards assigned for the middle watch that night is unknown.

One supposes that all stewards listed for the night watch assembled in the dining saloon towards midnight and then split up into the various areas, since the bedroom stewards' night watch changed daily. The night watchmen would then proceed to the pantries on the various decks, the pantries also being rest rooms for duty stewards. Here they waited to answer passengers' bells and also made their rounds.

The Stewardesses

There were twenty-three women amongst the 899 *Titanic* crew members. Nineteen of them were stewardesses, the other four worked in the Turkish bath and the à-la-carte restaurant. According to the crew lists seventeen were assigned to first class and two to second class. The pay for these fourteen stewardesses in first class was £3 10s:

Mabel Kate Bennett
Katherine Gold
Mary Josephine Gregson
Violet Constance Jessop
Elizabeth Mary Leather
Evelyn Marsden
Annie Martha Martin
Harriet Elizabeth McLaren
Alice Prichard
Mary Kezia Roberts
Annie Robinson
Mary Sloan
Kate Elizabeth Smith
Sarah Agnes Stap

The pay for these three stewardesses in first class was £3:

Emma Bliss
Elizabeth Lavington
Catherine Walsh

These two stewardesses signed on in second class, the latter as matron. Both were paid £3:

Lucy Violett Snape
Catherine Jane Wallis

All stewardesses survived except Catherine Walsh, Lucy Violett Snape and Catherine Jane Wallis. It is something of an enigma how these women were grouped and what their functions were. Therefore they will be considered here as a whole, regardless of the class they signed on.

The Wreck Commissioner's Inquiry took evidence from two stewardesses, Elizabeth Mary Leather and Annie Robinson. Leather was required to answer thirty rather mundane questions about the sinking, Robinson forty-three. All that can be gathered from their replies is that each stewardess was responsible for several female passengers. The memoir of Violet Jessop also enables nothing to be concluded about the division of work. Nevertheless, there are indications that the divisions into first and second class as per the muster list cannot be correct from what surviving stewardesses and passengers reported. Furthermore, the deck plans with the cabins intended for the stewardesses do not coincide with the muster list. Matron Catherine Jane Wallis worked in third class, not in second. According to reports, Catherine Walsh was said to have worked in second class,

Of the twenty-three women in *Titanic's* crew twenty survived, thirteen of whom are in this photograph, taken at their return in Plymouth. Possible identification, front row: possibly cashier restaurant, V.C. Jessop, M. Slocombe (Turkish bath stewardess), M. Sloan, M.K. Roberts, A. Prichard, H.E. McLaren (?). Aft row: possibly cashier restaurant, E.M. Leather (?), M.K. Bennett, A. Robinson, K. Gold, A. Martin. (Author's collection)

where four stewardesses were specified. It also seems to be obvious that the two other poorer remunerated stewardesses in first class per the muster list, Emma Bliss and Elizabeth Lavington, actually worked in second class, for there were not enough beds for all seventeen stewardesses supposedly in first class, and it is reasonable that the fourteen better-paid women all worked in first class. Sarah Agnes Stap told a journalist that she had been the senior stewardess. A confirmation of this claim may be the fact that she headed both the hiring and the paying-off lists. The corrected list would then look like this:

First Class: The senior stewardess was paid £3 10s.

Sarah Agnes Stap

First Class: The stewardesses in first class were all paid £3 10s.

Mabel Kate Bennett
Katherine Gold
Mary Josephine Gregson
Violet Constance Jessop
Elizabeth Mary Leather
Evelyn Marsden
Annie Martha Martin
Harriet Elizabeth McLaren
Alice Prichard
Mary Kezia Roberts
Annie Robinson
Mary Sloan
Kate Elizabeth Smith

Second Class: The stewardesses in second class were all paid £3.

Emma Bliss
Elizabeth Lavington
Lucy Violett Snape
Catherine Walsh

Third Class: The matron in third class was paid £3.

Catherine Jane Wallis

The stewardesses were competent to handle the special requirements of the female passengers and children on board scattered across the three classes. Their basic work was in

A White Star Line stewardess, around 1910. The photograph was probably taken on board the *Laurentic* or *Megantic*. (Author's collection)

the cabins and they were often to be found in the passenger cabin corridors, where they collaborated with the bedroom stewards and bath stewards (described ahead). They were well known to the ship's surgeons and, if required, performed a nursing role in the passenger cabins. Where necessary they mended and cleaned damaged clothing. In its publicity for the Australia service, White Star Line emphasised that a stewardess was aboard for the women and children, an important point for female travellers on long distance journeys, e.g. to help with dressing. In contrast to their male colleagues, stewardesses were all-rounders who primarily looked after female passengers. On several of the decks two stewardesses would always share an interior cabin so as to be near and of service to passengers around the clock. This is a further indication of the independence of the stewardesses in their work. A side effect of the accommodation arrangement was as a protection against undesirable advances being made by the male crew.

The Special Stewards in the Victualling Department

The bedroom stewards were not alone responsible for the needs of passengers, and were supported in some functions by special stewards. On board, for example, there were three laundry stewards, none of whom survived:

Ernest Roskelly Olive	£6	Clothes Presser Steward
Sidney Holloway	£3	Assistant Clothes Presser Steward
Thomas Ferguson Baxter	£4 10s	Linen Steward

These three looked after the laundry aboard *Titanic*. Passengers could have clothes washed and ironed for a fee. The bedroom stewards brought passengers' clothing for cleaning to the laundry on F-deck.

Bedsheets, table cloths, serviettes and so on were washed ashore, where the facilities were more efficient and fresh water was abundant. The linen steward's sole duty on board was to supply the bedroom and bath stewards with linen and towels; he would equip several smaller linen rooms throughout the ship. The bedsheets were changed daily in first and second class. The saloon stewards used hundreds of table cloths and napkins every day, the cooks and scullions a similar amount of kitchen towels and cook cloths. Everything was prepared for cleaning by drying them in a steam-heated room during the voyage to prevent putrefaction. The dirty laundry was stored in large cloth bags. The blankets of third class were exchanged at the destination, to be washed and disinfected. At the end of a journey, in New York or Southampton, many tons of dirty laundry were offloaded and brought into the White Star Lines own laundry.

The titles 'Chief Boots Steward' and 'Assistant Boots Steward' in the muster list were misleading. They were usually, at least in *Titanic* literature, misunderstood as shoe-shiner. However, nine shoe-shine boys for the two upper ship's classes seems a lot for a ship whose passengers spent most of their time inside. Their shoes were cleaned by the

The laundry was not washed on board the liners, but dried and offloaded after a round trip. Here the stewards of the *Aquitania* are offloading the laundry at Southampton. (Author's collection)

White Star Line laundry at Southampton in 1924; third-class blankets can be seen on the table on the left. (Author's collection)

bedroom steward. 'Boots' is an old English term for a servant. The cleaning crew handled all such work including the corridors, stairways and public rooms and receive herein the appropriate nomenclature. The chief cleaning steward received £4 15*s*:

Sidney Frederick Stebbing's

The cleaning stewards received £3 15*s*:

Alfred Fellowes
Edward John Guy
Cecil Jackson
William Henry Rattenbury
John Scott

The only survivor of the cleaning stewards was Edward John Guy. He was not required to appear before the boards of inquiry.

Only a few of the *Titanic* cabins had their own bath, and showers were not the mode of the time. Most passengers in cabins without baths had recourse on every deck to several bathrooms with tubs. If required, the bedroom steward would book a turn for a passenger with one of the five bath stewards, or with a stewardess for a female passenger. They ensured that baths and toilets were always kept clean – the bath tubs were disinfected

The only known photograph of a corridor on an *Olympic*-class liner. In this photograph it is a corridor on the starboard side on E-deck. Depending on the passenger ratio in first and second class it could be used alternately. In the foreground is the frame of a watertight door that, in case of emergency, was operated manually by the stewards. The corridors were kept tidy by the cleaning stewards; they were in the muster lists as 'boots' (i.e. hired as boot stewards). (Daniel Klistorner collection)

after each use. Bath stewards worked during the day and slept at night. Bath stewards were paid £3 15s:

Herbert George Broom
Thomas Edgar Major
Frank Herbert Morris
Thomas Frederick C. Pennal
Samuel James Rule

Frank Herbert Morris and Samuel James Rule survived. Both declared to the British Wreck Commissioner's Inquiry, but the questions and answers revolved almost exclusively around the evacuation of the ship and spending the night in the lifeboats, and made no mention of their activities aboard ship.

The five employees in the Turkish baths on F-deck assisted in the bodily hygiene of their guests. Passengers could receive a massage and spend time in sauna-like tempered rooms. The air in the Victorian Turkish bath was not humidified. Periods were set aside for male and female passengers. The adjacent swimming bath was also served by the Turkish-bath staff. In the electric bath, which was operated by the staff, the passengers lay in boxes heated by thermal lamps. These services were not included in the price of the voyage. A ticket for the Turkish bath (including swimming bath) cost 4s at the enquiry office, or 1s for the swimming bath only (free for men between 06:00 and 09:00hrs and for women between 10:00 and 12:00hrs). The three male attendants appear in the muster list for third class and kitchen. All were hired as Turkish bath attendants, Crosbie below receiving the prefix 'senior' by virtue of his higher remuneration. Of the listed staff, only the two women survived the loss of the ship:

A spartan first-class bathroom on *Olympic*. Next to the bath tub there was a mirror and a shelf for the clothes. (Daniel Klistorner collection)

A massage table on the *Olympic* in 1911, with a partly visible needle shower on the right. The marble massage tables in the shampooing rooms were where the Turkish bath staff worked. The adjustable nozzles of the Vichy shower and the shower stand could be used as needed. (Author's collection)

The cooling room of the Turkish bath was also used as the bath's reception and as a changing room. It was also where the passengers recovered after the hot room, the steam room or a massage. (Author's collection)

John Borthwick Crosbie	£6 10s	Senior Turkish Bath Attendant
Walter Ennis	£6	Turkish Bath Attendant
Leonard Taylor	£4	Turkish Bath Attendant
Annie Caton	£4	Turkish Bath Stewardess
Maud Louise Slocombe	£4	Turkish Bath Stewardess

There were a few other specialists with special functions. Besides the baths there was a squash court and a gymnasium. The squash court was on G-deck with an instructor, Frederick Wright. Hire of the court was 2s for 30 minutes and tickets were obtainable from the purser's office. Wright earned extra by the sale or hire of balls and racquets as stated on deck plans and in the information section of the first-class passenger list, whereas in a price list published by White Star Line in January 1912 the racquets were supposed to be included in the hire of the court.

Time in the gymnasium and the use of the apparatus were included in the cost of the voyage, although the instructor expected a tip. The room was on the boat deck and open during the day until 19:00hrs, children were only allowed admittance from 13:00–15:00hrs. The sports equipment was maintained by Thomas W. McCawley, who described himself on a business card as a 'Physical Educator'. Neither Wright nor McCawley survived:

Frederick Wright	£1/week	Racquet Steward
Thomas W. McCawley	£3 15s	Gymnasium Steward

In first class two barbers were available for passengers and appeared on the crew list for third class and kitchen irrespective of the class in which they worked. In the column of the hire fee was a symbol '/', interpreted later as a symbolic hire of 1s. However, it actually meant that White Star Line paid them nothing. Augustus Henry Weikman survived the tragedy and was the only crew member to be paid off with nothing. The symbol was repeated in

On the morning of approaching Queenstown on 11 April 1912, Francis Browne took this photograph of *Titanic's* gymnasium. The 'Hydraulic Rowing Apparatus' is demonstrated by Physical Educator Thomas W. McCawley and sitting on the 'Riding Apparatus' for men is William Henry Marsh Parr, an electrician from the Harland & Wolff guarantee group. The gymnasium was equipped with apparatus from the German Rossel, Schwarz & Co. Next to the world map stands the 'Universal Pull-Machine', on the left in the background is the 'Circling Rubbing of Abdomen' machine. (The Irish Picture Library/Father FM Browne SJ Collection)

the sign-off list for the six days aboard *Titanic*; perhaps he salvaged some of his takings in cash from the sinking ship.

The price was set by the White Star Line at 1*s* per shave, haircut and hair wash. The barbers kept the whole amount and paid no rent for their saloon. On a round trip they could earn from £10 to £20. So far as White Star Line was concerned, the barbers were not employees but independent. Most of the work was shaving the men: in contrast to other shipping lines, there were no ladies' hairdressers. Although the saloon was open from 07:00–19:00hrs, hair was only washed and cut between 12:00 and 17:30hrs, the rest of the time was for shaving. Besides their main commercial activity, the barbers sold souvenirs such as postcards, pin cushions, silver spoons and pins with the logo of the shipping company and the name of the ship, and other requirements, for example razor blades, powder, photographic glass plates or rolls of film:

Augustus Henry Weikman	./.	Barber
Arthur White	./.	Assistant Barber

The three lifts from A-deck to E-deck on *Titanic* were each attended by a lift steward, who responded when a passenger rang for attention, looked after the safety gate and brought the lift to the required deck. Presumably the three lift stewards organised it amongst themselves so that during the busy times before and after meals all three lifts would be in operation. The steward born as Frederick George Blades used the name Frederick George Allen to hire himself aboard *Titanic*. The surname Allen was that of the second husband of his grandmother, with whom he lived. None of the three lift stewards survived. The lift stewards earned £3 15*s*:

Frederick Charles Blades (Allen)
William Carney
Alfred John M. King

The Gastronomic Stewards

Besides the large group of saloon stewards, in the gastronomic area of first class there were other stewards with special functions. Drinks and snacks were also served in other sections of the ship. For this work, especially reliable and independent stewards were sought to work under the chief steward and his assistants. The special functions did not attract higher remuneration: such stewards each received £3 15*s* like most of their colleagues, but prospects for getting tipped were far better.

The major culinary offerings were in the lounge on A-deck. The responsibility devolved upon Lounge Steward Richard Edward J. Burke, with Charles Frederick Back at his side.

In the lounge, a third steward, Ernest Owen Abbott, was involved in the preparation of snacks. Therefore there was a spacious pantry behind the bar with a direct staircase and a dumb waiter into the main pantry, three decks below. The lounge stewards also organised the issue of reading material from the bookcase. At midday tea, and after dinner, coffee was served, but alcoholic beverages, cigarettes, cigars and postcards were also offered. The lounge was open from 08:00 until 23:30hrs.

In the smoke room a little farther astern, Brook Holding Webb and his assistant Ernest Hamilton worked. They offered drinks and tobacco goods. The bar was open from 08:00– 23:30hrs, the lights being extinguished at midnight.

Directly astern of the smoke room, at the end of A-deck, were the two verandah cafes, open from 08:00–23:00hrs and staffed by Athol Frederick Broome and John Stewart. Neither was described in the muster list as a chef or assistant – that was probably on account of there being two separate establishments; they were separated by the second-class staircase (which had no exit on A-deck). Broome and Stewart therefore managed one cafe each, the one on the starboard side only being accessible by passengers from outside along the promenade deck. The cafes did not have their own bar; the stewards used the one in

Card players in *Olympic*'s lounge, with the lounge steward on standby, *c.* 1924. (Author's collection)

A smoke room steward serving two passengers on *Olympic*, post 1920. (Author's collection)

the smoke room. In the muster lists each appears as a 'Verandah Steward' but the better designation is obviously 'Verandah Cafe Steward'.

Joseph Dolby and Thomas Holland attended to the requirements of passengers in the first-class reception room on D-deck. They were equals in the hierarchy. The reception room was separated by the smoke outlet of boiler rooms 3 and 4 and the forward stairway. Dolby and Holland must each have worked one side of the ship. Besides warm drinks they also served alcohol and cigarettes. The reception room was open until 23:00. The term 'Reception Room Steward' is used for clarity in place of the description in the muster list of 'Reception Steward'.

Especially on voyages at the milder times of year, many passengers preferred to take their midday tea outside in a deckchair. Ernest Edward Samuel Freeman and his assistants William John Boston and William Walter Hawkesworth worked as deck stewards.

On the muster roll Bugler Steward Percy William Fletcher is also listed together with the deck stewards. He summoned the passengers to their meals with the 'bugle call', and in the evening with 'dress call' advised the passengers that they had half an hour to dress for dinner. Of course, he did not only play a few bars on his trumpet each day. His position in the muster list shows that he was actually a deck steward, but was given the additional duty of being in charge of the bugle call, which he presumably also executed in second class.

The starboard verandah cafe on the *Titanic* was the only public room that was, for the passengers, only accessible from the outside. The assigned stewards shared the bar with their colleagues in the smoke room. (Author's collection)

Tea and coffee were served in the reception room, as seen in this photograph taken around 1924 on board *Olympic*. (Author's collection)

Tea and soup were served by the deck stewards. Wind-protected corners were also popular in wintertime. Deck chairs and steamer rugs could be hired from the enquiry office for 4s per crossing. The photograph was taken around 1910. (Author's collection)

Olympic's bugler steward around 1922 on B-deck. The 'Bugle Call' and the meals that followed were highlights of a monotonous day on any passenger liner. (Bruce Beveridge collection)

A musical first-class passenger of the Zeeland wrote down the daily bugle-call score on White Star Line stationery in 1910. (Author's collection)

When needed, the gastronomic stewards were supported by the saloon stewards. Aragõa Drummond Harrison said in an interview that he helped in the smoke room. The following list shows the special function of the various gastronomic stewards. All of them were hired at the rate of £3 15s:

Richard Edward J. Burke	Lounge Steward
Charles Frederick Back	Assistant Lounge Steward
Ernest Owen Abbott	Lounge Pantry Steward
Brook Holding Webb	Smoke Room Steward
Ernest Hamilton	Assistant Smoke Room Steward
Athol Frederick Broome	Verandah Cafe Steward
John Stewart	Verandah Cafe Steward
Joseph Dolby	Reception Room Steward
Thomas Holland	Reception Room Steward
Ernest Edward Samuel Freeman	Deck Steward
William John Boston	Assistant Deck Steward
William Walter Hawkesworth	Assistant Deck Steward
Percy William Fletcher	Bugler Steward

Of the above personnel only John Stewart survived, but he was not called upon by either inquiry committee. The staff of the Café Parisien is described in the chapter on the à-la-carte restaurant.

The Cooks and Butchers

In the monotony of shipboard life, undoubtedly the mealtimes represented the highlights of the day. The importance of the catering was reflected in the remuneration of the chef, Charles Proctor: he received £20 monthly, as did the purser and chief steward. The chef drew up the plans of meals (adhering to the purser's budget) and prepared the orders for the coming voyage. The kitchen lay between the dining saloons of the first and second class on D-deck – both classes were cooked for from one kitchen, the crew of the second-class kitchen will be described later. Cooking was carried out with steam or coals. Despite the high standards the food aboard the passenger liners was mass produced. Scarcely any electrical or mechanical kitchen device was absent from the *Titanic* if it made things easier or more economical.

Taken in Southampton in front of *Titanic*'s port-side verandah cafe, this photograph shows Chief Pantryman James Walpole in the centre with Chef Charles Proctor to the right of him. Behind Walpole is Sous-Chef Alexis Bochatay with other members of the kitchen staff. (Author's collection)

One of a few photographs taken inside of *Titanic*. In the foreground Sous-Chef Alexis Bochatay is at the stove. (Author's collection)

At Charles Proctor's side stood Alexis Joseph Bochatay, who according to the muster list was assistant chef taking on the role of sous-chef. He was responsible for supervising the cooks and jointly responsible for the quality of the courses:

Charles Proctor	£20	Chef
Alexis Joseph Bochatay	£10	Sous-chef

The *Titanic* cooks had some confusing work titles. As the passengers were accustomed to predominantly French cuisine, the research showed that many work titles were merely anglicised names for French specialist cooks. It seems as though *Titanic* cooks were hired to copy a major French kitchen and their various functions roughly translated into English. The following proves the point:

Sauce Cook	=	Saucier
Grill Cook	=	Grillardin
Roast Cook	=	Rôtisseur
Entre Cook	=	Entremetier

Larder Cook   = Garde Manger
Vegetable Cook = Légumier

Consequently, for the French gastronomy the French terms have been retained since they are less confusing than the White Star Line translations. The saucier was, as the name suggests, responsible for the sauces, but also for meat. Only an experienced cook would be appointed to this responsible post. Shortly before sailing, Alfred Edgar Windebank was hired for another cook, and shown in the muster list as an assistant cook, but he is listed as a sauce cook in the paying-off list and received the corresponding rate of pay. As a saucier he supervised the grillardins and rôtisseurs:

Alfred Edgar Windebank	£7	Saucier
William Ewart Caunt	£6 10s	Grillardin
John Lovell	£6 10s	Grillardin
Harry Owen G. Jones	£6 10s	Rôtisseur
William Barnett Bedford	£4 10s	Assistant Rôtisseur

The garnishing cook is called the entremetier in the trade jargon. According to the muster list, there was only one man to do this job; presumably he had several assistant cooks and scullions. Three assistant cooks on the muster list belonged to no stated section, and so it seems likely that they worked for the entremetier, who could not possibly have handled all the work himself. The entremetier also supervised the légumier (French, *légume* = vegetable):

Isaac Hiram Maynard	£7 10s	Entremetier
Augustus Charles Coombs	£4 10s	Assistant Cook
William Thorley	£4 10s	Assistant Cook
William Harold Welch	£4 10s	Assistant Cook

A rôtisseur at work on board *Olympic, c.* 1922. (Bruce Beveridge collection)

The grillardin on the *Olympic*, around 1922. (Bruce Beveridge collection)

Butchers at work in the cooling chamber of the North German Lloyd steamer *George Washington*. (Author's collection)

James Hutchinson	£6 10s	Légumier
John Bertie Ellis	£5	Assistant Légumier
Edwin George Ayling	£4 10s	Assistant Légumier
H. E. Buckley	£4 10s	Assistant Légumier
James Orr	£4 10s	Assistant Légumier

The other section within the kitchen was headed by the garde manger. He was responsible for the cold dishes, there principally for the hors d'oeuvre. Possibly some of the mentioned assistant cooks worked for him. As in every large kitchen, the butchers were assigned to him. It seems possible on account of their job description that the three butchers Maytum, Topp and Roberts had one ship's class each. Different meat had to be prepared in every class. Much of the butchery work was carried out in the refrigerated rooms on the Orlop-deck and G–deck.

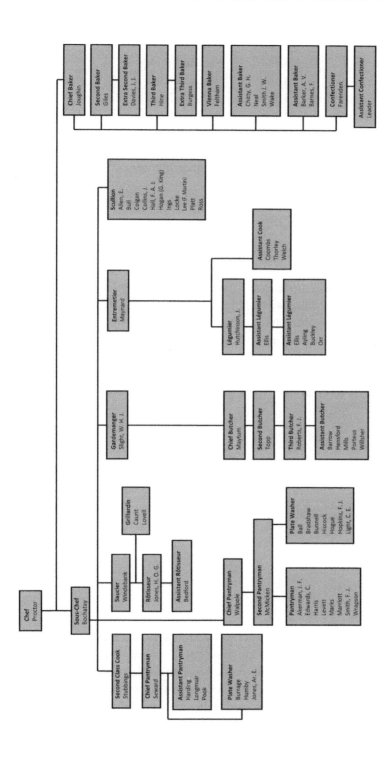

The complete organisation chart of the kitchen for first and second class, including the pantrymen, plate washers and bakers. (Diagram by author/Dominik Tezyk)

William Henry John Slight	£7	Garde Manger
Alfred Maytum	£6	Chief Butcher
Thomas Topp	£5 10s	Second Butcher
Frank John Roberts	£4 10s	Third Butcher
Charles Henry John Barrow	£4 10s	Assistant Butcher
Herbert George Hensford	£4 10s	Assistant Butcher
Christopher Mills	£4 10s	Assistant Butcher
Thomas Henry Porteus	£4 10s	Assistant Butcher
William Aubrey Willsher	£4 10s	Assistant Butcher

Of these twenty-five cooks and butchers, Windebank, Maynard, Ellis and Mills survived.

The Other Kitchen Employees

In the kitchen there were other assistants and men with special functions. They all came under Chef Charles Proctor and his sous-chef. The cooks included ten or eleven scullions, counting A. Locke, who was hired late. It is not known if he worked in first and second class for definite, as it is possible he worked in third class. It is also not known how the scullions were divided into groups, it would certainly have depended on the meal plan. They also worked outside the kitchen, as, for example, in the potato washing place on E-deck. Of the following, Colgan, Collins, Martin and Ross survived. Scullions earned £3 10s:

E. Allen
Walter Edward Bull
Joseph Colgan
John Collins
Frank Alfred J. Hall
John William Hogan (G. King)
William Ernest Ings
Henry Reginald Lee (F. Martin)
A. Locke
Wilfrid George Platt
Horace Leopold Ross

James Walpole and his assistant Benjamin Tucker McMicken had the major responsibility of managing the first-class pantry and were presumably skilled cooks who filled the orders. The saloon stewards placed the passengers' requirements in the pantry where the pantrymen had to have the various dishes ready for any particular table at the right time. The pantry also prepared hot drinks. The used dishes were brought from there to the scullery. The team was composed as follows:

| James Walpole | £7 | Chief Pantryman |
| Benjamin Tucker McMicken | £5 | Second Pantryman |

Assistant pantrymen, as below, were paid £3 10s:

Joseph Frank Akerman
Charles Edwards
Edward Matthew Harris
George Alfred Levett
James Marks
John William Marriott
Frederick John Smith
Frederick Bernard Wrapson

Plate washers, as below, were paid £3 15s:

Percy Ball
John Albert Perkin Bradshaw
Wilfred James Bunnell
Sydney George Hiscock
E. Hogue
Frederick James Hopkins
Charles Edward Light

The port pantry in first class of *Olympic*, seen from the pantrymen's perspective. On the left in the foreground is the servery for cold food, opposite the hot food. The saloon stewards fetched their dishes from the inside of the U-shaped pantry. (Author's collection)

Of all these men, only Percy Ball survived the sinking. Originally the plate washers were mustered as 'plate stewards', but Ball signed off as 'plate washer', which seems to be a more understandable description. It is noticeable that the plate washers were paid 5s more than the assistant pantrymen. For a reason unknown, they were included on the listing of stewards, who earned almost exclusively £3 15s, while the kitchen assistants earned only £3 10s. The pantrymen also earned 5s less than their colleagues in second class. Both the plate washers and pantrymen worked in the kitchen. The latter were only occupied there during mealtimes when they filled the plates; almost certainly they spent the rest of the time assisting the cooks. Plate Washer Frederick James Hopkins was the youngest crew member of *Titanic*. He was born in the last quarter of 1898 but at signing-on pretended he was 16. He was 13 years old at the time of his death.

The Bakers

The *Titanic* had numerous bakers aboard to supply the ship with bread and other bakery wares, including a Vienna baker who made rolls and pastries. Viennese bakeries had been popular in France since the 1840s. The importance of the bakery was reflected in the £12 remuneration of Chief Baker Charles John Joughin. He stated at the Wreck Commissioner's Inquiry that he had responsibility for thirteen bakers and confectioners. Therefore he led the bakeries of all three classes – the first- and second-class bakery on D-deck port side and the third class bakery on F-deck:

Charles John Joughin	£12	Chief Baker
John Robert Giles	£7	Second Baker
John James Davies	£5	Extra Second Baker

The following bakery jobs attracted a remuneration of £4 10s:

William Edward Hine	Third Baker
Charles Burgess	Extra Third Baker
George William Feltham	Vienna Baker
George Henry Chitty	Assistant Baker
Bentley Harold Neal	Assistant Baker
James William Smith	Assistant Baker
Percy Wake	Assistant Baker

Chief Baker Charles John Joughin, seen here after the disaster, was one of the best-paid crew members in the Victualling Department of *Titanic*. Of the surviving crew members, only the second officer and probably the maître d'hôtel earned more than Joughin. (Author's collection)

Olympic's bakery for first and second class, around 1922. (Bruce Beveridge collection)

A lesser remuneration of £4 was to be paid to two assistant bakers:

Albert Vale Barker
Frederick Barnes

The confectioners were hired at the following rates:

Ernest John Farenden	£8	Confectioner
Archibald Leader	£5 10s	Assistant Confectioner

The staff arrangement in the bakeries is not known. The ranks might be an indication of the working hours: the preparations and baking time for bread for all meals and everybody on board could not be completed in a single shift. Burgess, who survived with Joughin and Neal, said in an interview that his shift began at 21:00hrs, that he worked second class and was on D-deck with three colleagues when the collision happened. These colleagues included Joughin and Neal. This suggests that the bakers worked in shifts around the clock, and that the job title would not reflect the class they were working for. No further information has been found. Farenden and Leader made pies and fancy cakes in the confectionery near the bakery on D-deck.

The Service Crew of the À-la-carte Restaurant

The workforce of the à-la-carte restaurant had a special status aboard. Following the example of German liners, White Star Line wanted to offer its first-class passengers the

Several cooks and waiters worked in the noble Oddenino's Imperial Restaurant (photograph *c.* 1912) at Piccadilly Circus in London before they were taken along by the manager, Gaspare Antonio Pietro Gatti, and joined *Titanic*'s crew. (Author's collection)

opportunity to dine in a real restaurant in addition to the dining saloon. Thus there was such a restaurant aboard both *Olympic* and *Titanic* with a manager, the Italian Gaspare Antonio Pietro Gatti, known as Luigi Gatti, who had already successfully operated the restaurant aboard *Olympic* and had recruited most of his staff from his London Oddenino's Imperial Restaurant. The *Titanic* restaurant is often linked wrongly with the Ritz in London, or with the restaurants Gatti's The Strand and Gatti's Adelphi, whose owners also had the surname Gatti.

Gatti had his own cabin on C-deck located between that of the chief steward and those of the surgeons. He directed the restaurant as an independent organisation. No payments are entered on the muster list for the restaurant staff, presumably for reasons of discretion and to guard against the envy of other crew members. This led over the years to the myth that the staff was paid by Gatti himself and not the White Star Line. In contrast to the *Titanic*, the earnings of the *Olympic* restaurant crew were entered on the early hiring lists.

The outstanding due payments and the lists of the pensions paid to the surviving dependants by the '*Titanic* Relief Fund' provided further indications as to the hire pay. The Committee divided the deceased crew members into groups A to G. Group A has twelve names, nine of which earned more than £15 monthly. The other three were restaurant employees: Manager Gatti, Chef Rousseau and Head Waiter Nannini.

Thanks to these sources most of the rates of pay of the restaurant staff can be reconstructed. Most impressive is the income of Gatti, who earned £550 per year, or

Waiters from different countries created an international ambience in the à-la-carte restaurant. Of the sixty-nine employees in the *Titanic* restaurant, the two cashiers and the maître d'hôtel survived. This photograph was taken on *Olympic* after the 1913 refit – tablecloths, decoration and the two waiters were added by an artist for promotion publications. (Author's collection)

£45 16*s* 8*d* per month, the second highest salary after Captain Smith. Also very well paid were the chef and head waiter.

It is interesting that the restaurant staff of *Olympic* numbered forty-five men on her maiden voyage. Apparently this left them short-staffed, for in New York another four were taken on. From the second round trip there were around fifty men. The *Titanic* restaurant had eighteen more seats than the *Olympic*, and the new Café Parisien offered an additional sixty-eight places. Therefore sixty-nine men were hired for the *Titanic* instead of fifty.

The special situation of the restaurant staff explains the confusion surrounding Assistant Glass Washer Lazar Sartori. It cannot be confirmed that he was aboard, but in August 1915 the White Star Line informed the Board of Trade that he had gone down with the *Titanic*. Therefore he is included here.

The restaurant was open daily from 08:00–23:00hrs. For a supplement of 6*d* on the normal restaurant tariff, passengers could elect to have a Continental, English or American breakfast served in their cabin before 11:00hrs. In addition to the à-la-carte menu the restaurant offered a carte du jour for lunch and dinner. Passengers who had stated at booking or 12 hours after sailing that they wished to take all meals in the à-la-carte restaurant received a discount on their ticket of £3 (or £5 on a ticket costing from £35 per passenger).

Whilst non-British personnel were the exception amongst the *Titanic* crew, it was the reverse in the restaurant. Of its sixty-nine employees, only eight were originally from

Leaflets like this were handed out to first-class passengers to inform them about the restaurant, its dinner times and the option to have breakfast served in the cabin. (Author's collection)

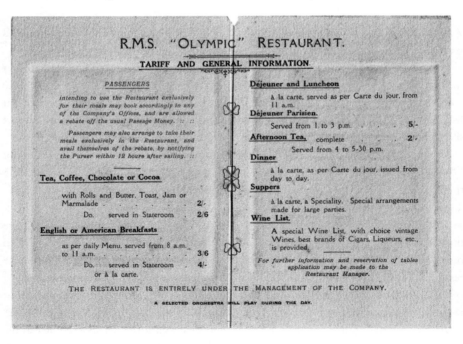

R.M.S. "OLYMPIC" RESTAURANT.

TARIFF AND GENERAL INFORMATION.

PASSENGERS

intending to use the Restaurant exclusively for their meals may book accordingly in any of the Company's Offices, and are allowed a rebate off the usual Passage Money.

Passengers may also arrange to take their meals exclusively in the Restaurant, and avail themselves of the rebate, by notifying the Purser within 12 hours after sailing.

Tea, Coffee, Chocolate or Cocoa

with Rolls and Butter, Toast, Jam or Marmalade	2/-
Do. served in Stateroom	2/6

English or American Breakfasts

as per daily Menu, served from 8 a.m. to 11 a.m.	3/6
Do. served in Stateroom	4/-
or à la carte.	

Déjeuner and Luncheon

à la carte, served as per Carte du jour, from 11 a.m.

Déjeuner Parisien.

Served from 1 to 3 p.m.	5/-

Afternoon Tea,   complete   2/-

Served from 4 to 5-30 p.m.

Dinner

à la carte, as per Carte du jour, issued from day to day.

Suppers

à la carte, a Speciality. Special arrangements made for large parties.

Wine List.

A special Wine List, with choice vintage Wines, best brands of Cigars, Liqueurs, etc., is provided.

For further information and reservation of tables application may be made to the Restaurant Manager.

THE RESTAURANT IS ENTIRELY UNDER THE MANAGEMENT OF THE COMPANY.

A SELECTED ORCHESTRA WILL PLAY DURING THE DAY.

Great Britain. White Star Line considered this international flair thoroughly desirable. Nevertheless, the shipping company placed value on having the restaurant under its own aegis. On *Titanic*, Purser McElroy represented the management and Gatti came under his jurisdiction even though he earned more than twice the salary of McElroy.

With the exception of Gatti, the restaurant staff was accommodated on E-deck, the two women analogous to stewardesses in a small cabin amongst the passengers. Three of the sixty-nine restaurant crew members survived, these being the two female cashiers and Paul Maugé, officially the 'kitchen clerk' and therefore the secretary for it: on the draft for expenses for the British inquiry he is described as the 'secretary to the chef'. In contrast to *Olympic*, this position was a new creation, presumably because the restaurant was bigger and as reinforcement for Gatti. All the same, it looks as though his function was more that of a maître d'hôtel, actually a representative of the management acting as host to his guests. At the time, the host was more important than the chef, who remained more in the background. Maugé's positition remains a matter of guesswork. It could be that he was not only assisting Gatti, but could have become his successor if Gatti was not on board. It seems that, with the introduction of *Titanic*, Gatti remained responsible for both Olympic-class restaurants, since he could not be present in both at the same time anyhow, and M. Pellegrin became the manager of *Olympic*'s restaurant. In general, the restaurant employees were comparably very well paid. That may have been the case with Maugé, who probably earned more than £15 per month. Maugé would therefore have been amongst the highest-earning survivors of the *Titanic* crew. That would explain why his salary is missing from the paying-off list – to avoid awkward questions about why he earned more than the second officer.

The two restaurant controllers occupied very modern positions that had first been introduced only a few years before in the largest American hotels. They oversaw the entire running of the restaurant, both the structure and the daily business, from the buying-in of goods and products to control of the warehousing aboard ship. They helped out in the peak hours, carried out spot checks in all areas of the business and tested the prepared foods for quality. They also audited the books. The area of monitoring is known today as Food and Beverage Controlling and, to reduce conflicts of interest, is often placed in the bookkeeping department. Presumably the two British employees had the strong perception that White Star Line was watching the foreign labour force very closely. For that reason they most probably reported directly to Gatti and were responsible for ensuring that everything in the restaurant was done exactly as it should have been.

Besides the two controllers, four of the five other British personnel had key positions. These were the two cashiers, the storekeeper and the barman. From that, one can infer how little foreigners were trusted – with these positions in British hands restaurant frauds were as good as eliminated. Whether this was the design of White Star Line or Gatti cannot be determined.

It is safe to assume that the restaurant management was composed according to the list below. Where the pay at hiring is indicated by (★), this is based on the *Olympic* muster

The organisation of the à-la-carte restaurant without the kitchen. The overview illustrates that the guests should not miss anything. (Diagram by author/Dominik Tezyk)

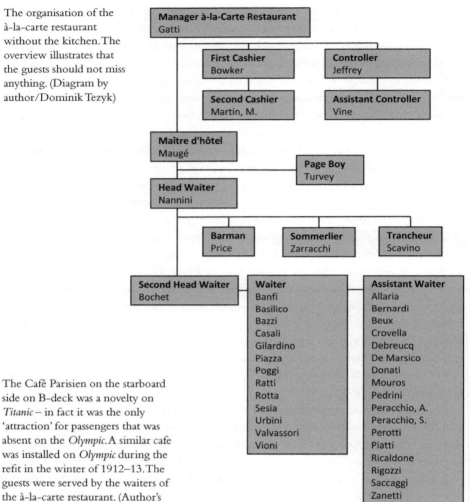

Manager à-la-Carte Restaurant
Gatti

First Cashier
Bowker

Controller
Jeffrey

Second Cashier
Martin, M.

Assistant Controller
Vine

Maître d'hôtel
Maugé

Page Boy
Turvey

Head Waiter
Nannini

Barman
Price

Sommerlier
Zarracchi

Trancheur
Scavino

Second Head Waiter
Bochet

Waiter	**Assistant Waiter**
Banfi	Allaria
Basilico	Bernardi
Bazzi	Beux
Casali	Crovella
Gilardino	Debreucq
Piazza	De Marsico
Poggi	Donati
Ratti	Mouros
Rotta	Pedrini
Sesia	Peracchio, A.
Urbini	Peracchio, S.
Valvassori	Perotti
Vioni	Piatti
	Ricaldone
	Rigozzi
	Saccaggi
	Zanetti

The Café Parisien on the starboard side on B-deck was a novelty on *Titanic* – in fact it was the only 'attraction' for passengers that was absent on the *Olympic*. A similar cafe was installed on *Olympic* during the refit in the winter of 1912–13. The guests were served by the waiters of the à-la-carte restaurant. (Author's collection)

lists. Since the settlement of the outstanding pay to the next of kin of Charles Turvey does not seem to fit either the weekly or monthly hire, it is therefore based on his hire for the corresponding position aboard *Olympic*. The rates of pay for the controller was possibly less aboard *Titanic* than *Olympic* because he had an assistant:

Gaspare Antonio Pietro Gatti	£550/year (*)	Manager, à-la-carte restaurant
Ruth Harwood Bowker	£7 10s	First Cashier
Mabel Elvina Martin	£3 15s	Second Cashier
William Alfred Jeffery	£130/year (*)	Controller
Herbert Thomas G.Vine	£3	Assistant Controller
Paul Achille Maurice Germain Maugé	more than £15	Maître d'hôtel
Charles Thomas Turvey	£1 10s (*)	Page Boy

Head Waiter Francesco Luigi Arcangelo Nannini and Second Head Waiter Pietro Giuseppe Bochet would have been under Maugé's control. They were in charge of thirty-one men. Attached to the restaurant was the Café Parisien, based on the design of a French street cafe. The restaurant waiters also served the clients of the cafe. The income of the head waiter on *Olympic* was £200 per annum, Nannini's next of kin received after his death 10s for every day worked, which would have been £182 10s for the year. Nevertheless, one can assume that the agreed annual salary was £200.

Nannini's service personnel were the sommelier hired as a wine butler, the trancheur (hired as carver, responsible to present, slice and serve precious meat at the table) and probably the barman. The pay for waiters and assistant waiters was variable initially on *Olympic*, on *Titanic* the workers within each respective group received the same. Based on the amounts paid over to the next of kin, the pay of service personnel is known. An exception is the estimate for the second head waiter based on the pension paid to his dependants. He was included in Group B of the *Titanic* Relief Fund (approximately £11 to £17), an amount including tips:

Francesco Luigi Arcangelo Nannini	£200/year	Head Waiter
Pietro Giuseppe Bochet	c. £11–17	Second Head Waiter
Ernest Cyril Price	£4	Barman
Luigi Zarracchi	£4	Sommelier
Candido Scavino	£4	Trancheur

Every waiter was paid £3:

Ugo Banfi	Enrico Rinaldo Ratti
Giovanni Cipriano Basilico	Angelo Mario Rotta
Narciso Bazzi	Giacomo Sesia
Giulio Casali	Roberto Urbini
Vincenzo Pio Gilardino	Ettore Luigi Valvassori
Pompeo Piazza	Roberto Vioni
Emilio Santo Attanasio Poggi	

Every assistant waiter was paid £2 2s:

Battista Antonio Allaria	Alberto Peracchio
Battista Bernardi	Sebastiano Peracchio
Davide Beux	Alfonso Perotti
Paolo Luigi Crovella	Louis Piatti
Maurice Emile Victor Debreucq	Rinaldo Renato Ricaldone
Giovanni De Marsico	Abele Rigozzi
Italo Francesco Donati	Giovanni Giuseppe Emilio Saccaggi
Javier Mouros	Mario Zanetti
Alessandro Pedrini	

The Kitchen Staff of the À-la-carte Restaurant

The muster list does not help to sort out the hierarchy in the restaurant kitchen. Gastronomy for the gourmet was not invented for the *Titanic* but certainly resembled the organisational chart of a top-class restaurant ashore. The *Titanic* restaurant had 140 seats. In contrast to the main kitchens, meals could not be prepared for a particular time: the courses were freshly prepared upon receipt of an order. According to the muster list, it was not intended to have a sous–chef: this would probably have been because specialist cooks were employed whose jobs were clearly defined.

The chef's remuneration (★) is taken from that of the *Olympic* in 1911. Compared to the main kitchen, the restaurant kitchen of *Titanic* had on top two poissonniers (fish cooks) and two potagers (soup cooks). Here the gastronomic terms were used as well, in the muster lists the men were hired as 'Roast', 'Soup', 'Fish' or 'Pastry' and the word 'cook' omitted. The rate of pay was calculated from payments made to the next of kin with reference to the *Olympic* lists. If the kitchen was organised after the fashion of French gourmet restaurants, the cooks under Rousseau would have been divided into the following category groups:

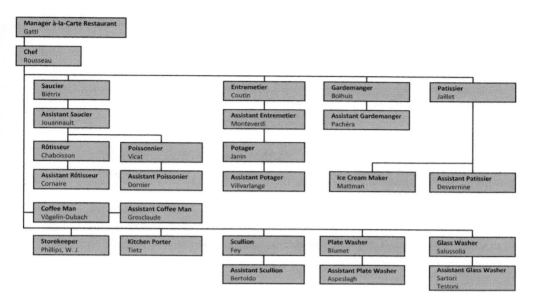

The organisation chart of the à-la-carte restaurant in first class. The restaurant on *Titanic* provided everything top gastronomy in 1912 could offer. (Diagram by author/Dominik Tezyk)

Pierre Rousseau	£425/year (★)	Chef
George Baptiste Biétrix	£3 10s/week	Saucier
Georges Jules Jouannault	£1 10s/week	Assistant Saucier
Adrien Firmin Chaboisson	£3/week	Rôtisseur
Marcel Raymond André Cornaire	£1 10s/week	Assistant Rôtisseur
Alphonse Jean Eugène Vicat	£3/week	Poissonnier
Louis Auguste Dornier	£1 10s/week	Assistant Poissonnier
Auguste Louis Coutin	£3/week	Entremetier
Giovanni Monteverdi	£1 10s/week	Assistant Entremetier
Claude Marie Janin	£3/week	Potager
Pierre Léon Gabriel Villvarlange	£1 10s/week	Assistant Potager
Hendrik Bolhuis	£3/week	Garde Manger
Jean-Baptiste Stanislas Pachéra	£1 10s/week	Assistant Garde Manger
Johannes Vögelin-Dubach	£1 15s/week	Coffee Man
Gérald Grosclaude	£1/week	Assistant Coffee Man

The restaurant kitchen was connected directly by a spiral staircase and a goods lift to the first- and second-class kitchen. Presumably there was some collaboration between the kitchens; for example, the meat was prepared by the butchers in the main kitchen and bread supplied from the bakery, although the restaurant had its own confectionery. Adolf Mattmann, trained as a patissier, was written up as 'Ice Man' in the hiring list: 'Ice Cream Maker' would have been more accurate:

Henri Marie Jaillet	£3/week	Patissier
Louis Gabriel Desvernine	£1 10s/week	Assistant Patissier
Adolf Mattmann	£1 10s/week	Ice Cream Maker

The kitchen brigade was fortified by several more men. There was no storekeeper on *Olympic*, and no documents could be found to confirm a payment to the next of kin of Walter John Phillips. He was included in Class E of the *Titanic* Relief Fund, giving equivalent monthly earnings of between £5 10s and £8:

Walter John Phillips	(*c.* £5 10s to £8)	Storekeeper
Karl Tietz	£1 5s/week	Kitchen Porter
Carlo Fey	£1 5s/week	Scullion
Fioravante Giuseppe Bertoldo	£1 2s 6d/week	Assistant Scullion
Jean Baptiste Blumet	£1 5s/week	Plate Washer
Georges Aspeslagh	£1 2s 6d/week	Assistant Plate Washer
Giovanni Salussolia	£1 5s/week	Glass Washer
Lazar Sartori	£1 2s 6d/week	Assistant Glass Washer
Ercole Testoni	£1 2s 6d/week	Assistant Glass Washer

The wages above were calculated on the outstanding amounts paid to next of kin. The exception is Lazar Sartori, whose next of kin received nothing initially. His pay was probably the same as that of Testoni. The plate and glass washers were originally signed on as platemen and glassmen, but for the sake of clarity their titles have been changed for the restaurant and main saloon listings here.

The Musicians

Titanic carried eight musicians for the entertainment of first- and second-class passengers. During the day they played in two groups, as a quintet and a trio. The White Star Line bypassed the hire fees set by the Amalgamated British Musicians Union and so the musicians were placed by the Liverpool music agency C.W. and F.W. Black. When the Union requested a contribution in March 1912 the shipping line reacted defiantly: the musicians received only £4 instead of £6. Their cabins were in second class anyhow and they were given a ticket for that class. When the *Olympic* left Southampton one week before *Titanic*, the musicians were mustered in the section of third class and galley. It seems that it was up to the purser how the musicians were listed in his books. Due to their status they were most probably subordinated to the purser's office. Therefore they are discussed here.

Seven of the eight musicians on *Titanic*. Top row: John Frederick Preston Clarke, Percy Cornelius Taylor; middle row: Georges Alexandre Krins, Wallace Henry Hartley, William Theodore Brailey; bottom row: John Law Hume, John Wesley Woodward. Not pictured here is Roger Marie Léon Joseph Bricoux. (Author's collection)

Steinway grand piano in *Olympic*'s first-class reception room, 1911. (Author's collection)

Just a few hours after the arrival of *Carpathia* in New York the legend surrounding the musicians was hardening. Errors fomented in the press of the time as to who played what and in which of the two groups remain uncorrected. The question of which musician played which instrument has caused confusion ever since.

The trio, a first compared to *Olympic*, played in the reception room in front of the à-la-carte restaurant on B-deck. Percy Cornelius Taylor, mostly identified as a pianist and violinist, was thought to have been a member of the trio. Since there was no piano in the foyer of the restaurant, there cannot have been two pianists but only William Theodore Brailey, who therefore formed a part of the quintet, while Taylor was a violinist and not a pianist. John Frederick Preston Clarke was said to play the viola – presumably 'Bass Viol' was interpreted as 'Viola' but means contrabass. On a business card found on his body it said 'Contra-Basso', and so therefore he belonged to the quintet.

Wallace Henry Hartley has gone down in history as bandleader of the quintet and is today an important historical figure in the *Titanic* legend; he became some kind of a national hero. Most would overlook the fact that in the trio, the first violinist was somehow another bandleader. This role is ascribed sometimes to Georges Krins, but he had no experience of the sea and this was his first voyage. On the other hand, John Law Hume was identified by stewardess Violet Constance Jessop and by Hume's father as the bandleader of the trio. As all the glory fell to Hartley, Hume's role as first violinist is still doubted today, even by his own family and even though he had been the bandleader on the *Carmania*. The Belgian Georges Alexandre Krins (violin) and the Frenchman Roger Marie Léon Joseph Bricoux (cello) fit well into the trio and underline the international flair of the restaurant upon which the White Star Line placed such value.

According to the foregoing, Percy Cornelius Taylor (violin) and John Wesley Woodward (cello) played in the quintet. The musicians therefore formed the following two groups. All lost their lives:

All musicians received the monthly remuneration of £4.

Wallace Henry Hartley	Violinist, Bandleader Quintet
Percy Cornelius Taylor	Violinist
William Theodore Brailey	Pianist
John Wesley Woodward	Cellist
John Frederick Preston Clarke	Contra-Bassist
John Law Hume	First Violinist, Trio
Georges Alexandre Krins	Violinist
Roger Marie Léon Joseph Bricoux	Cellist

The passengers usually arranged a collection for the musicians. According to their contract all tips were equally split through the number of musicians plus one, and the bandleader was given two shares. Aboard *Olympic* in 1911 the quintet played at the following times:

Second class, aft reception room, C-deck: 10:00–11:00, 17:00–18:00
    and 21:15–22:15hrs
First class, staircase, entrance, boat deck: 11:00–12:00hrs
First class, reception room, D-deck, 16:00–17:00 and 20:00–21:15hrs

Musicians in the aft reception room in *Olympic*'s second class, around 1924. Before the First World War there were no saxophones played on British liners and the passengers would not dance. (Author's collection)

The Post Office Clerks

The RMS (Royal Mail Ship) *Titanic* was licensed to carry letters and packets. She was also a 'United States Mail Steamer'. Although the postal clerks did not work for any of the three shipboard classes, they could move about in first class and so are treated here.

On smaller ships the mail was locked away, and only the captain had access to the mail room. In order not to leave the material untouched for the duration of the crossing, *Titanic* carried post-office staff to sort the mail. For this purpose there was a post office on G-deck connected by steps to the mail room on the Orlop-deck. The United States Post Office Department employed three postal clerks and Royal Mail the other two. Their consultant on board would have been the first-class purser – the post was enormously important for the image of the White Star Line and also as a source of income, and therefore it was made a principal business.

On the westward passage the responsibility was with the British, on the return the Americans handled it. This might be surprising, but it was the duty of the sending postal authorities to sort the letters for the different states and countries. On F-deck directly above the post office were two two-bed cabins for the post-office clerks. Normally only four postal clerks would travel, but this time William Logan Gwinn had asked to go by an earlier ship than planned for America because his wife was ill there. He was put on the *Titanic* and presumably given a first-class cabin.

The postal clerks took their meals, which came by a dumb waiter from the main kitchen, in a dining room on C-deck that they shared with the wireless operators. It would be no surprise that these 'hired-in' shipboard staff should be associated in this way, for in those times the mail companies worked closely with the telegraph companies.

The post clerks were the only people aboard *Titanic* who were neither mentioned on passenger or crew lists. Other external crew members were named on the muster list

The sorting room of the *Oceanic*, around 1909. Since the journey over the Atlantic took several days, the post was sorted during the passage. (Author's collection)

(radio operators) or the passenger list (musicians). To the present day the number of crew members aboard *Titanic* is often given as 885 persons. This figure omits the five postal clerks, eight musicians and the Assistant Glass Washer Lazar Sartori – 899 persons in all.

Nevertheless, White Star Line soon included the postal clerks in the crew total, although the remuneration is not recorded. Seagoing US postal clerks received at least US$1,200 annually, equivalent to about £20 per month. This figure applies to Oscar Scott Woody; John Starr March and William Logan Gwinn earned at least as much.

The remuneration figures shown below for the two British employees have been supplied by Royal Mail. There would have been about 20 per cent extra in allowances. For the round trip originally £6 expenses were intended in order to make the work more attractive and compensate for Sunday working. White Star Line informed the postal authorities that stewards were not to be tipped, at which the expenses paid were reduced to £5 5s:

John Richard Jago Smith	£2 7s 6d/week	Royal Mail Clerk
James Bertram Williamson	£2 13s 6d/week	Royal Mail Clerk
William Logan Gwinn	not less than US$1,200/year	US Post Office Clerk
John Starr March	not less than US$1,200/year	US Post Office Clerk
Oscar Scott Woody	US$1,200/year	US Post Office Clerk

All post office clerks lost their lives.

8

THE VICTUALLING DEPARTMENT – SECOND CLASS

The structure of second class was fairly similar to first class, though with fewer personnel and specialists. Some areas (such as the Turkish baths or restaurant) were absent from second class. Numerous tasks (in the kitchen, bakery, printing shop, etc.) were carried out by the staff of first class. Below Purser McElroy was a second purser, Reginald Lomond Barker, who was competent for second and third class. He earned £15 and had his office on E-deck next to his cabin. He was assisted by the clerk Donald S. Campbell who earned £5, as did his colleagues in first class. Naturally, the infrastructure of first class was also available to Barker.

The senior crew structure in second and third class was as follows:

Reginald Lomond Barker	£15	Purser
Donald S. Campbell	£5	Clerk
John William Hardy	£10	Chief Second Class Steward
James Kieran	£8	Chief Third Class Steward
William John T. Simmons	£7	Passenger Cook (Third Class)

Above: Reginal Lomond Barker was, as purser, responsible for second and third class. (Author's collection)

The second-class purser of *Olympic* in his office on E-Deck, around 1924. (Author's collection)

John William Hardy, the only man of the above five to survive the sinking, had sixty-six men and two women under him. His office was at the second-class foyer on E-deck. The staff complement was appropriate to the simpler environment and the smaller number of passengers. After the complex organisation of first class, the Victualling Department of second class seems even simple and clearly arranged.

The Saloon Stewards

The meal times in second class were about one hour earlier than in first class, which reduced peak time pressures in the combined kitchen, but prolonged the working hours of the respective staff. The breakfast was served at 08:00hrs, lunch at 12:30hrs and dinner at 18:00hrs.

The responsibility for the dining room lay with the Chief Second Class Steward John William Hardy and Second Class Saloon Steward Henry Thomas Jenner, with charge of forty-three stewards. As with first class, these are referred to as saloon stewards for clarity. In contrast to first class, it is known who was active as a saloon steward and assistant saloon steward, therefore waiter and assistant waiter, the assistant serving two saloon stewards. Remuneration was unchanged for all of them:

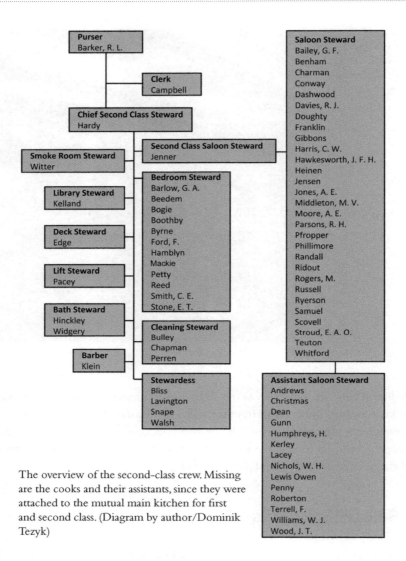

The overview of the second-class crew. Missing are the cooks and their assistants, since they were attached to the mutual main kitchen for first and second class. (Diagram by author/Dominik Tezyk)

Henry Thomas Jenner   £4 5s   Second Class Saloon Steward

Saloon stewards were paid £3 15s:

George Francis Bailey	Richard John Davies
Fred John Benham	Walter Thomas Doughty
John James Charman	Alan Vincent Franklin
Percy Walter Conway	Jacob William Gibbons
William George Dashwood	Charles William Harris

Olympic's dining room for the second-class passengers. (Author's collection)

John Fisher Henry Hawkesworth	Walter George Ridout
Joseph Dominikus Heinen	Michael Rogers
Charles Valdemar Jensen	Boysie Richard Russell
Albert Edward Jones	William Edwy Ryerson
Mark Victor Middleton	Owen Wilmore Samuel
Alfred Ernest Moore	Robert Scovell
Richard Henry Parsons	Edward Alfred Orlando Stroud
Richard Paul Josef Pfropper	Thomas Moore Teuton
Harold Charles William Phillimore	Alfred Henry Whitford
Frank Henry Randall	

Assistant saloon stewards were also paid £3 15s:

Charles Edward Andrews	Walter Henry Nichols
Herbert Edward Christmas	Lewis Owen
George H. Dean	William Farr Penny
Joseph Alfred Gunn	George Edward Roberton
Humphrey Humphreys	Frank Terrell
William Thomas Kerley	Walter John Williams
Bertie Leonard Lacey	James Thomas Wood

Eight of these men survived: Andrews, Gibbons, Nichols, Pfropper, Phillimore, Ryerson, Terrell and Williams. There were also night watchmen in second class. It is not known if some of the saloon stewards worked in the dining room at night instead of by day or if only the bedroom stewards kept the night watch. It is also unknown if the saloon stewards similar to first class helped; for example, if needed in the smoke room or library.

The Bedroom Stewards

Each of the twelve bedroom stewards of second class looked after twelve cabins. As in first class, they worked independently and came under the chief second class steward directly. None of them survived, and only for two of them does an indication exist of which cabins they served. Bedroom stewards earned £3 15s:

George Arthur Barlow   Ernest William Hamblyn
George Arthur Beedem   George William Mackie
Norman Leslie Bogie   Edwin Henry J. Petty, cabin F33
Walter Thomas Boothby   Thomas Charles Prowse Reed
James Edward Byrne   Charles Edwin Smith
Francis Ford   Edward Thomas Stone, cabins E99 to E107

It is certain that the second-class bedroom stewards also acted as night watchmen to attend to passengers' requirements. After lights-out at 23:00hrs, four remained on station until midnight. Then two came on for the middle watch until 04:00hrs. The others took over until 05:30hrs, then all reported for duty (apart from the middle watch, not until 07:30hrs). Which stewards had middle watch on the night of the sinking is not known.

A steward with two passengers in their D-deck cabin on *Olympic*, around 1924. (Author's collection)

Specialist Stewards in the Victualling Department

There were comparatively few stewards with a specialist function in second class, and they are all grouped together here since any further sub-division makes little sense. All the following stewards earned £3 15s:

James William Cheetham Witter	Smoke Room Steward
Thomas Kelland	Library Steward
Frederick William Edge	Deck Steward
Reginald Ivan Pacey	Lift Steward
Henry Ashburnham Bulley	Cleaning Steward
Joseph Charles Chapman	Cleaning Steward
William Charles Perren	Cleaning Steward
George Herbert Hinckley	Bath Steward
Isaac George Widgery	Bath Steward

The stewardesses earned £3:

Emma Bliss	Stewardess
Elizabeth Lavington	Stewardess
Lucy Violett Snape	Stewardess
Catherine Walsh	Stewardess

The barber was not paid by the shipping company:

Herbert Klein	Barber

Bliss, Chapman, Lavington, Widgery and Witter survived the sinking.

A second-class deck steward approaching passengers on *Olympic*, *c*. 1924. (Author's collection)

The library steward not only loaned books and games, but also served tea. Shown here is the second-class bookcase on *Olympic*, around 1924. (Author's collection)

Corner of the second-class smoke room on *Olympic* in the early 1920s. (Author's collection)

The library steward was the only position exclusive to second class, as there was no equivalent position in first class. Although first class had a large bookcase in the lounge, second class had a room designated as a library. Besides immigrants of reasonable means (who expected a more pleasant journey and simpler arrival formalities than third-class passengers), the classic middle classes travelled second class, amongst them businessmen, teachers and clergymen. These erudite clients expected a library. Although the bookcase was smaller than that in the first-class lounge, it gave the room the name. The library was located astern on C-deck and was also used as a writing and reading room. Library Steward Thomas Kelland lent books and games, served tea and distributed arrival forms for the destination port, which could be completed immediately at a writing table.

The lift from F-deck up to the boat deck was operated by Lift Steward Reginald Ivan Pacey. Presumably his reliefs were arranged with a saloon or bedroom steward.

In charge of the smoke room was James William Cheetham Witter. He opened his bar at 08:00hrs and closed it at 22:30hrs; the lights were extinguished at midnight.

The second-class barber shop of the *Olympic*, around 1919. As well as providing haircuts, souvenirs and articles for daily use were sold here. (Author's collection)

After the loss of the *Titanic*, the widow of Herbert Klein, barber, sued White Star Line for a pension as a dependent. The shipping line refused, since it did not pay the barbers. The court decided, however, that compensation was due based on an income of about £10 to £20 per round trip.

As explained in regard to the first-class stewardesses, according to the muster list only Stewardess Lucy Snape and Matron Wallis worked in second class, but it seems much more plausible as explained that Emma Bliss, Elizabeth Lavington, Lucy Snape and Catherine Walsh worked there instead. Chief Second Class Steward John Hardy strengthens this assumption by his statement to the US Senate hearing. To better understand what is said, it should be pointed out that in the following quote from Hardy the word 'men' includes 'women', though not stated. Hardy said to Senator Duncan Upshaw Fletcher (page 594): 'I have 14 men out of 70. That is all I did save, sir.' In Hardy's sphere of jurisdiction, according to the muster list he had only sixty-eight persons, of whom eleven survived. The discrepancy is explained as follows: The Matron worked not in second but third class, despite what the muster list might say. Additionally, three stewardesses on the muster list as first class worked in second class. Since two of the three supposedly first-class stewardesses survived, that would make the fourteen survivors, including Hardy himself.

The Cooks and Other Kitchen Employees

The second-class kitchen was integrated into that of first class. A common kitchen for the two classes meant greater efficiency both in purchasing and storing equipment. Although there were enough passengers travelling in the two upper classes to justify separate kitchens operating, there was naturally no objection to there being similar items on the menu. On the evening of 14 April 1912, for example, there were nearly identical dishes served in the

The cooks of first and second class worked together in the kitchen on D-deck. Note the impressive mortar and pestle in the foreground. This photograph was taken on *Olympic* in 1911. (Author's collection)

first- and second-class dining saloons: beef soup (two variations), lamb with mint sauce, roast potatoes (called Chateau potatoes in first class), rice and green peas. Other parallels between the various work steps can be recognised. Presumably the first-class menu was drawn up first, then individual items taken for the second-class menu so as to co-ordinate and even out the workload.

The cook in second class, Harry Robert Stubbings, worked closely with the cooks of first class but had responsibility for his own area. He earned more than most cooks in first class. That arose from his being responsible not only for a section, but for the whole second-class kitchen. Above him were Chef Charles Proctor and Sous-Chef Alexis Bochatay. There would have been no point in assigning him to the second-class purser because the splitting of jurisdiction would have frustrated the advantage of combining kitchens. It is also not a contradiction that the pantrymen and plate washers were used indirectly to work for both first and second class: this work was organised through separate foremen.

As mentioned, the following men did not amount to the full complement to cook for second class, but drew help from other quarters. Pantrymen and plate washers could be called up for all possible kitchen work, only during food preparation and washing up were their roles clearly defined:

| Harry Robert Stubbings | £7 10s | Second Class Cook |
| Wilfred Deable Seward | £4 10s | Chief Pantryman |

The following assistant pantrymen and plate washers all earned £3 15s:

Alfred John Harding	Assistant Pantryman
John Dickson Longmuir	Assistant Pantryman
Percy Robert Pook	Assistant Pantryman
Arthur Victor Edward Burrage	Plate Washer
Frederick Humby	Plate Washer
Arthur Ernest Jones	Plate Washer

Only Seward and Burrage of the kitchen brigade in second class survived.

9

THE VICTUALLING DEPARTMENT – THIRD CLASS

Even easier to work out than the organisation of second class was that of third class. Here the passengers enjoyed none of the costly extravaganzas. It is obvious that the purser of second class, Reginald Lomond Barker, also looked after third class. For one thing, he was hardly overburdened with just second class, while the purser in first class had more than enough work, and from that one can assume that Barker kept McElroy's back free. The management of the crew in third class was undertaken mainly by the chief third-class steward and his assistant:

A corner of the generous third-class dining room. About twenty-five of the third-class stewards served the meals here. Unlike in the upper classes, the meals here were not served on plates. The stewards placed the pots and dishes on the tables and the passengers helped themselves. (Author's collection)

| James Kieran | £8 | Chief Third Class Steward |
| Sidney Francis Sedunary | £5 | Second Third Class Steward |

No third-class stewards were hired with specialist functions. They kept the place orderly but naturally did not offer the service that the other two ship's classes did. Service in the dining saloon was reduced to the minimum. The kitchen area of third class shows that, in comparison to the other classes, nobody was hired for washing up, a job handled by the stewards afterwards. The bedroom stewards also had comparatively more cabins each to service. Besides cleaning work they disinfected the cabins and sanitary installations several times on a crossing. The following forty-three stewards worked in third class; only a few of them can be split into bedroom or saloon stewards. All the following stewards earned £3 15s:

Albert Edward Akerman
Sidney John Barton
Harry Ross Baxter
Robert Charles Bristow
John Cress Brookman
Charles Thomas Cecil
Archibald George Chitty
William Denton Cox
Sidney Edward Daniels
Francis Samuel Jacob Edbrooke
George Bulkeley Ede
William Henry Egg
Henry Herman Finch
William C. Foley
Ernest Ford
William Thomas Fox
Edwin Henry Halford
John Edward Hart
Henry Parkinson Hill
James Leo Hyland
Henry Ingrouille
Leonard George Knight

Matthew Leonard
Arthur Ernest Read Lewis
John Charles Mabey
Roland Frederick Mantle
Thomas A. Mullin
Arthur D. Nichols
Alfred Ernest Pearce
Frank Port
John Arthur Prideaux
Harold John Prior
Alfred Pugh
Percy Rice
Thomas Ryan
Charles James Savage
William Sivier
Harry John Slight
George Frederick Charles Talbot
Bernard Cuthbert Taylor
Montague Donald Thaler
W. Willis
Rowland Winser

Daniels, Foley, Halford, Hart, Hyland, Lewis, Port, Prior and Pugh survived the sinking; Daniels probably became the last surviving crew member of the *Titanic*, he died in May 1983. How were the stewards divided into groups? Of the survivors, only John Hart delivered testimony at the British inquiry. To Solicitor General John Simon and Attorney William Dawson Harbinson, he answered:

| Simon (9919): | How many third-class stewards would there be who would have charge of rooms in the after end of the ship? |
| Hart: | Eight. |

...

| Harbinson (10215): | Who else besides you, then, were bringing the people from their berths – rousing them and bringing them up to the boat deck? How many others? |
| Hart: | Almost eight. A portion of the third-class stewards were room stewards, of whom I am the only survivor. |

From that it can be deduced that the other eight surviving stewards from third class were not bedroom stewards.

Presumably eight to ten stewards were responsible for the cabins of the men travelling alone in the bow. On the night of the disaster these all had their hands full. The other eight survivors must have been saloon stewards and possibly the stewards of the two bars in third class – one in the bow on D-deck, the other in the stern of C-deck near the Smoke Room. Also, in third class the bedroom stewards alternated in the middle watch from 00:00–04:00hrs, but which they were on during the fateful night is not known:

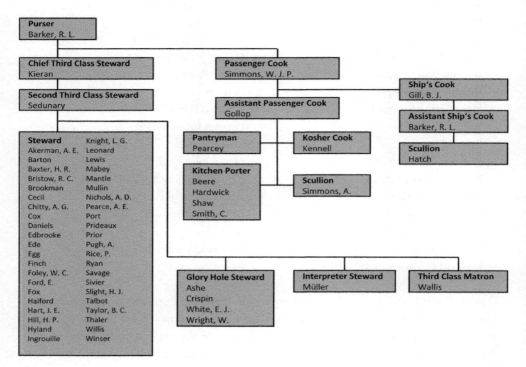

The third-class crew. The crew cooks and the stewards for the crew quarters were also affiliated to third class. (Diagram by author/Dominik Tezyk)

| Louis Müller | £4 10s | Interpreter Steward |
| Catherine Jane Wallis | £3 | Third Class Matron |

In order to master the confusion of languages in third class, the White Star Line hired the interpreter Louis Müller for £4 10s. Besides German and English, presumably he also spoke a Scandinavian language. He would often have been in the company of Chief Third Class Steward Kieran, Second Third Class Steward Sedunary, Matron Catherine Jane Wallis and Kosher Cook Charles Kennell.

An American immigration official described the interpreter on board a White Star Liner in 1909 in an interesting but not very flattering way:

An interpreter who spoke English, Swedish, Norwegian, and some German was on board to serve when needed. He was, however, not at all conscientious in the performance of any duties and evidently not very capable. His price for granting privileges, performing favors and overlooking abuses was a mug of stout. I know him to have openly asked one passenger for such a treat and, judging from the number of treats he received and the reputation given him by others of the crew, he did not hesitate to solicit free drinks from everyone. He was generally present in the dining room during meals, though he did nothing. To young women passengers his manner could be most friendly and gracious. To others he was positively rude. He made most disparaging remarks about a German who merely refused to buy favor with drinks.

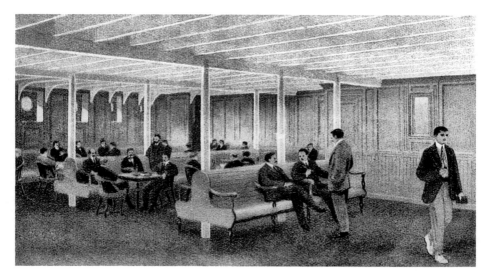

This artist's impression of the third-class smoke room of the *Olympic* and *Titanic* was created in 1911. Just outside of the smoking room was one of two bars in third class. (Author's collection)

Catherine Jane Wallis was hired as matron for second class, but reports agree that she was active in third class. What was her function? There is no paperwork on the subject from the *Titanic*. In Britain, the matron was the most senior nursing sister in a hospital, or the superintendent of an almshouse or children's home. On ships she attended women travelling alone. She instructed women passengers how keep a cabin orderly. Those unable to take their meals in the dining room were provided with food by the matron. During the meals she handed out milk to the children and served bouillon to women and children in the morning. She visited the sick passengers several times a day in their cabins. Many third-class passengers would not have been familiar with the modern sanitary installations of the *Titanic* (e.g. running water, flush toilets) and so Matron Wallis would certainly have helped them in this respect. She had to keep an eye open to ensure that unrelated men and women met only in the community rooms. Unmarried men had their quarters in the bow, the women at the stern – men in the women's cabin corridors at the stern would have been noticed at once.

That might give the impression that the matron was a strict overseer who restricted the freedom of the women. The contrary was the case. The matron protected the women against the unwelcome interest of male passengers and crew members. The shipping company had made a point of protecting the women on its ships. If a woman from third class was examined by the surgeon, the matron would be present. She was certainly alert to the early signs of illnesses and relayed her observations to the doctors.

To complete the medical picture, the hospital steward, William Dunford, must be mentioned. His name has already come up previously for he was assigned to the surgeons attached to the Deck Department. Therefore, although he was on the muster list as third class, he is not counted in here. None of the specialised third-class crew members survived.

The Kitchen Brigade

The third-class kitchen was on the starboard side of F-deck. In contrast to the major kitchen of first and second class, only steam was used to cook in third, for which four 360-litre boilers were available. No cooks appear in the muster lists for third class.

The *Titanic* had been declared officially to be an emigrant ship. According to the New Passenger Act of 1849, such a ship with more than 100 passengers had to carry a passenger cook. On the muster list there was a 'Passg. Cook' and his assistant. The abbreviation was interpreted as 'Passage Cook' or 'Passenger Cook', the latter being required by law and so assigned to third class. The implementation of this law, intended for the protection of emigrants, was for long a matter of course, but nevertheless the term was retained for decades. For the preparation of comparatively simple meals in third class, the following men were hired aboard *Titanic*:

William John T. Simmons	£7	Passenger Cook
Percival Salisbury Gollop	£4 10s	Assistant Passenger Cook

| Charles Kennell | £4 | Kosher Cook |
| Albert Victor Pearcey | £4 | Pantryman |

The following men were all hired at the rate of £3 10s:

Andrew Simmons	Scullion
William Beere	Kitchen Porter
Reginald Hardwick	Kitchen Porter
Henry Shaw	Kitchen Porter
Charles Smith	Kitchen Porter

Hardwick, Pearcey and A. Simmons survived. It is not certain from the muster lists whether the scullion and four kitchen porters were assigned to third class. In the lists, the kitchen porters are listed immediately before the passenger cooks, the scullion follows the kosher cook. On account of the number of passengers to be cooked for and the size of the kitchen, the number of kitchen employees seems appropriate. Certain preparatory work may have been done by the main kitchen.

In connection with the third-class kitchen, a design flaw can be seen from a study of the deck plans: all provisions had to be brought from the stores by lift to E-deck, and from there everything had to be carried down a stairway to the kitchen in the deck below. This meant that the scullions and storekeepers spent a large part of the day in transport work. During *Olympic*'s later career this was not corrected, and so the food for hundreds of people had to be brought into the kitchen down a stairway every day.

The galley of an unknown steamer, around 1910. The three huge steam cookers are an indication that this photograph was taken in third class. (Author's collection)

Close by the kitchen was the third-class bakery. Although all bakers answered to Chief Baker Joughin, some were delegated to Passenger Cook William John T. Simmons, though who they were is not known. A question that remains is to whom the third-class cooks reported. The chef is, by tradition, a member of the upper hierarchy, and so it seems as though the burden fell on Purser Barker, who was partially responsible for third class.

The *Titanic* had a kosher cook, Charles Kennell. In the muster list he is described as 'Hebrew Cook'. In the linguistic usage of the time 'Hebrew' was equal to 'Jewish'. The Jewish-prescribed method of food preparation for kosher eating was then, as now, very strict. Kennell would have needed his own kitchen, but all he had was a wooden chest with cooking utensils and cutlery. His area of operations was basically in third class and he was not just a cook but the intermediary between the Jewish passengers and the crew. An American immigration official described this position in 1909:

The Hebrew steerage passengers were looked after by a Hebrew who is employed by the company as a cook, and is at the same time appointed by Rabbi as guardian of such passengers. This particular man told me that he is a pioneer in this work. He was the first to receive such an appointment. It is his duty to see that all Jewish passengers are assigned sleeping quarters that are as comfortable and good as any, to see that kosher food is provided and to prepare it. He has done duty on most ships of the White Star Line. On each he has instituted this system of caring for the Hebrews and then has left it to be looked after by some successor.

10

THE CREW'S CREW

It seems logical that a crew of 899 men and women must have its own crew to cater for the crew areas. For example, the Deck and Engine departments had their own cooks and the captain had his own steward, as described in the corresponding chapters.

The higher-ranking crew members of the Victualling Department received their meals from the main kitchen. This raises the questions with regard to the almost 500 other crew members of this department: who cooked for them and where? Where did they eat their food? There is no sure indication. On the *Titanic* there was no kitchen or mess for the complement of the Victualling Department. The Merchant Shipping Act 1906 provided that the crew's cook was to be specified as 'Ship's Cook' on the muster list. There actually is one such on the muster list, together with his assistant and one scullion:

Patrick Joseph Gill	£5 10s	Ship's Cook
Harry Thorn (Johnson)	£4	Assistant Ship's Cook
Hugh Vivian Hatch	£3 10s	Scullion

But where did they work? To where was the prepared food brought? The Victualling Department made up around 56 per cent of the total crew. That all workers of this section fed on the leftovers of the upper-class passengers is unthinkable, since in that case more high-value food would have had to be carried. It is possible that, after the passengers had dined, the crew took over the dining rooms and ate there, but that would have meant 'driving out' first-class passengers. This would leave one imagining crew members waiting outside the dining room ravenously hungry until it cleared. It is inconceivable that the saloon stewards waited to lay places for the crew after a long day, and, furthermore, there would have had to have been separate crew crockery.

Because of the way the decks were divided up it can be ruled out that the Victualling Department used the firemen's mess – the three-watch system of the Engine Department would have made this impossible. It is more probable that the Victualling Department (presumably in two groups one after the other) used the third-class dining room. That would make sense of having the meals prepared in third class, and in reality the crew's food would have resembled that of third class more than the higher classes. It would seem reasonable that these large groups of staff had fixed mealtimes before or after the passengers, allowing the use of cheaper and more sturdy crockery, and nobody would have been disturbed, bearing in mind the location of the F-deck dining room. Similar to the other departments, the crew of the Victualling Department would have been catered for in the immediate vicinity of their accommodation. To solve the lack of an official mess for the stewards on *Olympic*, the former port-side, third-class open space on D-deck was turned into a steward's mess in 1920. In 1928 an even more logicical solution was found, when the forward starboard quarter of the third-class dining room was changed into a steward's mess.

The third-class kitchen seems very small for the possible 1,134 passengers in third class. It is difficult to imagine that almost 500 crew members were also cooked for there. Even less likely is that the food was cooked in the main kitchen or crew galley and carried down without the use of a lift. The first- and second-class kitchen was not laid out for mass-produced simple meals. Logistically the simplest solution was to cook everything in third class. The third-class kitchen actually resembled the crew galley on C-deck in its fittings and equipment. Ship's Cook Patrick Gill and his men would therefore probably have come under the cook of third class.

Most crew members involved with food preparation and serving on *Titanic* had their quarters amidships on E-deck at 'Scotland Road', the corridor from the bow to the stern. The crew shared these corridors with third-class passengers. Therefore it is not surprising that the four stewards responsible for order and cleanliness in the crew quarters appeared in the third-class muster lists and came under the chief third-class steward. The term 'glory hole' was applied to crew quarters aboard ship. Glory holes were traditionally lumber rooms aboard ship in which useless material was stowed. Therefore the origin of the term for crew quarters is probably a linguistic joke, for crew members that were 'stowed' after their duty in tight quarters – the so-called glory holes. Glory hole stewards were all paid £3 15s:

Henry Wellesley Ashe
William Crispin
Edward Joseph White
William Wright

Of these, only William Wright survived. The stewards cleaned the toilets and floors and made the crew's beds for a tip. They had hot drinks ready and were presumably responsible for the purchase of alcoholic drink and tobacco for the crew. They would have reported necessary repairs to the chief steward.

That completes the description of the organisation of the *Titanic* crew.

11

STATISTICS

The following statistics take into account all crew members who sailed on the *Titanic* after leaving Queenstown, therefore including the five postal clerks and eight musicians but leaving aside the fireman, John Coffey, who deserted. This leaves a total of 899. The captain's steward, hospital steward and the two radio operators are reckoned with the Deck Department for reasons described previously, some statistics appear on page 24 lacking these corrections:

Percentages of Crew in Each Department

Deck Department	70 men	7.8%
Engine Department	325 men	36.1%
Victualling Department	504 men and women	56.1%
Total	899 men and women	100%

Survival Rates

Deck Department	44 men	62.9%
Engine Department	71 men	21.8%
Victualling Department	97 men and women	19.2%
(Victualling Department	77 men	16.0%)
(Victualling Department	20 women	87.0%)
Total	212 men & women	23.6%

Survival Rate Boiler Rooms

The boiler-room crew who were on watch at the time of the collision had the lowest survival rate, while those who were preparing to come on watch had the best. Not included are the seven firemen and five trimmers hired at the last minute:

	Watch	Watch	Watch	Total
	00:00–04:00	04:00–08:00	08:00–12:00	
	12.00–16:00	16:00–20:00	20:00–24:00	
Engineers	0% (0/3)	0% (0/3)	0% (0/3)	0% (0/9)
Ldg. Firemen	20% (1/5)	40% (2/5)	20% (1/5)	26.7% (4/15)
Firemen	38.5% (20/52)	32.7% (17/52)	12.5% (6/48)	28.3% (43/152)
Trimmers	41.7% (10/24)	22.7% (5/22)	18.2% (4/22)	27.9% (19/68)
Total	36.9% (31/84)	29.3% (24/82)	14.1% (11/78)	27% (66/244)

Statistic of Survivors and Victims

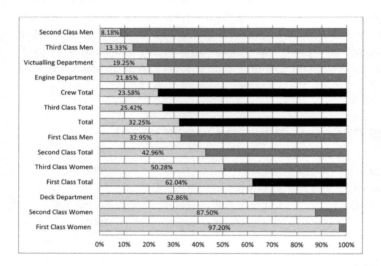

Statistics of survivors and victims (without children). The light band (left) shows the rate of survival in the respective group, the darker band (right) the percentage of victims. (Graphic by author/Corina Amrein)

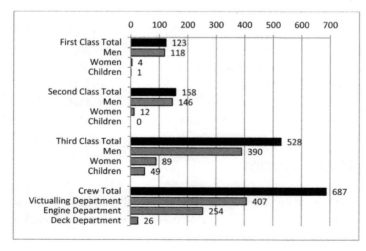

The effective number of victims, sorted by classes and crew – 45.9 per cent of the *Titanic* victims were crew members. (Graphic by author/Corina Amrein)

Crew Origins

The crew of the *Titanic* consisted overwhelmingly of men and women from Great Britain. It would require another work of its own to establish the precise origin, since the place of birth is not conclusive by itself. The ethnic origin must also be taken into account. Of the 899 crew members, around eighty-four were foreigners, about 9 per cent. Most of them, actually sixty-two, worked in the à-la-carte restaurant. If one discounts the restaurant, then in the remainder of the crew of 830 there were about twenty-two foreigners, around 2.6 per cent, the bulk being British, 97.4 per cent.

The Monthly Hire of the *Titanic* Crew

In the following table showing the remuneration of crew members, a weekly income has been rounded up to a thirty-day month; similarly, the annual salary of the captain and some restaurant workers has been rounded down. The captain's bonus for accident-free voyaging and the unpaid supplements to the lookouts have been discounted. The US Post Office clerks allegedly earned US$1,200 annually, equivalent to £20 per month, although we only have one document to confirm that fact. The outstanding hire of the radio operators, post-office clerks and musicians was not settled by White Star Line. For numerous crew members, details such as tips (which are not recorded in the ledgers of the shipping company) are missing. The number of crew members performing the same job is shown in brackets: for the Victualling Department, Roman numerals show which of the three ship's classes are involved, or (R) for restaurant in first class. Some restaurant workers whose hire was assumed as an equivalent from the *Olympic* are denoted with an asterisk ★. The maître d'hôtel, the second head waiter and the storekeeper have been omitted from the restaurant crew because their salaries are not known. Here is the 'ranking list' by remuneration:

£104 3s 4d	Master/Captain
£45 16s 8d	Manager à-la-carte Restaurant (R★)
£35 8s 4d	Chef (R★)
£35	Chief Engineer
£25	Chief Officer
£22	Senior Second Engineer
£20	Purser (I,II+III), Chief Steward (I), Chef (I+II), US Post Office Clerk (3)
£18	Second Engineer, Junior Second Engineer
£17 10s	First Officer
£16 13s 4d	Head Waiter (R★)
£16 10s	Senior Third Engineer
£15 10s	Junior Third Engineer

£15	Purser (II+ III), Saucier (R)
£14	Second Officer, Senior Fourth Engineer
£13 10s	Junior Fourth Engineer
£13	Senior Assistant Second Engineer
£12 17s 2d	Entremetier (R), Garde Manger (R), Patissier (R), Poissonnier (R), Potager (R), Rôtisseur (R)
£12 10s	Junior Assistant Second Engineer (2)
£12	Senior Assistant Third Engineer, Boilermaker, Chief Electrician, Chief Baker (I,II+III)
£11 15s	Senior Radio Operator (incl. £1 15s/week from Marconi Company)
£11 10s	Junior Assistant Third Engineer (2)
£11 9s 3d	Royal Mail Clerk
£11	Senior Assistant Fourth Engineer, Junior Boilermaker, Second Electrician
£10 16s 8d	Controller (R★)
£10 10s	Junior Assistant Fourth Engineer (2), Deck Engineer, Extra Assistant Fourth Engineer (Refrigeration)
£10 3s 7d	Royal Mail Clerk
£10	Surgeon, Senior Fifth Engineer, Second Steward (I), Chief Second Class Steward (II), Sous-Chef (I+ II)
£9 10s	Third Officer, Carpenter, Junior Fifth Engineer, Extra Fifth Engineer (Turbine), Assistant Deck Engineer
£9	Fourth Officer, Senior Sixth Engineer, Plumber
£8 10s	Fifth Officer, Sixth Officer, Boatswain, Assistant Surgeon, Junior Sixth Engineer
£8	Assistant Electrician (4), Assistant Second Steward (2, I), Chief Third Class Steward (III), Confectioner (I)
£7 10s	Entremetier (I+ II), First Cashier (R), Second Class Cook (II), Coffee Man (R)
£7	Storekeeper (2), Passenger Cook (III), Saucier (I+II), Garde Manger (I+II), Second Baker, Chief Pantryman (I)
£6 10s	Leading Fireman (15), Greaser (33), Senior Turkish Bath Attendant (I), Rôtisseur (I+II), Grillardin (2, I+II), Légumier (I+II)
£6 8s 7d	Ice Cream Maker (R), Assistant Entremetier (R), Assistant Garde Manger (R), Assistant Patissier (R), Assistant Poissonnier (R), Assistant Potager (R), Assistant Rôtisseur (R), Assistant Saucier (R)
£6 8s 3d	Junior Radio Operator (incl. £1/week from Marconi Company)
£6	Joiner, Fireman (159), Assistant Storekeeper (2), Crew Cook/Engine Department (3), Engineers' Secretary, Printer Steward (I,II+III), First Saloon Steward (I), Clothes Presser Steward, (I,II+III), Turkish Bath Attendant (I), Chief Butcher (I,II+III), Chief Storekeeper (I,II+III)
£5 10s	Boatswain's Mate, Master-at-Arms (2), Trimmer (73), Second Butcher (I,II+III), Assistant Confectioner (I+II), Ship's Cook
£5 7s 2d	Glass Washer (R), Kitchen Porter (R), Scullion (R), Plate Washer (R)

£5 5s	Quartermaster (7), Lamp Trimmer, Storekeeper
£5 1s 6d	Assistant Scullion (R), Assistant Glass Washer (2, R), Assistant Plate Washer (R)
£5	A.B. Seaman (29), Seaman (2), Lookout (6), Crew Cook/Engine Department, Clerk (4, I+II), Second Third Class Steward (III), Assistant Légumier (I+II), Extra Second Baker (I,II+III), Second Pantryman (I)
£4 10s	Hospital Steward, Stenographer (I), Second Saloon Steward (I), Linen Steward (I,II+III), Interpreter Steward (III), Assistant Passenger Cook (III), Assistant Rôtisseur (I+II), Assistant Cook (3, I+II), Assistant Légumier (3, I+II), Third Butcher (I,II+III), Assistant Butcher (5, I,II+III), Chief Pantryman (II), Third Baker (I,II+III), Extra Third Baker (I,II+III), Assistant Baker (4, I,II+III), Vienna Baker (I)
£4 5s 9d	Racquet Steward (I), Assistant Coffee Man (R)
£4 5s	Chief Cleaning Steward (I), Second Class Saloon Steward (II), Second Storekeeper (I,II+III)
£4	Window Cleaner (2), Crew Cook/Deck Department (2), Assistant Printer Steward (I,II+III), Musicians (8, I+II), Baggage Steward (I), Third Saloon Steward (I), Turkish Bath Attendant (I), Turkish Bath Stewardesses (2, I), Kosher Cook (III), Assistant Baker (2, I,II+III), Assistant Ship's Cook, Pantryman (III), Barman (R), Sommelier (R), Trancheur (R)
£3 15s	Captain's Steward, Mess Steward (2), Saloon Steward (135, I+II excl. Night Watchman), Bedroom Steward (47, I+II), Third Class Steward (43, III), Gastronomy Steward with specific function (15, I+II), Telephone Steward (I), Bugler Steward (I), Lift Steward (4, I+II), Bath Steward (7, I+II), Cleaning Steward (8, I+II), Night Watchman (5, I), Gymnasium Steward (I), Glory Hole Steward (4), Assistant Pantryman (3, II), Plate Washer (10, I+II), Storekeeper (6, I,II+III), Second Cashier (R)
£3 10s	Stewardess (14, I), Assistant Pantryman (8, I), Scullion (13, I,II+III & Crew), Kitchen Porter (4, III)
£3	Assistant Clothes Presser Steward (I,II+III), Stewardess (4, II), Matron (III), Waiter (13, R), Assistant Controller (R)
£2 2s	Assistant Waiter (17, R)
£2	Bell Boy Steward (3, I)
£1 10s	Page Boy (R★)
./.	Barber (3, I+II)

Wage Comparison

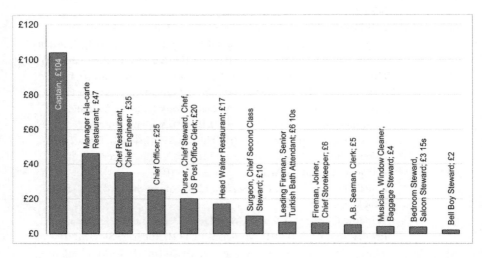

Comparison of the wages of some jobs on *Titanic*. Monthly payments above £10 are rounded. Not considered are possible tips for many of the crew members. (Graphic by author/Corina Amrein)

Wage Bill Per Month

In the following table of the wage bill three restaurant workers are excluded, all three US Post Office clerks are reckoned as earning US$1,200 per annum:

Deck Department	£532 1s
Engine Department	£2,151 10s
Victualling Department	£2,282 1s
Total (month of 30 days)	£4,965 12s

Wage Bill Round Trip

Most crew members' wages in the muster lists were given on a monthly basis, not an annual wage. The calculation of the wage bill per round trip is based on a month of 30 days and the length of a round trip between two departures from Southampton:

Deck Department	£372 10s
Engine Department	£1506 1s
Victualling Department	£1,597 9s
Total	£3,476

PERCEPTIONS

Those parties interested in the *Titanic* will have drawn many and varied conclusions from the foregoing work. The intention with this book was to create a fresh approach for exploitation by other researchers.

At this point, however, there follow a number of matters that were realised during the course of the work and provide a look in depth into the White Star Line in general, and the *Titanic* in particular.

- In general it can be said that the *Titanic* hierarchy was much more perpendicular in structure than accepted previously. Most leaders or foremen had fewer workers beneath them, and so the latter had relatively little independence. Accordingly, their superiors were not overburdened with leadership tasks and knew their men. (An exception was the large groups of cabin and saloon stewards whose work was clearly defined, who knew their trade, and for whom no instructions were needed in the real sense, only supervision.)
- The White Star Line was a conservative firm. That is clear not only from the design of its ships, but even from how it saw its crews. Many job titles came from the age of sail. The watch system provided other indications that new trends were only introduced hesitantly. The shipping line was not au fait with modern terms in use in gastronomy. The to some extent incorrect and misleading job titles were an impediment to understanding the crew organisation. Not to be underestimated as a pointer to its conservatism was such a 'minor thing' as the failure to have a ladies' hairdresser aboard (women do not appear to have been a target group for their custom). On the other hand, the separate à-la-carte restaurant had many more modern structures.
- For the first time it was possible to reconstruct practically all the remuneration of the *Titanic* crew. Particularly for the restaurant staff, little of it was documented, but now the pay of almost everybody aboard is known, with the exception of three restaurant staff and two US Post Office clerks.
- If one discounts special names for individual functions, then there were around forty different trades represented, even though (especially in the passenger

areas) many employees were hired for a special function (such as lift stewards, pantrymen, etc.).

- Owing to the steep leadership structure of White Star Line that had developed over decades, few crew members had a picture of the organisational structure of a ship. New entrants could be familiarised quickly with their points of intersection. The overview over most shipboard activities was presumably reserved for the captain, the senior officers, the pursers and the surgeons.

- Comparing the muster lists of *Olympic* and *Titanic* indicates how independently the pursers worked and how they solved the listing of some less clear crew members; they chose different lists and job titles for some positions.

- It was possible to establish those responsible for cleaning ship. The day hands of the seaman branch were responsible for the outer areas, the greasers for the engine-room installation. The cleaning stewards (boots) swept the interior of first and second class. In the third class it was the stewards, and in the crew spaces the glory hole stewards, who did the work. Elsewhere there were window cleaners, cooks, bath stewards, bedroom stewards, etc.

- By an analysis of the various watches certain conclusions can be drawn regarding events on the night of the sinking. Thus a comparison of survival rates led to the supposition that the greasers had substantially less chance than other trade groups of surviving by reason of where their accommodation was located.

- From the British point of view the à-la-carte restaurant was staffed almost exclusively by foreigners. Their mistrust of foreigners is clear when it is seen that almost all key positions aboard ship were occupied by persons of British nationality.

- Certain crew members did not work at the jobs described in the muster lists. Mess stewards worked as crew cooks, the kosher cook was not a cook, the boots steward was not a shoeshine boy and some saloon stewards were actually night watchmen.

- Numerous engineers worked not in the engine room but with the boilers. All engineers knew their precise task despite their confusing job titles.

- Obvious organisational improvements were not seen. One has the impression that everything was a shade more complicated than necessary. Thus it is incomprehensible why, for example, the boat assignments for emergencies did not coincide with the seamen's watch system.

- Some crew members were hired on a 'false' muster list – the nine lists prepared should have had a more logical system of allocation.

- From an analysis of the statements to the official inquiries twenty different integral watch arrangements can be defined. On the other hand, individual working hours (particularly in the kitchen area) are not documented.

- Numerous crew members worked to a very strict watch system. When the collision occurred, many were working their 12th or 14th hour of duty on that day. During the intended one-week long crossing, important crew members such as junior officers, quartermasters, lookouts and seamen never had more than 4 hours rest. The maximum period for sleep was therefore about 3.5 hours. Fatigue probably played a bigger part in the sinking than previously assumed.

- The tasks involved in numerous traditional trades or callings, or new ones, were described for the *Olympic*-class positions.
- The watch system of the stewards with varied duties by night was one of the reasons why only a few statements identifying people could be made in relation to the evacuation of the ship on the night of the accident.
- Although a majority of the seamen survived the sinking, it is not possible to ascertain the composition of the various watches.
- Taking into account the almost obligatory custom of tipping, the remuneration can be seen in another light. The really poorly paid crew members were a small minority (low hire without the prospect of tips, e.g. scullions).

These and many other perceptions made in this book should lead us to take a fresh look at the numerous matters and open questions about the *Titanic* and its loss. With knowledge of the organisation the ship comes more to life, for it was the crew that breathed life into the technological marvel to make it a ship.

On the whole this was a well-organised concern, with 899 workers divided into three departments and numerous divisions. The smooth interaction of all was the precondition for a successful voyage.

The collision with an iceberg in the night hours made new demands of an organisation that was running a normal routine. The crew did their jobs, not of the daily routine but for the first time an emergency drill that was the real thing. Many found their true selves for the first time under these circumstances. Not all knew how they were supposed to act in this situation. They did what they considered to be their duty.

Six-hundred and eighty-seven crew members did not survive the night. Almost 46 per cent of all *Titanic* lives lost belonged to the crew.

WHITE STAR LINE UNIFORMS

There are some misunderstandings and misinformation about the uniforms of White Star Line crew members. In general, these uniforms were based on the uniform of the Royal Navy. Most photographs of White Star Line officers and engineers show them in their full dress uniform, but at sea during the daily routine they looked much less fancy. Most crew members had to purchase their uniform themselves (the exceptions are mentioned below). Usually the uniforms were purchased from specialised tailors. It seems that Miller & Sons was the preferred tailor – one Southampton branch was located at 3, 4, 6 Canute Road, right across the street from the White Star Line offices.

This appendix focuses more on the different insignia than the use of the different uniform types used for different occasions and the fabrics from which they were made. Nevertheless, here is a short overview of the different uniform types. Postal workers and Marconi operators donned the uniforms of their respective employers.

Full Dress

The full dress uniform was the most formal clothing for ceremonies and receptions. The civilian equivalent was the frock coat. During embarkation and disembarkation of passengers, when leaving and arriving a port and during Sunday's divine service full dress was worn. Only crew members with an officer's rank had a full dress uniform. No full dress was necessary on steamers with few or no passengers.

Undress

The undress uniform was less formal and was worn by officers at sea at all other occasions when no full dress was required. Since it was a working uniform the fabric used varied on the season to keep the men warm in the cold season. In addition, there was a white

The tailor company Miller & Sons specialised in uniforms, and with its shop opposite the White Star Line office at Southampton it was the house tailor for many crew members. (Author's collection)

version for routes with a warmer climate. For the insignia, black mohair braids were used instead of gold.

Mess Dress

Only those entitled to dine with passengers needed a mess dress. It was based on the full dress uniform; a bow tie instead of necktie was used.

The above uniform types were of importance for the higher-ranking crew members only, but there were rules for every one of the crew who could cross the paths of passengers, therefore basically only greasers, firemen, trimmers and kitchen staff had no rules in respect of their clothing. There is no uniform regulation known for the à-la-carte restaurant staff; most probably they were dressed as waiters in a fancy restaurant. What follows is an overview of the different ranks' uniforms, based on the White Star Line uniform regulations from 1907, updated in 1908 and *c.* 1912. In these regulations the doctor was listed in the Victualling Department. The stewards were given a badge with a number for identification in case of praise or complaint.

Deck Department

For passengers and crew, it was equally important to recognise the captain. Also, the captain's uniform is the most complex one. After its detailed description many other uniform descriptions will refer to this uniform without repeating all details.

Captain
Full Dress Coat: blue cloth, double breasted, same cut, standard of length and number of buttons (company's pattern, bright, gilt) as navy frock coat; cuffs trimmed with four rows of ½in gold lace, straight, with circle at top of upper row.

Full Dress Vest: blue cloth, same cut and number of buttons as navy vest.

Full Dress Trousers: blue cloth.

Undress Jacket: double-breasted, same cut and number of buttons as navy undress jacket, with cuffs trimmed similar to full dress, but black mohair braid.

Undress Vest and Trousers: all to be of dark-blue pilot cloth or serge, according to the season. In services where hot weather is prevalent white drill suits of navy pattern may be worn. Rank stripes in gold lace on shoulder straps.

Captain Edward John Smith in his full dress uniform. The captain had the most complex uniform, many of the others can be imagined by removal of some insignia. The photograph was taken on 10 April 1912 on *Titanic's* boat deck in front of the officers' quarters. (Author's collection)

Cap: shape and style that of Royal Navy captain, blue cloth with leather chin stay, black mohair braid band 1½in wide, blue cloth peak embroidered with gold leaves, company's badge. White ribbed cap covers to be used in the summer.

Overcoat: same cut, standard of length and number of buttons as navy overcoat, with plain cuffs, rank stripes in gold lace on shoulder straps.

Boots: black boots only to be worn with uniform, or white in summer.

Gloves: to be plain brown buckskin or dogskin.

Necktie: black.

Chief Officer

All uniform items identical to captain, except three rows gold lace. Cap with leather peak, without embroidery.

First Officer

All uniform items identical to captain, except two rows gold lace. Cap with leather peak, without embroidery.

The leading officers of each department, besides the captain. This photograph of the chief engineer, the chief officer and the purser of the *Canopic* was taken in 1911 and illustrates the difficulty of recognising the rank insignia on the daily use undress uniform. Instead of the golden laces a black mohair braid was used, which can hardly be seen on the blue cloth. Only the white stripe on the purser's cuff is clearly visible, but only traces of the black mohair can be seen on his and the chief engineer's undress uniform. (Author's collection)

Second Officer

All uniform items identical to captain, except one row gold lace. Cap with leather peak, without embroidery.

Third and other Junior Officers

All uniform items identical to second officer, except one row ⅜in gold lace.

Surgeon

All uniform items identical to first officer, but no gold circle with rank stripes and on full dress ¼in red velvet between gold laces, on undress cloth in lieu of lace and velvet. (Temporary assistant surgeons require undress uniform only, with one gold stripe only, red cloth below.)

Boatswain and Boatswain's Mate

Blue navy cap, blue jacket, with six company's buttons and anchor on left sleeve.

Carpenter and Joiner

Same as boatswain, without anchor.

First Officer William McMaster Murdoch, Captain Edward John Smith, Purser Hugh Walter McElroy and Doctor William Francis O'Loughlin in their full dress uniform on the *Olympic* in 1911. (Author's collection)

Quartermaster

The quartermasters were given the following uniform items twice a year (except the white shirt, which was only given once) by the White Star Line: blue navy serge shirt with White Star Line badge and good conduct stripe on sleeve; white drill navy shirt with White Star Line and good conduct stripe in blue on sleeve; flannel singlet, navy pattern; black neck handkerchiefs; White Star cap and ribbon; blue serge trousers, navy pattern; cloth jacket as required.

Able Seaman and Seaman

Guernsey, embroidered 'White Star Line' on breast; man-of-war cap, with ribbon, having 'White Star Line' in gold thread; blue serge trousers. All uniform parts were sold by the boatswain.

Lookout

Same as seaman, jackets provided free of charge by company.

Engine Department

Chief Engineer

All uniform items identical to captain, but no gold circle in rank insignia. Cap with leather peak, without embroidery.

Second Engineer

All uniform items identical to chief engineer, except three rows gold lace.

Third Engineer

All uniform items identical to chief engineer, except two rows gold lace.

Fourth Engineer and all Assistant Engineers

All uniform items identical to chief engineer, except one row gold lace.

Fifth and Sixth Engineer, Boilermaker

All uniform items identical to chief engineer, except cuffs without gold lace.

Electrician

All uniform items identical to fifth engineer. Title worked in gilt wire on both sides of collar on full dress coat and undress jacket.

Victualling Department

Purser
All uniform items identical to first officer, but no gold circle with rank stripes and on full dress ¼in white velvet between gold laces, on undress cloth in lieu of lace and velvet.

Assistant Purser
All uniform items identical to purser, except one row gold lace, on full dress ⅛in white velvet below gold lace, on undress cloth in lieu of lace and velvet.

Purser's Clerk
All uniform items identical to assistant purser, without gold lace; no full dress coat.

Stewards
The stewards' uniforms existed in too many variations to describe them individually. Therefore it is easier to describe the different uniform parts, as each uniform item contains all the variations for the different stewards:

Jacket: Chief Steward (except when in saloon during meal times): blue superfine serge, double-breasted, five buttons (company's standard pattern) each side of front, three on each cuff, cuffs trimmed with one row ¼in gold braid, straight. Overcoat of company's regulation pattern without shoulder straps.

A group of White Star Line stewards, most probably on the deck of the *Celtic* in New York. Sitting in the centre is the first saloon steward, behind him is likely to be the second saloon steward. The men with the white jackets are most probably the second steward and the assistant second steward. They are surrounded by saloon stewards. (René Bergeron collection)

Chief Steward (when in saloon during meal times): blue cloth tuxedo jacket, two cross pockets, long roll black silk collar, no buttons in front. Cuffs trimmed with one row of ¼in gold lace straight round, and three small buttons.

Second Steward, Storekeeper and Turkish Bath Attendant: same as chief steward but single-breasted, without gold braid on cuffs. Cuffs and edges of jacket to be trimmed with black braid as per standard pattern.

First Class Stewards (excepting stewards waiting in saloon in Liverpool and Southampton services): same serge, close fitting, cut short with point at back, five buttons down front, three buttons on each cuff, with black braid on cuffs and edges, two buttons and link for button holes at top.

First Class Stewards (when waiting in saloon in Liverpool and Southampton services): same serge, close fitting, cut short with point at back, four buttons down front, three buttons on each cuff on blue silk navy slashes, roll collar with blue silk facings, and silver embroidered White Star on each side of roll.

Chief Second Class Steward and Chief Third Class Steward: same as chief steward, but single-breasted without any braid.

Second Class Stewards: same as first class stewards, but without any braid.

Third Class Stewards: coarser serge, of same cut and finish as second-class stewards.

Second Steward: to wear a short, close fitting, double-breasted jacket, with point at back, during dinner in saloon.

Second Steward, Assistant Second Steward, First Class Saloon Steward, Chief Second Class Steward, Chief Third Class Steward, Deck Steward, Library Steward, Smoke Room Steward, Lounge Attendant, Lift Attendant, Gymnasium Attendant, Bath Steward, Barber, Bugler, Chief Boots and Interpreter to have their titles worked in gilt wire on right and left sides of collar.

(White suits may be worn in hot weather by chief and second stewards, without shoulder straps.)

Vest: Same material as jacket, cut for six buttons, except in case of first-class saloon steward, which is to be made for four buttons only.

First-class stewards to have black braid on edges.

The third-class chief steward of the *Laurentic* with his title worked in gilt wire into the collar. (Ioannis Georgiou Collection)

This photograph of a first-class steward and two stewardesses was taken in early 1912 on the *Olympic* at New York. Under his jacket the steward wears the blue vest, which was only worn from October to April. On his arm a black braid is visible, a rare detail of the stewards' uniform vest. The stewardess in the middle wears her blue morning dress and the one on the right has her linen apron with the White Star Line burgee, collar and cuffs, with the unfolded nurse's cap in her hand. (René Bergeron collection)

Chief stewards to wear white vest cut for four buttons only when in saloon during meal times.

First- and second-class stewards to wear white vests from 1 May to 30 September, inclusive.

Second Steward to wear white vest cut for four buttons, during dinner in saloon at all seasons.

Trousers: Plain, of same material as jacket, cross pockets.

Cap: Navy-blue cloth, blue cord chin-stay, no band, cloth peak, the chief steward to have a badge with White Star flag in wreath laurel leaves, others an enamel White Star.

Collars: Collars to be turned down all round, black satin made-up bows of about 3in to be worn, except at dinner time, when white bows of the same size will be worn by saloon waiters.

Boots: Only black boots to be worn with uniform.

Stewardesses
Afternoon: Tailor-made navy-blue serge. Plain round bodice fastened in front with buttons (15–18 according to height) of approved pattern for stewardesses, plain skirt clear of the ground, collar of dress to stand up, sleeves quite plain with a little fullness on shoulder. Linen turned-down collar, cuffs, and cap, as per pattern to be seen at White Star works. Short muslin apron, as per approved pattern, with house flag worked on bands at points of shoulders. For warm weather, the dress may be of blue cambric instead of serge.

Morning: Blue-striped print, of approved pattern, made same as serge, with collar, cuffs, and cap, and a linen apron 4in longer than muslin apron.

Bandmaster
Blue serge tuxedo jacket: two cross pockets, long roll green cloth collar, two jacket-size gilt buttons to link in front. Cuffs trimmed with gold Russia braid forming a crow's-toe knot, and two small gilt buttons: small gilt lyre on left arm.

Vest: blue serge or white Marcella without collar. Six gilt buttons.

Trousers: blue serge.

Cap: blue serge, mohair band, gilt lyre.

Bandsmen
Same as bandmaster, without the gold Russia braid.

DUTIES AT BERTHING AND CASTING-OFF

An outline of the tasks and duties of the crew when berthing the ship and casting-off provides a further impression of crew life. The following is a short, incomplete compilation from the White Star Line regulations for the crews of their steamers, in force from 1 July 1907.

General

Any leave of absence in a home port will be arranged by the superintendents of each department. When absent on leave, addresses must always be left.

Leave of absence is only to be granted by the commander or officer in charge, in case of engineers also by chief engineer. Return to duty must be duly reported.

No leave of absence is to be granted for the night preceding day of sailing from any foreign port.

When in port, whether at home or abroad, at least one officer and two quartermasters must be in charge of the deck and one engineer in charge of the engine room and stokehold. In addition, the night watchman must visit all parts of the vessel on an hourly basis to safeguard against fire.

In a foreign port, a senior and junior officer as well as the chief or a second engineer and a junior engineer to be aboard at all times.

In port, the ensign and company's signal are to be hoisted at 08:00 and hauled down at sunset. In stormy weather small flags should be used.

All company's steamers in ports in Great Britain must be dressed on the King's birthday and Empire Day, in ports of the United States on Washington's birthday and on the 4th of

July, in Belgium on the King's birthday. Rule is to be extended to any other nation in whose waters the ship may be on similar occasions or on special instructions from the management or agents.

No visitor may remain on board later than 21:00 on any day without special permission of the commander.

Under no circumstances are relatives or friends allowed the day and night before sailing.

No alcohol is to be brought on board by crew.

No matches are to be brought on board, other than the company's safety matches. Anyone breaking this rule is to be reported to the commander.

If a man shall be confined or punished in port, the local authorities must be informed.

A strict search must be made for stowaways before leaving port, and should any be found they must be reported immediately to the commander.

Crew for each department must be mustered at least an hour before leaving port in order that any vacancies may be identified and filled.

Deck Crew
Every Sunday in port abroad the crew is to be mustered and inspected at 09:00. The inspection is to consist of mustering at boat and fire stations only.

Captain
Commanders will report to the management or agents verbally, and in writing if required, any particular incident on the voyage. They must attend the company's office, wherever they may be, at 11:00 daily, unless otherwise instructed. When on leave of absence they will furnish their addresses to the marine superintendent.

The commander shall give at least 18 hours' notice to the chief engineer before requiring the use of the main engines.

The commanders and chief officers of vessels in the United States trade are required to attend the Office of the American Consul before each voyage for the purpose of verifying signatures upon certificates lodged with the consul.

Commanders, officers, engineers and others must wear the company's full dress uniform when passengers embark and while leaving port.

As far as possible, departures from ports should take place in daylight. Prior to each voyage, commanders should familiarise themselves with details of vessels that they are likely to meet in the channel, leaving port and at sea.

Chief Officer

When in port, the chief officer has general responsibility for the supervision of the ship. He will pay strict attention to the moorings, gangways, etc.

In port a thorough inspection is to be made by the chief officer each morning at 10:30, when the crew are on board. Particular attention must be paid to the sanitary condition of the ship.

Will see that none of the crew leaves the ship on sailing day.

Under the direction of the chief officer, an officer must be placed in charge of the passengers' baggage. Care must be taken to keep baggage from all classes separate.

Immediately before leaving port the chief officer must renew the water in the water breaker in each lifeboat. The airtight biscuit tins in the stern of the boats must also be checked and refreshed as necessary.

Station when leaving port: forecastle head.

First Officer

The first officer will, under the direction of the chief officer, share with the second officer the responsibility for the holds, will examine them carefully after cargo has been discharged and see that holds, bilges, etc. are properly cleaned. Great care must be exercised to see that no packages are overlooked between ports. He will give a written report of his examination to the chief officer. He will be responsible for any items designated by the management as 'special cargo' and stowed in the holds under his charge. He will watch such cargo carefully until it is locked or covered up, and the same officer who has seen it loaded must see it unloaded at the port of discharge.

The first officer will ensure that the engine room and deck times agree.

Station when leaving port: docking bridge, where he will be responsible for the unmooring of the ship. He will pay particular attention to the propellers to see that nothing fouls them when leaving the dock. He will ensure that his men are on stations, signal flags (red and white) ready, and will himself attend the docking telegraph where there is no junior officer to do so.

Second Officer
Station when leaving port: in crow's nest.

Officer of Watch
The officer of watch will be responsible for the closing of all coal, cargo and any other ports near the water when work ceases, and for the closing of all coal ports as soon as coaling has been completed.

Junior Officers
Junior officers must supervise the holds during loading to control the stowage, and prevent stealing and the improper use of hooks and crowbars by the stevedores.

Stations when leaving port: third officer at standard compass and fourth officer on the Bridge with Commander, in charge of the telegraph.

Surgeon
He must not absent himself from the ship without permission of the management, commander of officer in charge. In foreign ports he must depute a fully qualified surgeon, approved by the commander.

Chief Engineer
The chief engineer will supervise personally the coaling of the steamer, both at home and abroad. By measuring and weighing he will satisfy himself that the proper quantity and quality of coal has been received on board.

The chief engineer is expected to be on board while chilled or frozen meat is being received, and to inspect personally the condition and stowage of same. Should matters be unsatisfactory in either respect, he is to notify the commander at once so that, in conjunction with the management of agent, he will take such steps as may be necessary to protect the company's interests.

Will see that none of the crew leave the ship on sailing day.

His presence in the engine room when the ship is leaving port, undocking or in any other circumstance is imperative.

As soon as the order 'stand by' is received from the bridge, he will see that all members of his department are on their respective stations. It shall be the duty of the junior engineers to keep a careful records of all orders transmitted from bridge to engine room.

Purser

Except on sailing day the purser will join the commander daily at 11:00 at the company's office.

He must not absent himself from the ship without permission of the management, commander or officer in charge.

The purser is responsible for seeing that no passenger, on any pretext whatever, is allowed to proceed in the steamer without either having paid the fare, settled the balance of deposit or produced a written order for his or her passage from the managers or agents.

Duties after Departure

When leaving port, care must be taken that the salutes of passing vessels are answered promptly, and that all government vessels are saluted.

When passing tows or deeply laden small craft, the commander must see that a very moderate rate of speed is maintained or that his ship is kept at such a distance as to prevent injury to these boats.

No transfers in saloon accommodation, with or without payment, are to be made after leaving port without reporting same to the commander. All changes in cabins on the voyage are to be reported to the office in Liverpool or other home port.

In case of any death occurring, the purser is required to report the same to the head office of the company in Liverpool or other home port, or its agents abroad as the case may be, handing in a complete list of effects immediately on the ship's arrival. In the case of the New York service the purser shall, after conference with the doctor, state in the telegram from Queenstown or Plymouth homewards, on the form provided, the cause of death, or in case of sickness the nature of the illness, so that the customs authorities may be contacted to prevent delay in the disembarkation of passengers. The purser is also to make an inventory of the effects of the deceased at once, in the presence of the doctor and second steward, and for it to be delivered to the agent at the port for which the passenger had booked, if abroad; if booked for England the effects are to be handed over to the company's office at the port of arrival. The effects of deceased officers or men belonging to the crew are to be treated as above, except that in all such cases, in accordance with the regulations of the Board of Trade, the inventory must be entered in the official log, and the effects, with balance of pay due, handed over to the Board of Trade authorities on arrival in Britain.

Seventy-fifth meridian time must be used from the time of arrival at and departure from Sandy Hook Lightship, Five Fathom Bank Lightship, and other points of arrival and departure in the United States and Canada. Greenwich Mean Time must be used in abstract logs after making English or Irish landfall. When passing points and ships at sea, either eastbound or westbound, Greenwich Mean Time, as well as the ship's time, must be used.

A thorough search must be made for stowaways before leaving port and also in the Atlantic trade on the westbound journey before arriving at Queenstown, Flushing, the Needles or other points, and on the eastbound journey before reaching Sandy Hook, the Breakwater or other point of departure; and should any be found, they must be reported immediately to the commander, and a report also made to the office at the end of the voyage. Westbound, on the arrival of the vessel in the United States or Canadian port, the stowaway must be locked up prior to being handed over to the immigration authorities, and a man placed on watch to prevent his escape.

The chief officer will pay strict attention to the holds. He will also have the steam fire extinguishers tested each voyage by the officer of the hold, accompanied by an engineer and the carpenter.

Regular sea watches are to be undertaken from the time the ship leaves the port of departure until reaching the port of arrival.

In case of an accident to the ship, the commander must regard it as of secondary importance to the lives of the passengers and crew.

Heads of each department will carry out searches for alcohol and enter results in the logbook. Any alcohol found must be confiscated, thrown overboard and its owner logged.

No man shall be confined or punished at sea without the commander's order. Punishment must be recorded in the logbook.

On all occasions at sea, the company's undress uniform must be worn, except for the Sunday service. The commander, officers, engineers and crew must always be properly and uniformly dressed.

Whenever any repairs are required in the passenger department for which the chief steward is responsible, the chief engineer must be informed immediately by written report. He will initial the same and ensure that the repairs are attended to promptly.

Duties before Arrival

All ports should be entered in daylight as far as possible.

The chief engineer will carefully prepare a list of all necessary repairs, alterations or changes that may be required for the proper and efficient working of the department for the ensuing voyage. He must make out a written report on any article that it not up to the usual standard required in service. He will also make a written report explaining any exceptional repairs made, or stores supplied at the previous port or ports.

The ship must be searched for contraband before entering any port and the result is to be entered in the logbook.

More especially, before entering a port in the United States, a very thorough search of crew quarters must be undertaken.

Once a week and before arrival the commander must inspect and sign the crew's wine books. No alcohol must be sold to crew for cash to avoid excess. The commander must pay attention to the consumption of each individual.

The commander will sign the cards for wines required for visitors and officials entertained by him or under his authority. The cards thus signed must be handed in with the wine account, which is to contain a statement of all such issues to visitors, made on the form supplied for the purpose. The purser will sign for wines required for cooking purposes and for consumption by quarantine and other port officials. These cards must be counter-signed by the commander at the end of the voyage.

On approaching port, the commander will have the passengers' baggage brought on deck in order that no delay may arise in landing passengers. The utmost haste must always be used in landing the mail bags, and in the case of an accident to the ship, the commander must regard them as next in importance to the lives of the passengers and crew. Baggage on deck must be stowed and kept protected by tarpaulin. Baggage is not to be brought on deck in rain or in storm.

Upon nearing Queenstown or Plymouth the doctor will advise the purser of any cases of sickness.

Commanders, officers, engineers and others must wear the company's full dress uniform while entering port and until the passengers have disembarked.

Stations when entering port: same as departure.

Duties after Arrival

Same as duties before sailing, plus: The first officer in twin-screw ships will see that propeller spars are placed around the stern as soon as the ship is moored, and that the propeller notice boards are hung over the quarter.

Immediately upon arrival the chief officer must hand to the marine superintendent all ordinary requisitions for improvements, repairs and supplies for the deck department.

The chief engineer must carefully prepare detailed particulars of the consumption of fuel and stores during the passage, and also a list of what will be required on the next passage. The requisitions must be handed to the superintendent engineer immediately upon arrival.

The commander shall be responsible for the safe custody and due delivery of the mail bags, as well as the punctual rendering of the various returns required by the British and US Post Office authorities. The usual documents are to be made out and sent to the managers by the purser upon the ship's arrival at New York and Liverpool or Southampton.

In all cases, commanders are required to report personally the arrival of their ships at all ports and, except with special permission or instructions, they and all members of the crew are to remain by the ship whilst passengers are still aboard.

At the end of the voyage the logbook must be delivered to the marine superintendent, signed by the commander and chief officer. The course book is to be submitted voyage by voyage to the marine superintendent. Commanders will present themselves at the company office and the customs house as soon as possible after arrival, bringing with them all necessary papers.

The doctor is to keep a journal of his practice in which at the time he is to detail the treatment employed in every case under his care, and hand the same to the passenger department on arrival home. In addition to the journal, the doctor is to report at the company's office as soon as possible after the steamer's arrival and give full information regarding any cases of sickness or deaths on the voyage. At New York it is to be understood that any sick passengers must be taken to Ellis Island.

On the return of the steamer, the purser is to make a general report of the voyage, touching on all matters of interest relating to his department.

Under no circumstances are relatives or friends allowed on board on the day of arrival.

In the home port after discharge of the crew, the chief engineer is responsible for ensuring that, having been thoroughly cleaned and prepared to receive the crew shipped for the ensuing voyage, crew quarters are to be locked up and kept so until required for occupation by the new crew.

The purser is required to hand over journals, receipt books and all money received by the cashier punctually, on the day of arrival if possible, at Liverpool or other home port.

In a home port, as soon as the deck department has done with the engines, they are to be thoroughly examined. When the engines are cleaned down, the line of shafting and crank shafts are to be examined with the utmost care, the chief engineer reporting the result to the superintendent engineer. In a foreign port the same examination is to take place, and the fact noted in the engineers' logbook. An account is to be kept by the second engineer of the work done by the engineers' staff whilst in foreign ports. Advantage shall be taken of every opportunity which may occur, whilst lying in a foreign port, to open up or repair such parts of the engines as may require attention, and the boilers shall receive such cleaning and sealing as time will allow.

When any portion of the machinery has been opened up for examination, it must not be closed up again until the second engineer has thoroughly satisfied himself that everything is in proper order.

DAILY ROUTINE ABOARD A WHITE STAR LINER

The following daily routine was taken from the White Star Line crew regulations valid from 1 July 1907 pertaining to when at sea. Every captain could impose additional regulations for his ship. The list is only what was laid down by the shipping company and is therefore incomplete.

00:00hrs

Officer of Watch	Eight bells, to be answered by lookout. Signals the end and beginning of the old/new watch respectively.
	Lights in smoking room to be extinguished.
	Send man to check livestock (if being carried): hourly (listed once only).
Chief Engineer	Record the temperature of refrigerated store. Every four hours (listed once only).
Junior Officer	Watch begins (until 04:00 hrs).
Carpenter	Sound the wells and report to chief officer and engine room. Every six hours (listed only once). To be accompanied by a junior officer once a day.

00:30hrs

Officer of Watch	One bell, to be answered by lookout.

01:00hrs

Officer of Watch	Two bells, to be answered by lookout.

01:30hrs

Officer of Watch	Three bells, to be answered by lookout.

02:00hrs

Officer of Watch	Four bells, to be answered by lookout.
Chief Officer	Watch begins (until 06:00hrs).

02:30hrs

Officer of Watch	Five bells, to be answered by lookout.

03:00hrs

Officer of Watch	Six bells, to be answered by lookout.

03:30hrs

Officer of Watch	Seven bells, to be answered by lookout.

04:00hrs

Officer of Watch	Eight bells, to be answered by lookout. (Every thirty minutes 1 to 8 bells as between 00:00 and 04:00hrs, not listed going forward, and exception during second dog watch from 18:00–20:00hrs only four bells, starting with one bell at 18:30hrs).
Junior Officer	Watch begins (until 08:00hrs).

06:00hrs

Officer of Watch	All clocks set for noon before 06:00hrs. Engine room and wheelhouse time must agree.
Second Officer	Watch begins (until 10:00hrs), relieved by first officer for breakfast.
Carpenter	Sound ballast and fresh water tanks and report to chief officer and engine room. Twice daily, once accompanied by a junior officer.

08:00hrs

Captain	Commander to inspect and sign chief officer's soundings book.
Chief Officer	Responsible for ensuring that the decks are clean and dry and that paint and brasswork is cleaned before 08:00hrs. All work that may inconvenience passengers must be complete before 08:00hrs.
First Officer	Wind and compare all chronometers and wind all clocks. Keep a chronometer comparison book.
Junior Officer	Watch begins (until 12:00hrs).

10:00hrs

First Officer	Watch begins (until 14:00hrs), relieved by second officer for lunch.

10:30hrs

Captain	Daily except Sunday. Thorough inspection of ship (with the exception of occupied state rooms) with chief engineer, purser, surgeon and

chief steward. If circumstances or weather do not allow commander or chief officer to participate, the others will report to him later.

Daily except: Sunday:	Inspection of engine room with chief engineer. All watertight bulkhead and fire doors to be examined, opened and shut. Inspection on Sunday to take place without commander. To be entered in logbook and mentioned in commander's report.
Daily:	Inspection of mail room with purser.
Sunday:	Divine service for passengers. If weather or other duties prevent the commander from officiating, the service is to be taken by the purser or surgeon. A service is only to be held on steamers trading with British or United States ports. All crew must wear full dress uniform.

12:00hrs

Officer of Watch Captain	Whistle to be sounded, except in narrow waters: The bridge and engine room telegraphs to be tested, tests to be entered in logbook. Discussion with officer of watch re ship's position and course to be steered, the effect of tides and currents should be considered, particularly if in a channel or in the vicinity of land. A track must be posted in the companionways of all classes showing progress and position of ship.
Officers	As soon as is practical after noon, the ship's position is to be calculated and taken to the commander. Position to be posted in the chart room.
Junior Officer	Watch begins (until 16:00hrs).
Chief Engineer	As soon as is practical after noon, the chief engineer must provide the commander with a signed report detailing an estimate of coal used and the mileage travelled since noon the previous day. Quantity of remaining coal and estimated amount required to complete the voyage to also be recorded. Company's printed form to be used for this report. Quantities on daily reports must agree with those in engineers' log.

Lunch

Purser/Surgeon	Alternately the purser and surgeon must take their midday meal in the second class saloon. If a ship carries an assistant purser, he will take his meals with second class passengers.

14:00hrs

Chief Officer	Watch begins (until 18:00hrs).

16:00hrs

Junior Officer   Watch begins (until 18:00hrs).

18:00hrs

Second Officer   Watch begins (until 22:00hrs).
Junior Officer   Watch begins (until 20:00hrs).
Carpenter   Sound ballast and fresh water tanks and report to chief officer and
                        engine room. Twice daily, once accompanied by a junior officer.

Sunset

Officer of Watch   The side, masthead and stern lights must be lit. Spare oil lamps must
                        always be kept ready. If there are two masts, one must always have an
                        oil lamp, except in channels. On the nights after departure and before
                        arrival, as well as in fog and misty weather, only oil lamps must be
                        used for the side and masthead lights. Report to the bridge every 30
                        minutes all lights burning brightly (not listed going forward).

                        The globe lights in the two emergency boats must be trimmed and
                        lit. Red oil lamps are to be hung in passageways of passenger areas and
                        at the foot of each staircase, and must burn until sunrise.

Captain   Before retiring, the commander must enter the course to be steered
                        and all other necessary instructions in the night order book in ink.
                        Night order book must be handed over to next officer of watch and
                        initialled for his watch.

20:00hrs

Captain   Commander to inspect and sign chief officer's soundings book.
Chief Officer   The Chief Officer to inspect the ship. Inspection to include readiness
                        of fire gear, sluice valves shut, fire detectors in order, emergency boats
                        ready. If open, all side ports on cattle decks should be made ready to be
                        closed. Report to the commander as soon as possible after inspection.
                        Inspection to be done by officer of watch if chief officer has been
                        relieved.
Junior Officer   Watch begins (until 24:00hrs).

21:00hrs

Purser/Surgeon/   Inspection of passenger areas. The evening inspection may be replaced
Chief Steward   by an alternate inspection at 10:30hrs.

22:00hrs

First Officer   Watch begins (until 02:00hrs).

Officer of Watch   All lights in third class and the forecastle to be extinguished except those required by law. Exceptions require the permission of the commander or chief officer. Between 22:00 and 06:00hrs ship's time must be changed. Engine room and wheelhouse time must agree.

23:00hrs

Officer of Watch   Lights in saloon or library, on deck and in companionways must be extinguished. Exceptions require the permission of the commander or chief officer.

APPENDIX D

REVIEW OF WATCH SCHEME AND WORK HOURS

There follows an extract of the various watch schemes aboard *Titanic*. In the Deck and Engine departments nearly all crew members could be integrated into a watch system. A few personnel remained 'idlers' and had arranged their working hours to suit themselves since they remained on call for 24 hours.

In the Victualling Department, in contrast to the other departments, few positions were occupied around the clock. Working hours were dependent on mealtimes and the daily routine of the passengers. Controller staff had the responsibility to ensure that all work was done to schedule – the chief baker divided up his men, the chef the cooks. The exceptions were the few personnel whose working hours are known by the opening times of their areas: although there might have been preparatory and clearing up work only the opening times are given.

As mentioned in the introduction, for reasons of complexity the watch periods were calculated without taking account of the daily adjustments to the clock. Every ship had its own shipboard time, heading westwards every day was 30–50 minutes longer dependent on the speed of the ship and its course. During the eastward passage the day shortened correspondingly. These changes were spread across two watches at 22:00hrs. Thus at the time of the collision the men of the starboard watch were already into their fifteenth working hour on 14 April 1912.

Deck Department

Chief Officer
02:00–06:00 and 14:00–18:00hrs

First Officer
10:00–14:00 and 22:00–02:00hrs

Second Officer
06:00–10:00 and 18:00–22:00hrs

Third Officer, Fifth Officer, Quartermasters, Boatswain, Seamen (port watch)
Even dates in April 1912:   04:00–08:00, 12:00–16:00 and 18:00–20:00hrs
Odd dates in April 1912:   00:00–04:00, 08:00–12:00, 16:00–18:00 and 20:00–24:00hrs

Fourth Officer, Sixth Officer, Quartermasters, Boatswain's Mate, Seamen (starboard watch)
Even dates in April 1912:   00:00–04:00, 08:00–12:00, 16:00–18:00 and 20:00–24:00hrs
Odd dates in April 1912:   04:00–08:00, 12:00–16:00 and 18:00–20:00hrs

Day Hands, Window Cleaners
06:00–17:00hrs

Lookouts
00:00–02:00, 06:00–08:00, 12:00–14:00 and 18:00–20:00hrs
02:00–04:00, 08:00–10:00, 14:00–16:00 and 20:00–22:00hrs
04:00–06:00, 10:00–12:00, 16:00–18:00 and 22:00–24:00hrs

Senior Radio Operator
20:00–02:00hrs and rotating watches during day

Junior Radio Operator
02:00–08:00hrs and rotating watches during day

Engine Department

Third Engineers (or Fourth), Electricians, Greasers, Leading Firemen, Firemen, Trimmers
04:00–08:00 and 16:00–20:00hrs

Second Engineers, Electricians, Greasers, Leading Firemen, Firemen, Trimmers
08:00–12:00 and 20:00–24:00hrs

Fourth Engineers (or Third), Electricians, Greasers, Leading Firemen, Firemen, Trimmers
00:00–04:00 and 12:00–16:00hrs

Senior Fifth Engineer, Senior Sixth Engineer
Even dates in April 1912:   08:00–12:00 and 16:00–20:00hrs
Odd dates in April 1912:   02:00–08:00, 12:00–16:00 and 20:00–02:00hrs

Junior Fifth Engineer, Junior Sixth Engineer
Even dates in April 1912:   02:00–08:00, 12:00–16:00 and 20:00–02:00hrs
Odd dates in April 1912:   08:00–12:00 and 16:00–20:00hrs

Victualling Department

Barbers
07:00–19:00hrs

First Class Saloon Stewards
c. 07:00–11:00, 12:00–16:00 and 18:00–23:00hrs

Second Class Saloon Stewards
c. 07:00–10:00, 11.30–15:00 and 17:00–23:00hrs

Reception Room Stewards, Verandah Cafe Stewards
08:00–23:00hrs

Lounge Stewards
08:00–23:30hrs

Smoke Room Stewards
08:00–24:00hrs

Night Watchmen
23:00–07:30hrs

Bedroom Stewards (not daily, alternated, when on night watch)
Until 21:00, 00:00–04:00 and from 07:30hrs

THE TITANIC CREW LIST

Hermann Söldner's *Titanic* crew list, published in 2000, was updated for this book in 2013, and minor corrections have been made up to this edition in 2016 and 2019. Much new information such as corrected ages and the manner of writing the name were included but only when confirmed by official documents.

The following list includes the whole crew of the *Titanic* on 10 April 1912, also the musicians, post-office clerks and deserter John Coffey. Therefore, the list, in alphabetical order, contains 900 names. The survivors are highlighted. The age of each individual at the time of the departure follows the name in parentheses; at the time of the sinking Allen Mardon Baggott, Giulio Casali, John Haggan, John George Phillips, Joseph Thomas Wheat and Oscar Scott Woody were one year older.

In the penultimate column the actual work undertaken aboard is given. This may vary from the job shown on the muster list but provides the better indication. In the last column the department to which the person was assigned is shown as per the original muster lists:

1. Deck Department
2. Engineer (Engine Department)
3. 4-8 (Engine Department – Book 1)
4. 8-12 (Engine Department – Book 2)
5. 12-4 (Engine Department – Book 3)
6. First Class (Victualling Department)
7. Second Class (Victualling Department)
8. Third Class & Galley Staff (Victualling Department)
9. Restaurant (Victualling Department)
10. Substitute engaged

Surname/ Forenames/Age	Abode	Trade/Calling	Section
Abbott, Ernest Owen (21)	Southampton	Lounge Pantry Steward	6
Abrams, William Thomas (33)	Southampton	Fireman	3
Adams, Robert John (26)	Southampton	Fireman	4
Ahier, Percy Snowden (20)	Southampton	Saloon Steward	6
Akerman, Albert Edward (28)	Southampton	Steward	8
Akerman, Joseph Frank (37)	Southampton	Assistant Pantryman	6
Allan, Robert Spencer (35)	Shirley	Bedroom Steward	6
Allaria, Battista Antonio (22)	Southampton	Assistant Waiter	9
Allen, Ernest (24)	Southampton	Trimmer	5
Allen, E. (26)	Southampton	Scullion	8
Allen, Henry (30)	Southampton	Fireman	5
Allsop, Frank Richard (43)	Southampton	Saloon Steward	6
Allsopp, Alfred Samuel (35)	Southampton	Second Electrician	2
Anderson, James (40)	Southampton	A.B. Seaman	1
Anderson, Walter Yuill (48)	Southampton	Bedroom Steward	6
Andrews, Charles Edward (19)	Southampton	Assistant Saloon Steward	7
Archer, Ernest Edward (36)	Woolston	A.B. Seaman	1
Ashcroft, Austin Aloysius (26)	Seacombe	Clerk	6
Ashe, Henry Wellesley (32)	Liverpool	Glory Hole Steward	8
Aspeslagh, Georges (26)	London	Assistant Plate Washer	9
Avery, James Albert (21)	Southampton	Trimmer	5
Ayling, Edwin George (22)	Southampton	Assistant Légumier	8
Back, Charles Frederick (37)	Southampton	Assistant Lounge Steward	6
Baggott, Allen Mardon (27)	Itchen	Saloon Steward	6
Bagley, Edward Henry (33)	Southampton	Saloon Steward	6
Bailey, George Francis (36)	Shepperton	Saloon Steward	7
Bailey, George Frank W. (46)	Woolston	Fireman	4
Bailey, Joseph Henry (46) (born as Bailey, Job H.)	Southampton	Master-at-Arms	1
Baines, Richard (54)	Southampton	Greaser	5
Ball, Percy (18)	Southampton	Plate Washer	6
Banfi, Ugo (24)	London	Waiter	9
Bannon, John Joseph (33)	Southampton	Greaser	4
Barker, Albert Vale (18)	Winchester	Assistant Baker	8
Barker, Ernest Thomas (40)	London	Saloon Steward	6
Barker, Reginald Lomond (40)	Southampton	Purser	6

Surname/ Forenames/Age	Abode	Trade/Calling	Section
Barlow, Charles Henry (30)	Southampton	Fireman	4
Barlow, George Arthur (38)	Southampton	Bedroom Steward	7
Barnes, John (39)	Woolston	Fireman	3
Barnes, Frederick (40)	Southampton	Assistant Baker	8
Barnhouse, Robert (42) (signed on as Barnes, Charles)	Southampton	Fireman	5
Barratt, Arthur Jr. (15)	Southampton	Bell Boy Steward	6
Barrett, Frederick W. (29)	Southampton	Leading Fireman	4
Barrett, Frederick William (33)	Southampton	Fireman	4
Barringer, Arthur William (34)	Southampton	Saloon Steward	6
Barrow, Charles Henry John (35)	Southampton	Assistant Butcher	8
Barrows, William (32)	N. London	Saloon Steward	6
Barton, Sidney John (26)	Southampton	Steward	8
Basilico, Giovanni Cipriano (27)	London	Waiter	9
Baxter, Harry Ross (53)	Southampton	Steward	8
Baxter, Thomas Ferguson (55)	Southampton	Linen Steward	6
Bazzi, Narciso (33)	London	Waiter	9
Beattie, Joseph (41)	Belfast	Greaser	3
Beauchamp, George William (25)	Southampton	Fireman	4
Bedford, William Barnett (31)	Itchen	Assistant Rôtisseur	8
Beedem, George Arthur (35)	Harlesden N.W.	Bedroom Steward	7
Beere, William (19)	Southampton	Kitchen Porter	8
Bell, Joseph (50)	Southampton	Chief Engineer	2
Bendell, Frank (23)	Southampton	Fireman	5
Benham, Fred John (29)	Wokingham	Saloon Steward	7
Bennett, George Alfred (30)	Southampton	Fireman	5
Bennett, Mabel Kate (33)	Southampton	Stewardess	6
Benville, Edward (48)	Southampton	Fireman	5
Bernardi, Battista (21)	London	Assistant Waiter	9
Bertoldo, Fioravante Giuseppe (23)	London	Assistant Scullion	9
Bessant, Edward (31)	Southampton	Baggage Steward	6
Bessant, William Edward L. (39)	Southampton	Fireman	5
Best, Edwin Alfred (39)	Southampton	Saloon Steward	6
Beux, Davide (25)	London	Assistant Waiter	9
Bevis, Joseph Henry (21)	Southampton	Trimmer	4
Biddlecombe, Reginald Arthur Charles (36)	Southampton	Fireman	4

Surname/ Forenames/Age	Abode	Trade/Calling	Section
Biétrix, George Baptiste (28)	London	Saucier	9
Biggs, Edward Charles (20)	Southampton	Fireman	4
Billows, James (20)	Southampton	Trimmer	3
Binstead, Walter William (20)	Southampton	Trimmer	3
Bird, Charles Frederick (42) (signed on surname Morgan)	Birkenhead	Storekeeper	6
Bishop, Walter Alexander (33)	Southampton	Bedroom Steward	6
Black, Alexander (28)	Southampton	Fireman	4
Black, David (41)	Southampton	Fireman	10
Blackman, Albert Edward (23)	Southampton	Fireman	5
Blades, Frederick Charles (17) (signed on surname Allen)	Southampton	Lift Steward	6
Blake, Percival Albert (22)	Southampton	Trimmer	5
Blake, Stanley (26)	Southampton	Crew Cook/Engine Dept.	2
Blake, Thomas Henry (36)	Southampton	Fireman	4
Blaney, James (29)	Southampton	Fireman	3
Blann, Eustace Horatius (21)	Southampton	Fireman	4
Bliss, née Junod, Emma (45)	New Southgate	Stewardess	6
Blumet, Jean Baptiste (26)	Southampton	Plate Washer	9
Bochatay, Alexis Joseph (30)	Southampton	Sous-Chef	8
Bochet, Pietro Giuseppe (43)	London	Second Head Waiter	9
Bogie, Norman Leslie (57)	Eastleigh	Bedroom Steward	7
Bolhuis, Hendrik (27)	Southampton	Garde Manger	9
Bond, William John (40)	Southampton	Bedroom Steward	6
Boothby, Walter Thomas (37)	Shirley	Bedroom Steward	7
Boston, William John (32)	Southampton	Assistant Deck Steward	6
Bott, William Thomas (45)	Southampton	Greaser	5
Boughton, Bernard John (24)	Southampton	Saloon Steward	6
Bowker, Ruth Harwood (28)	Little Sutton	First Cashier	9
Boxhall, Joseph Groves (28)	Hull	Fourth Officer	1
Boyd, John (35)	Southampton	Saloon Steward	6
Boyes, John Henry (35)	Southampton	Saloon Steward	6
Bradley, Patrick (39)	Southampton	Fireman	3
Bradley, Thomas Henry (29)	Southampton	A.B. Seaman	1
Bradshaw, John Albert Perkin (43)	Southampton	Plate Washer	6
Brailey, William Theodore (24)	London	Musician, Pianist	2nd Cl.
Brewer, Matthew Henry (41)	Southampton	Trimmer	4

Surname/ Forenames/Age	Abode	Trade/Calling	Section
Brewster, George Henry (52)	Southampton	Bedroom Steward	6
Briant, Albert (34) (signed on as Stafford, Michael)	Southampton	Greaser	3
Brice, Walter Thomas (42)	Southampton	A.B. Seaman	1
Bricoux, Roger Marie Léon Joseph (20)	Southampton	Musician, Cellist	2nd Cl.
Bride, Harold Sydney (22)	Southampton	Junior Radio Operator	6
Bright, Arthur John (42)	Southampton	Quartermaster	1
Bristow, Robert Charles (39)	Southampton	Steward	8
Bristow, Harry (38)	Shortland, Kent	Saloon Steward	6
Brookman, John Cress (28) (born surname Pibworth)	Southampton	Steward	8
Brooks, Sidney (25)	Southampton	Trimmer	4
Broom, Herbert George (33)	East Cowes	Bath Steward	6
Broome, Athol Frederick (30)	Bitterne Park	Verandah Cafe Steward	6
Brown, Edward (34)	Southampton	Saloon Steward	6
Brown, John Alfred (26)	Southampton	Fireman	5
Brown, Joseph (30)	Eastleigh	Fireman	10
Brown, Walter James (28)	Bitterne Park	Saloon Steward	6
Buckley, H. E. (34)	Southampton	Assistant Légumier	8
Buley, Edward John (26)	Southampton	A.B. Seaman	1
Bull, Walter Edward (36)	Southampton	Scullion	8
Bulley, Henry Ashburnham (21)	Southampton	Cleaning Steward	7
Bunnell, Wilfred James (20)	Southampton	Plate Washer	6
Burgess, Charles (18)	Southampton	Extra Third Baker	8
Burke, Richard Edward J. (32)	Chandler's Ford	Lounge Steward	6
Burke, William (31)	Southampton	Second Saloon Steward	6
Burr, Ewart Sydenham (29)	Woolston	Saloon Steward	6
Burrage, Arthur Victor Edward (20)	Southampton	Plate Washer	7
Burroughs, Arthur Peel (35)	Southampton	Fireman	5
Burton, Edward John (35)	Southampton	Fireman	5
Butt, Robert Henry (21)	Southampton	Saloon Steward	6
Butt, William John (31)	Southampton	Fireman	3
Butterworth, John (23)	Southampton	Saloon Steward	6
Byrne, James Edward (44)	Ilford	Bedroom Steward	7
Calderwood, Hugh (32)	Belfast	Trimmer	3
Campbell, Donald S. (28)	'At sea'	Clerk (Second Class)	6

Surname/ Forenames/Age	Abode	Trade/Calling	Section
Canner, John (40)	Woolston	Fireman	5
Carney, William (35)	Liverpool	Lift Steward	6
Carr, Richard Stephen (27)	Southampton	Trimmer	5
Carter, James (35) (signed on as Ball, W.)	Southampton	Fireman	4
Cartwright, James Edward (32)	London	Saloon Steward	6
Casali, Giulio (33)	London	Waiter	9
Casey, Thomas (44)	Southampton	Trimmer	5
Casswill, Charles (34)	Southampton	Saloon Steward	6
Castleman, Edward (37)	Southampton	Greaser	4
Caton, Annie (33)	N. London	Turkish Bath Stewardess	6
Caunt, William Ewart (27)	Southampton	Grillardin	8
Cave, Herbert (39)	Southampton	Night Watchman	6
Cavell, George Henry (22)	Sholing	Trimmer	4
Cecil, Charles Thomas (21)	Southampton	Steward	8
Chaboisson, Adrien Firmin (25)	London	Rôtisseur	9
Chapman, Joseph Charles (32)	Southampton	Cleaning Steward	7
Charman, John James (25)	Southampton	Saloon Steward	7
Cherrett, William Victor (24)	Southampton	Fireman	4
Cheverton, William Frederick (27)	Newport, I.O.W.	Saloon Steward	6
Chisnall, George Alexander (36)	Itchen	Boilermaker	2
Chitty, Archibald George (28)	Southampton	Steward	8
Chitty, George Henry (50)	Southampton	Assistant Baker	8
Clarke, John Frederick Preston (29)	Southampton	Musician, Contrabassist	2nd Cl.
Clench, Frederick Charles (33)	Southampton	A.B. Seaman	1
Clench, George James (31)	Southampton	A.B. Seaman	1
Chorley, John Henry (25)	Southampton	Fireman	4
Christmas, Herbert Edward (33)	Southampton	Assistant Saloon Steward	7
Clark, William (40)	Southampton	Fireman	5
Coe, Harry (21)	Southampton	Trimmer	4
Coffey, John (23)	Southampton	Fireman, deserted	(5)
Coleman, Albert Edward (29) (born as Albert Edwin)	Bitterne Park	Saloon Steward	6
Coleman, John (58)	Itchen	Crew Cook/Engine Dept.	2
Colgan, E. Joseph (33)	Southampton	Scullion	8
Collins, John (17)	Belfast	Scullion	8
Collins, Samuel J. (35)	Southampton	Fireman	5

Surname/ Forenames/Age	Abode	Trade/Calling	Section
Combes, George (34)	Southampton	Fireman	3
Conway, Percy Walter (25)	London	Saloon Steward	7
Cook, Gilbert William (32)	Weymouth	Saloon Steward	6
Coombs, Augustus Charles (45)	Southampton	Assistant Cook	8
Cooper, Henry William (28)	Southampton	Fireman	4
Cooper, James (25)	Southampton	Trimmer	5
Copperthwaite, Albert Harry (28)	Southampton	Fireman	3
Corben, Ernst Theodore (27)	Southampton	Assistant Printer Steward	6
Corcoran, Denis (33)	Southampton	Fireman	4
Cornaire, Marcel Raymond André (19)	London	Assistant Rôtisseur	9
Cotton, Alfred (30)	Southampton	Trimmer	10
Couch, Frank (27)	Port Isaac	A.B. Seaman	1
Couch, Joseph Henry (49)	Southampton	Greaser	5
Couper, Robert Frederick W. (29)	Southampton	Fireman	3
Coutin, Auguste Louis (28)	Southampton	Entremetier	9
Cox, William Denton (30)	Southampton	Steward	8
Coy, Francis Ernest George (26)	Southampton	Junior Assistant Third Engineer	2
Crabb, Henry James (23)	Southampton	Trimmer	5
Crafter, Frederick Horace (21)	Southampton	Saloon Steward	6
Crawford, Alfred James (36)	Southampton	Bedroom Steward	6
Creese, Henry Philip (44)	Woolston	Deck Engineer	2
Crimmins, James (22)	Southampton	Fireman	4
Crisp, Albert Hector (39)	Southampton	Saloon Steward	6
Crispin, William (32)	Eastleigh	Glory Hole Steward	8
Crosbie, John Borthwick (45)	London	Senior Turkish Bath Attendant	8
Cross, William Alfred (44)	Southampton	Fireman	5
Crovella, Paolo Luigi (16)	Southampton	Assistant Waiter	9
Crowe, George Frederick (30)	Southampton	Saloon Steward	6
Crumplin, Charles George C. (35)	Southampton	Bedroom Steward	6
Cullen, Charles James (49)	Liverpool	Bedroom Steward	6
Cunningham, Andrew O. (39)	Southampton	Bedroom Steward	6
Cunningham, Bernard William (34)	Southampton	Fireman	4
Curtis, Arthur (25)	Southampton	Fireman	5
Daniels, Sidney Edward (18)	Southsea	Steward	8
Dashwood, William George (18)	Southampton	Saloon Steward	7

Surname/ Forenames/Age	Abode	Trade/Calling	Section
Davies, Gordon Raleigh (32)	Southampton	Bedroom Steward	6
Davies, John James (27)	Southampton	Extra Second Baker	8
Davies, Richard John (27)	Southampton	Saloon Steward	7
Davies, Thomas (33)	Southampton	Leading Fireman	3
Davis, Stephen James (39)	Portsmouth	A.B. Seaman	1
Dawson, Joseph (23)	Southampton	Trimmer	5
Dean, George H. (19)	Shirley	Assistant Saloon Steward	7
Debreucq, Maurice Emile Victor (18)	London	Assistant Waiter	9
Deeble, Alfred Arnold (34)	Southampton	Saloon Steward	6
De Marsico, Giovanni (20)	London	Assistant Waiter	9
Derrett, Alfred Henry (28)	Southampton	Saloon Steward	6
Deslandes, Percival Stainer (37)	Southampton	Saloon Steward	6
Desvernine, Louis Gabriel (20)	Southampton	Assistant Patissier	9
Diaper, John Henry E. (27)	Southampton	Fireman	3
Dickson, William (37)	Southampton	Trimmer	10
Dilley, John Arthur Christopher (29)	Southampton	Fireman	3
Dillon, Thomas Patrick (33)	Southampton	Trimmer	4
Dinenage, James Richard (50)	Southampton	Saloon Steward	6
Dodd, Edward Charles (38)	Southampton	Junior Third Engineer	2
Dodd, George Charles (44)	Southampton	Second Steward	6
Dodds, Henry Watson (27)	Southampton	Junior Assistant Fourth Engineer	10 (2)
Doel, Frederick Olive (22)	Southampton	Fireman	5
Dolby, Joseph (38)	Southampton	Reception Room Steward	6
Donati, Italo Francesco (17)	London	Assistant Waiter	9
Donoghue, Thomas Francis (35)	Southampton	Bedroom Steward	6
Dore, Albert James (22)	Southampton	Trimmer	4
Dornier, Louis Auguste (20)	Southampton	Assistant Poissonnier	9
Doughty, Walter Thomas (22)	London	Saloon Steward	7
Doyle, Laurence (27)	Southampton	Fireman	5
Duffy, William Luke (31)	Itchen	Engineers' Secretary	2
Dunford, William (47)	Southampton	Hospital Steward	8
Dyer, Henry Ryland (24)	Southampton	Senior Assistant Fourth Engineer	2
Dyer, William Henry (33)	Southampton	Saloon Steward	6
Dymond, Frank (35)	Southampton	Fireman	5
Eagle, Alfred James Jacob (27)	Southampton	Trimmer	3

Surname/ Forenames/Age	Abode	Trade/Calling	Section
Eastman, Charles (44)	Southampton	Greaser	3
Edbrooke, Francis Samuel Jacob (23)	Landport	Steward	8
Ede, George Bulkeley (22)	Southampton	Steward	8
Edge, Frederick William (39)	Southampton	Second Class Deck Steward	7
Edwards, Charles (42)	Southampton	Assistant Pantryman	6
Egg, William Henry (34)	London	Steward	8
Elliott, Everett Edward (23)	London	Trimmer	5
Ellis, John Bertram (30) (born as John Bertie)	Southampton	Assistant Légumier	8
Ennis, Walter (34)	Southport	Turkish Bath Attendant	8
Ervine, Albert George (18)	Belfast	Assistant Electrician	2
Etches, Henry Samuel (43)	Southampton	Bedroom Steward	6
Evans, Alfred Frank (24)	Southampton	Lookout	1
Evans, Frank Olliver (27)	Southampton	A.B. Seaman	1
Evans, George Russell (33)	Southampton	Saloon Steward	6
Evans, William Robert (29)	Southampton	Trimmer	5
Fairall, Henry Charles (40)	Ryde, I.O.W.	Saloon Steward	6
Farenden, Ernest John (22)	Emsworth	Confectioner	8
Farquharson, William Edward (39)	Southampton	Senior Second Engineer	2
Faulkner, William Stephen (35)	Southampton	Bedroom Steward	6
Fay, Thomas Joseph (30)	Southampton	Greaser	5
Fellowes, Alfred (28)	Southampton	Cleaning Steward	6
Feltham, George (36)	Southampton	Vienna Baker	8
Ferrary, Antonio (34)	Southampton	Trimmer	4
Ferris, William (39)	Southampton	Leading Fireman	4
Fey, Carlo (30)	London	Scullion	9
Finch, Henry Herman (18)	Southampton	Steward	8
Fitzpatrick, Cecil William (21)	Southampton	Mess Steward	2
Fitzpatrick, Hugh Joseph (27)	Belfast	Junior Boilermaker	2
Flarty, Edward (50)	Southampton	Fireman	5
Fleet, Frederick (24)	Southampton	Lookout	1
Fletcher, Percy William (25)	London	Bugler Steward	6
Foley, John (46)	Southampton	Storekeeper	1
Foley, William C. (27)	Southampton	Steward	8
Ford, Ernest (32)	Southampton	Steward	8
Ford, Francis (44)	Southampton	Bedroom Steward	7

Surname/ Forenames/Age	Abode	Trade/Calling	Section
Ford H. (22)	Southampton	Trimmer	3
Ford, Thomas Henry (34)	Southampton	Leading Fireman	5
Forward, James (27)	Southampton	A.B. Seaman	1
Foster, Albert George (39)	Southampton	Storekeeper	2
Fox, William Thomas (28)	Ealing	Steward	8
Franklin, Alan Vincent (28)	Southampton	Saloon Steward	7
Fraser, James Cameron (29)	Southampton	Junior Assistant Third Engineer	2
Fraser J. (30)	Southampton	Fireman	4
Fredericks, Walter Francis (20)	Southampton	Trimmer	5
Freeman, Ernest Edward Samuel (45)	Southampton	Deck Steward	6
Fryer, Albert Ernest (26)	Southampton	Trimmer	4
Gatti, Gaspare Antonio Pietro (37)	Southampton	Manager Restaurant	9
Geddes, Richard Charles (31)	Southampton	Bedroom Steward	6
Geer, Alfred Ernest (26)	Southampton	Fireman	10
Gibbons, Jacob William (36)	Studland Bay	Saloon Steward	7
Gilardino, Vincenzo Pio (31)	Southampton	Waiter	9
Giles, John Robert (32)	Southampton/ Liverpool	Second Baker	8
Gill, Joseph Stanley (39)	Southampton	Bedroom Steward	6
Gill, Patrick Joseph (41)	Southampton	Ship's Cook	8
Godley, George Auguste (38)	Southampton	Fireman	5
Godwin, Frederick Charles (35)	Totton	Greaser	3
Gold, née Cook, Katherine (42)	Southampton	Stewardess	6
Golder, William Lewis (36) (signed on as Golder, M.W.)	Southampton	Fireman	4
Gollop, Percival Salisbury (29)	Southampton	Assistant Passenger Cook	8
Gordon, John Dowie (29)	Southampton	Trimmer	10
Goree, Frank (40)	Southampton	Greaser	4
Goshawk, Alfred James (40)	Southampton	Third Saloon Steward	6
Gosling, Bertram James (22)	Southampton	Trimmer	4
Gosling, Sidney (26)	Southampton	Trimmer	5
Gradidge, Ernest Edward (22)	Southampton	Fireman	3
Graham, Thomas G. (28)	Belfast	Leading Fireman	3
Green, George (20)	Southampton	Trimmer	5
Gregory, David (43)	Southampton	Greaser	4
Gregson, Mary Josephine (45)	Southampton	Stewardess	6

Surname/ Forenames/Age	Abode	Trade/Calling	Section
Grosclaude, Gérald (24)	London	Assistant Coffee Man	9
Gumery, George (24)	Southampton	Mess Steward	2
Gunn, Joseph Alfred (29)	Southampton	Assistant Saloon Steward	7
Guy, Edward John (29)	Milton Abbas	Cleaning Steward	6
Gwinn, William Logan (36)	Asbury Park, USA	US Post Office Clerk	–
Haggan, John (34)	Belfast	Fireman	3
Haines, Albert (31)	Southampton	Boatswain's Mate	1
Halford, Edwin Henry (22)	Southampton	Steward	8
Hall, Frank Alfred J. (38)	London	Scullion	8
Hall, J. (32)	Southampton	Fireman	4
Hallett, George Alexander (23)	Southampton	Fireman	5
Hamblyn, Ernest William (46)	Southampton	Bedroom Steward	7
Hamilton, Ernest (26)	Southampton	Assistant Smoke Room Steward	6
Hands, Bernard (53)	Southampton	Fireman	4
Hannam, George Herbert (27)	Southampton	Fireman	3
Harder, William (39)	Southampton	Window Cleaner	1
Harding, Alfred John (20)	Swaythling	Assistant Pantryman	7
Hardwick, Reginald (21)	Southampton	Kitchen Porter	8
Hardy, John William (40)	Southampton	Chief Second Class Steward	7
Harris, Amos Fred (23)	Southampton	Trimmer	3
Harris, Charles William (18)	Southampton	Saloon Steward	7
Harris, Clifford Henry (16)	Southampton	Bell Boy Steward	6
Harris, Edward Matthew (17)	Winchester	Assistant Pantryman	6
Harris, Edward John (28)	Southampton	Fireman	3
Harris, Frederick (39)	Gosport	Fireman	4
Harrison, Aragõa Drummond (40)	Southampton	Saloon Steward	6
Harrison, Norman John (38)	Southampton	Junior Second Engineer	2
Hart, John Edward (31)	Southampton	Steward	8
Hart, James (53)	Southampton	Fireman	4
Hartley, Wallace Henry (33)	Dewsbury	Musician, Leader Quintet	2nd Cl.
Hartnell, Frederick (21)	Bitterne Park	Saloon Steward	6
Harvey, Herbert Gifford (34)	Belfast	Junior Assistant Second Engineer	2
Haslin, James (45)	Liverpool	Trimmer	5
Hatch, Hugh Vivian (20)	Southampton	Scullion	8

Surname/ Forenames/Age	Abode	Trade/Calling	Section
Hawkesworth, James (38)	Southampton	Saloon Steward	7
Hawkesworth, William Walter (43)	Southampton	Assistant Deck Steward	6
Hayter, Arthur (44)	Southampton	Bedroom Steward	6
Head, Alfred Charles (22)	Southampton	Fireman	3
Hebb, Albert W. (22)	Southampton	Trimmer	3
Heinen, Joseph Dominikus (30)	Lewisham	Saloon Steward	7
Hemming, Samuel Ernest (43)	Southampton	Lamp Trimmer	1
Hendrickson, Charles Oscar (29)	Southampton	Leading Fireman	3
Hensford, Herbert George (26)	Southampton	Assistant Butcher	8
Hendy, Edward Martin (39)	Southampton	Saloon Steward	6
Hesketh, John Henry (33)	Liverpool	Second Engineer	2
Hewitt, Thomas (37)	Southampton	Bedroom Steward	6
Hichens, Robert (29)	Southampton	Quartermaster	1
Hill, Henry Parkinson (36)	Southampton	Steward	8
Hill, James (25)	Southampton	Trimmer	3
Hill, James Colston (40)	Southampton	Bedroom Steward	6
Hinckley, George Herbert (39)	Southampton	Bath Steward	7
Hine, William Edward (36)	Bruckley	Third Baker	8
Hinton, William Stephen (30)	Southampton	Trimmer	5
Hiscock, Sidney George (24)	Southampton	Plate Washer	6
Hoare, Leonard James (18)	Southampton	Saloon Steward	6
Hodge, Charley (29)	Woolston	Senior Assistant Third Engineer	2
Hodges, William John (24)	Southampton	Fireman	5
Hodgkinson, Leonard (46)	Southampton	Senior Fourth Engineer	2
Hogan, John William (20) (signed on as King, G.)	Southampton	Scullion	8
Hogg, Charles William (43)	Liverpool	Bedroom Steward	6
Hogg, George Alfred (29)	Southampton	Lookout	1
Hogue, David Lees (E.) (24)	London	Plate Washer	6
Holland, Thomas (28)	Liverpool	Reception Room Steward	6
Holloway, Sidney (23)	Southampton	Assistant Clothes Presser Steward	6
Holman, Harry (28)	Southampton	A.B. Seaman	1
Hopgood, Roland (29)	Woolston	Fireman	3
Hopkins, Frederick James (13)	Southampton	Plate Washer	6
Hopkins, Robert John (40)	Southampton	A.B. Seaman	1
Horswill, Albert Edward James (33)	Southampton	A.B. Seaman	1

Surname/ Forenames/Age	Abode	Trade/Calling	Section
Hosgood, Richard William (22)	Southampton	Fireman	10
Hosking, George Fox (36)	Itchen	Senior Third Engineer	2
House, William Robert Henry (39)	Southampton	Saloon Steward	6
Howell, Arthur Albert (31)	Itchen	Saloon Steward	6
Hughes, William Thomas (34)	Southampton	Assistant Second Steward	6
Humby, Frederick (16)	Southampton	Plate Washer	7
Hume, John Law (21)	Dumfries	Musician, First Violinist, trio	2nd Cl.
Humphreys, Humphrey (31)	Southampton	Assistant Saloon Steward	7
Humphreys, Sidney James (56)	Southampton	Quartermaster	1
Hunt, Sylvanus Alfred (22)	Southampton	Trimmer	3
Hunt, Thomas (28)	Southampton	Fireman	4
Hurst, Charles John (40)	Southampton	Fireman	4
Hurst, Walter (28)	Southampton	Fireman	5
Hutchinson, James (28)	Liverpool	Légumier	8
Hutchinson, John Hall (28)	Southampton	Joiner	1
Hyland, James Leo (19)	Southampton	Steward	8
Ide, Harry John (31)	Southampton	Bedroom Steward	6
Ingram, George (19)	Southampton	Trimmer	5
Ings, William Ernest (20)	Southampton	Scullion	8
Ingrouille, Henry (21)	Southampton	Steward	8
Instance, Thomas (31)	Southampton	Fireman	4
Jackopson, John Henry (29)	Southampton	Fireman	3
Jackson, Cecil (21)	Southampton	Cleaning Steward	6
Jago, Joseph (58)	Southampton	Greaser	5
Jaillet, Henri Marie (28)	London	Patissier	9
James, Thomas (35)	Southampton	Fireman	3
Janaway, William Frank (35)	Southampton	Bedroom Steward	6
Janin, Claude Marie (29)	London	Potager	9
Jeffery, William Alfred (28)	Southampton	Controller	9
Jenner, Henry Thomas (55)	Southampton	Second Class Saloon Steward	7
Jensen, Charles Valdemar (25)	Southampton	Saloon Steward	7
Jessop, Violet Constance (24)	London	Stewardess	6
Jewell, Archie (23)	Southampton	Lookout	1
Joas, N. (38)	Southampton	Fireman	3
Johnston, James (41)	Southampton	Night Watchman	6
Jones, Albert Edward (17)	Southampton	Saloon Steward	7

Surname/ Forenames/Age	Abode	Trade/Calling	Section
Jones, Arthur Ernest (38)	Woolston	Plate Washer	7
Jones, Harry Owen G. (36)	Alresford	Rôtisseur	8
Jones, Victor Reginald (20)	Southampton	Saloon Steward	6
Jones, Thomas William (32)	Liverpool	A.B. Seaman	1
Jouannault, Georges Jules (24)	Southampton	Assistant Saucier	9
Joughin, Charles John (32)	Southampton	Chief Baker	8
Judd, Charles Edward (32)	Southampton	Fireman	5
Jukes, Henry James (38)	Southampton	Greaser	3
Jupe, Boykett Herbert (30)	Southampton	Assistant Electrician	2
Kasper, Fredrik (42)	Southampton	Fireman	5
Kearl, Charles Henry (44)	Southampton	Greaser	3
Kearl, George Edward (25)	Sholing	Trimmer	3
Keegan, James (38)	Southampton	Leading Fireman	5
Keen, Percy Edward (31)	Southampton	Saloon Steward	6
Kelland, Thomas (18)	Southampton	Library Steward	7
Kelly, James (44)	Southampton	Greaser	4
Kelly, William P. (23)	Dublin	Assistant Electrician	2
Kemish, George (22)	Southampton	Fireman	4
Kemp, Thomas Hulman (43)	Southampton	Extra Assistant Fourth Engineer (Refrigeration)	2
Kenchenten, Frederick Charles (36)	Southampton	Greaser	3
Kennell, Charles (30)	Southampton	Kosher Cook	8
Kenzler, August (43)	Southampton	Storekeeper	2
Kerley, William Thomas (28)	Salisbury	Assistant Saloon Steward	7
Kerr, Thomas (26)	Southampton	Fireman	5
Ketchley, Harry (35)	Southampton	Saloon Steward	6
Kieran, James (32)	Southampton	Chief Third Class Steward	8
Kieran, Edgar Michael (33)	Southampton	Storekeeper	6
King, Alfred John M. (18)	Southampton	Lift Steward	6
King, Ernest Waldron (28)	Clones	Clerk	6
King, Thomas Walter (43)	Great Yarmouth	Master-at-Arms	1
Kingscote, William Ford (47)	Freemantle	Saloon Steward	6
Kinsella, Louis (30)	Southampton	Fireman	10
Kirkaldy, Thomas Benjamin (35) (signed on surname Clark)	Southampton	Bedroom Steward	6
Kirkham, James (41)	Southampton	Greaser	5
Kitching, Arthur Alfred (30)	Southampton	Saloon Steward	6

Surname/ Forenames/Age	Abode	Trade/Calling	Section
Klein, Herbert (33)	Southampton	Barber (Second Class)	8
Knight, George (44)	Woolston	Saloon Steward	6
Knight, Leonard George (21)	Bishopstoke	Steward	8
Knowles, Thomas (42)	Lymington	Crew Cook/Engine Dept.	2
Krins, Georges Alexandre (23)	London	Musician, Violinist	2nd Cl.
Lacey, Bertie Leonard (21)	Salisbury	Assistant Saloon Steward	7
Lally, Thomas Louis (32)	East Dulwich	Fireman	4
Lake, William (35)	Southampton	Saloon Steward	6
Lane, Albert Edward (33)	Woolston	Saloon Steward	6
Latimer, Andrew J. (55)	Liverpool	Chief Steward	6
Lawrance, Arthur (36)	Southampton	Saloon Steward	6
Lavington, Elizabeth (40)	Winchester	Stewardess	6
Leader, Archibald (22)	W. Southbourne	Assistant Confectioner	8
Leather, née Edwards, Elizabeth Mary (51)	Port Sunlight	Stewardess	6
Lefebvre, Paul Georges (35)	Southampton	Saloon Steward	6
Lee, Henry Thomas (18)	Southampton	Trimmer	4
Lee, Henry Reginald (29) (signed on as Martin, F.)	Fareham	Scullion	8
Lee, Reginald Robinson (41)	Southampton	Lookout	1
Leonard, Matthew (25)	Southampton	Steward	8
Levett, George Alfred (25)	New Southgate	Assistant Pantryman	6
Lewis, Arthur Ernest Read (27)	Southampton	Steward	8
Light, Christopher William (21)	Southampton	Fireman	5
Light, Charles Edward (23)	Christchurch	Plate Washer	6
Light, W. (47)	Southampton	Fireman	3
Lightoller, Charles Herbert (38)	Netley Abbey	Second Officer	1
Lindsay, Charles William (30)	Southampton	Fireman	3
Littlejohn, Alexander James (40)	Southampton	Saloon Steward	6
Lloyd, Humphrey (33)	Southampton	Saloon Steward	6
Lloyd, William (29)	Southampton	Fireman	10
Locke A. (33)	Worthing	Scullion	10 (8)
Long, Frank (31)	Southampton	Trimmer	3
Long, William (36)	Southampton	Trimmer	5
Longmuir, John Dickson (19)	Eastleigh	Assistant Pantryman	7
Lovell, John (35)	Southampton	Grillardin	8

Surname/ Forenames/Age	Abode	Trade/Calling	Section
Lowe, Harold Godfrey (29)	Barmouth	Fifth Officer	1
Lucas, William Watson (31)	Southampton	Saloon Steward	6
Lucas, William Arthur (25)	Southampton	A.B. Seaman	1
Lydiatt, Charles (45)	Southampton	Saloon Steward	6
Lyons, William Henry (26)	Southampton	A.B. Seaman	1
Mabey, John Charles (23)	Southampton	Steward	8
Mackie, George William (34)	Southampton	Bedroom Steward	7
Mackie, William Dickson (32)	S.E. London	Junior Fifth Engineer	2
Major, Thomas Edgar (35)	London	Bath Steward	6
Major, William James (32)	Southampton	Fireman	5
Mantle, Roland Frederick (39)	Southampton	Steward	8
March, John Starr (50)	Newark, USA	US Post Office Clerk	–
Marett, George John (26)	Southampton	Fireman	4
Marks, James (26)	Southampton	Assistant Pantryman	6
Marriott, John William (20)	Southampton	Assistant Pantryman	6
Marsden, Evelyn (28)	Southampton	Stewardess	6
Marsh, Frederick Charles (39)	Southampton	Fireman	3
Martin, née Woodland, Annie Martha (39)	Portsmouth	Stewardess	6
Martin, Mabel Elvina (20)	London	Second Cashier	9
Maskell, Leopold Adolphus L. (26)	Southampton	Trimmer	4
Mason, Frank Archibald Robert (32)	Southampton	Fireman	5
Mason, J. (39)	Southampton	Leading Fireman	4
Matherson, David (33)	Southampton	A.B. Seaman	1
Mathias, Montague Vincent (28)	Southampton	Crew Cook/Deck Dept.	1
Mattmann, Adolf (20)	Southampton	Ice Cream Maker	9
Maugé, Paul Achille Maurice Germain (25)	London	Maître d'Hôtel	9
Maxwell, John (29)	Southampton	Carpenter	1
May, Arthur William (Jr.)	Southampton	Fireman	4
May, Arthur William (Sr.)	Northam	Crew Cook/Engine Dept.	2
Maynard, Isaac Hiram (31)	Southampton	Entremetier	8
Mayo, William Peter (27)	Southampton	Leading Fireman	3
Maytum, Alfred (52)	Southampton	Chief Butcher	8
Mayzes, Thomas Jubilee (25)	Bitterne	Fireman	3
McAndrew, Thomas Patrick (37)	Southampton	Fireman	4
McAndrews, William Airley (23)	Wigan	Fireman	3

Surname/ Forenames/Age	Abode	Trade/Calling	Section
McCarthy, Frederick James (38)	Southampton	Bedroom Steward	6
McCarty, William (47)	Southampton	A.B. Seaman	1
McCastlan, W. (38)	Southampton	Fireman	4
McCawley, Thomas W. (36)	Southampton	Gymnasium Steward	6
McElroy, Hugh Walter (37)	Southampton	Purser	6
McGann, James (26)	Southampton	Trimmer	5
McGarvey, Edward Joseph (34)	Southampton	Fireman	5
McGaw, Eroll Victor (30)	Southampton	Fireman	3
McGough, George Francis (36)	Southampton	A.B. Seaman	1
McGrady, James (27)	Southampton	Saloon Steward	6
McInerney, Thomas Arthur (37)	Southampton	Greaser	5
McIntyre, George William (21)	Southampton	Trimmer	5
McKay, Charles Donald (30)	Southampton	Saloon Steward	6
McLaren, née Allsop, Harriet Elizabeth (40)	Southampton	Stewardess	6
McMicken, Arthur (26)	Southampton	Saloon Steward	6
McMicken, Benjamin Tucker (21)	Southampton	Second Pantryman	6
McMullin, John Richard (36)	Southampton	Saloon Steward	6
McMurray, William (43)	Liverpool	Bedroom Steward	6
McQuillan, William (26)	Belfast	Fireman	4
McRae, William Alexander (32)	Southampton	Fireman	4
McReynolds, William (22)	Belfast	Junior Sixth Engineer	2
Mellor, Arthur (34)	Southampton	Saloon Steward	6
Middleton, Alfred Pirrie (26)	Ballysadare	Assistant Electrician	2
Middleton, Mark Victor (24)	S.W. London	Saloon Steward	7
Milford, George (28)	Southampton	Fireman	4
Millar, Robert (26)	Alloa	Extra Fifth Engineer (turbine)	2
Millar, Thomas (33)	Belfast	Assistant Deck Engineer	2
Mills, Christopher (51)	Southampton	Assistant Butcher	8
Mintram, William (46)	Southampton	Fireman	5
Mishellany, Abraham Mansoor (53)	W. London	Printer Steward	6
Mitchell, Lorenzo Horace (18)	Southampton	Trimmer	3
Monteverdi, Giovanni/Jean (23)	London	Assistant Entremetier	9
Moody, James Paul (24)	Grimsby	Sixth Officer	1
Moore, Alfred Ernest (38)	Southampton	Saloon Steward	7
Moore, George Alfred (32)	Southampton	A.B. Seaman	1

Surname/ Forenames/Age	Abode	Trade/Calling	Section
Moore, John William (29)	Southampton	Fireman	3
Moore, Ralph William (21)	Headbourne Worthy	Trimmer	3
Moores, Richard (44)	Southampton	Greaser	4
Morgan, Arthur Herbert (25)	Southampton	Trimmer	4
Morgan, Thomas A. (26)	Southampton	Fireman	5
Morrell/Morrill, Ronald Samuel (21)	Southampton	Trimmer	4
Morris, Arthur (32) (born as Briant, Arthur)	Southampton	Greaser	3
Morris, Frank Herbert (28)	London	Bath Steward	6
Morris, William (24)	Southampton	Trimmer	3
Moss, William Stephen (35)	Southampton	First Saloon Steward	6
Mouros, Jean/Javier (20)	London	Assistant Waiter	9
Moyes, William Young (23)	Stirling	Senior Sixth Engineer	2
Müller, Louis (37)	Southampton	Interpreter Steward	8
Mullin, Thomas A. (20)	Southampton	Steward	8
Murdoch, William John (33)	Belfast	Fireman	5
Murdoch, William McMaster (39)	Southampton	First Officer	1
Nannini, Francesco Luigi Arcangelo (42)	London	Head Waiter	9
Neal, Henry (25)	Southampton	Assistant Baker	8
Nettleton, George Walter (29)	Southampton	Fireman	3
Newman, Charles Thomas N. (32)	Southampton	Assistant Storekeeper	2
Nicholls, S. (39)	Southampton	Saloon Steward	6
Nichols, Alfred W. S. (46)	Shirley	Boatswain	1
Nichols, Arthur D. (36)	Southampton	Steward	8
Nichols, Walter Henry (35)	Southampton	Assistant Saloon Steward	7
Niven, John Brown (30) (signed on as McGregor, J.)	Southampton	Fireman	4
Noon, John Thomas (42)	Southampton	Fireman	4
Norris, James Edward (23)	Southampton	Leading Fireman	3
Noss, Bertram Arthur (21)	Southampton	Fireman	4
Noss, Henry (30)	Southampton	Fireman	5
Nutbean, William (30)	Southampton	Fireman	3
O'Connor, John (29)	Southampton	Trimmer	10
O'Connor, Thomas Peter (44)	Liverpool	Bedroom Steward	6
Olive, Charles (31)	Southampton	Greaser	3
Olive, Ernest Roskelly (26)	Southampton	Clothes Presser Steward	6

Surname/ Forenames/Age	Abode	Trade/Calling	Section
Oliver, Harry (32)	Southampton	Fireman	5
Olliver, Alfred John (27)	Southampton	Quartermaster	1
O'Loughlin, Dr. William Francis Norman (62)	Southampton	Surgeon	1
Orpet, Walter Hayward (31)	Southampton	Saloon Steward	6
Orr, James (40)	Southampton	Assistant Légumier	8
Osborne, William Henry (32)	Southampton	Saloon Steward	6
Osman, Frank (28)	Itchen	A.B. Seaman	1
Othen, Charles Alfred (36)	Southampton	Fireman	3
Owen, Lewis (49)	Southampton	Assistant Saloon Steward	7
Pacey, Reginald Ivan (17)	Southampton	Lift Steward (Second Class)	7
Pachéra, Jean-Baptiste Stanislas (19)	Southampton	Assistant Garde Manger	9
Paice, Richard Charles John (32)	Southampton	Fireman	3
Painter, Charles Frederick (31)	Southampton	Fireman	3
Painter, Frank (29)	Southampton	Fireman	5
Paintin, James Arthur (29)	Southampton	Captain's Steward	6
Palles, Thomas Henry M. (45)	Liverpool	Greaser	3
Parsons, Edward (37)	Southampton	Chief Storekeeper	6
Parsons, Frank Alfred (26)	Southampton	Senior Fifth Engineer	2
Parsons, Richard Henry (18)	Ashbrittle	Saloon Steward	7
Pascoe, Charles Henry (44)	Southampton	A.B. Seaman	1
Pearce, Alfred Ernest (24)	Southampton	Steward	8
Pearce, John (34)	Southampton	Fireman	5
Pearcey, Albert Victor (24)	Southampton	Pantryman	8
Pedrini, Alessandro (21)	Southampton	Assistant Waiter	9
Pelham, George (39)	Southampton	Trimmer	5
Pennal, Thomas Frederick C. (34)	Shirley	Bath Steward	6
Penny, William Farr (31)	Southampton	Assistant Saloon Steward	7
Penrose, John Poole (49)	Southampton	Bedroom Steward	6
Peracchio, Alberto (20)	London	Assistant Waiter	9
Peracchio, Sebastiano (17)	London	Assistant Waiter	9
Perkins, Lawrence Alexander (21)	Soberton	Telephone Steward	6
Perkis, Walter John (37)	Bitterne	Quartermaster	1
Perotti, Alfonso (20)	London	Assistant Waiter	9
Perren, William Charles (38)	Southampton	Cleaning Steward	7
Perriton, Hubert Prouse (31)	Southampton	Saloon Steward	6
Perry, Edgar Lionel (19)	Southampton	Trimmer	5

Surname/ Forenames/Age	Abode	Trade/Calling	Section
Perry, Henry F. L. (23)	Southampton	Trimmer	4
Peters, William Chapman (26)	Woolston	A.B. Seaman	1
Petty, Edwin Henry J. (25) (born surname Mason)	Southampton	Bedroom Steward	7
Pfropper, Richard Paul Josef (30)	Southampton	Saloon Steward	7
Phillimore, Harold Charles William (23)	Southampton	Saloon Steward	7
Phillips, George Albert (27)	Southampton	Greaser	3
Phillips, John George (24)	Godalming	Senior Radio Operator	6
Phillips, Walter John (37)	Southampton	Storekeeper	9
Piatti, Louis (17)	London	Assistant Waiter	9
Piazza, Pompeo (32)	London	Waiter	9
Pitfield, William James (25)	Southampton	Greaser	3
Pitman, Herbert John (34)	Castlecary	Third Officer	1
Platt, Wilfred George (17)	Southampton	Scullion	8
Podesta, Alfred John Alexander (24)	Southampton	Fireman	3
Poggi, Emilio Santo Attanasio (28)	Southampton	Waiter	9
Poingdestre, John Thomas (33)	Southampton	A.B. Seaman	1
Pond, George (32)	Southampton	Fireman	5
Pook, Percy Robert (35)	Plymouth	Assistant Pantryman	7
Port, Frank (22)	Southampton	Steward	8
Porteus, Thomas Henry (33) (signed on surname Parker)	Southampton	Assistant Butcher	8
Prangnell, George Alexander (30)	Southampton	Greaser	3
Prentice, Frank Winnold (22)	Southampton	Storekeeper	6
Preston, Thomas Charles Alfred (20)	Southampton	Trimmer	5
Price, Ernest Cyril (17)	London	Barman	9
Prichard, née Friend?, Alice Maud (36)	London	Stewardess	6
Prideaux, John Arthur (23)	Bournemouth	Steward	8
Priest, Arthur John (24)	Southampton	Fireman	5
Prior, Harold John (21)	Southampton	Steward	8
Proctor, Charles (45)	Southampton	Chef	8
Proudfoot, Richard Royston (21)	Southampton	Trimmer	4
Pryce, Charles William (22)	Southampton	Saloon Steward	6
Pugh, Alfred (20)	Southampton	Steward	8
Pugh, Arthur Percy (31)	Northam	Leading Fireman	4
Pusey, William Robert H. (22)	Southampton	Fireman	3

Surname/ Forenames/Age	Abode	Trade/Calling	Section
Puzey, John Edward (43)	Itchen	Saloon Steward	6
Randall, Frank Henry (29)	Southampton	Saloon Steward	7
Ranger, Tom (29)	Sholing	Greaser	3
Ransom, James (49)	Bristol	Saloon Steward	6
Ratti, Enrico Rinaldo (21)	London	Waiter	9
Rattenbury, William Henry (37)	Southampton	Cleaning Steward	6
Ray, Frederick Dent (32)	Reading	Saloon Steward	6
Raymond, Philip (26) (signed on as Sullivan, S.)	Southampton	Fireman	4
Read, Joseph Alfred (21)	Southampton	Trimmer	4
Reed, Thomas Charles Prowse (54)	Southampton	Bedroom Steward	7
Reeves, Frederick Ernest (31)	Southampton	Fireman	3
Reid/Read, Robert Thomas (30)	Southampton	Trimmer	4
Revell, William James Francis (31)	Southampton	Saloon Steward	6
Ricaldone, Rinaldo Renato (22)	London	Assistant Waiter	9
Rice, Charles (32)	Southampton	Fireman	4
Rice, John Reginald (25)	Crosby	Clerk	6
Rice, Percy (19)	Southampton	Steward	8
Richards, Joseph James (29)	Southampton	Fireman	5
Rickman, George Albert D. (36)	Southampton	Fireman	3
Ricks, Cyril Gordon (23)	Southampton	Storekeeper	6
Ridout, Walter George (29)	Southampton	Saloon Steward	7
Rigozzi, Abele (22)	London	Assistant Waiter	9
Rimmer, Gilbert (28)	Southampton	Saloon Steward	6
Roberts, Frank John (36)	Farnborough	Third Butcher	8
Roberts, Hugh Henry (45)	Liverpool	Bedroom Steward	6
Roberts, née Humphreys, Mary Kezia (41)	Nottingham	Stewardess	6
Roberts, Robert George (35)	Southampton	Fireman	4
Roberton, George Edward (19)	Southampton	Assistant Saloon Steward	7
Robinson, James William (30)	Southampton	Saloon Steward	6
Robinson, née Bastin, Annie (45)	Southampton	Stewardess	6
Rogers, Edward James William (31)	Southampton	Storekeeper	6
Rogers, Michael (27)	Winchester	Saloon Steward	7
Ross, Horace Leopold (38)	Woolston	Scullion	8
Rotta, Angelo Mario, (23)	London	Waiter	9
Rous, Arthur John (26)	Southampton	Plumber	2

Surname/ Forenames/Age	Abode	Trade/Calling	Section
Rousseau, Pierre (49)	London	Chef	9
Rowe, Edgar Maurice (31)	Southampton	Saloon Steward	6
Rowe, George Thomas (31)	Gosport	Quartermaster	1
Rudd, Henry (24)	Southampton	Assistant Storekeeper	2
Rule, Samuel James (58)	Southampton	Bath Steward	6
Russell, Boysie Richard (17)	Redbridge	Saloon Steward	7
Rutter, Sidney Frank (26) (signed on as Graves, Sidney)	Southampton	Fireman	3
Ryan, Thomas (27)	Southampton	Steward	8
Ryerson, William Edwy (32)	London	Saloon Steward	7
Saccaggi, Giovanni Giuseppe Emilio (24)	London	Assistant Waiter	9
Salussolia, Giovanni (25)	London	Glass Washer	9
Samuel, Owen Wilmore (43)	Southampton	Saloon Steward	7
Sangster, Charles Edward (30)	Southampton	Fireman	5
Sartori, Lazar (24)	London	Assistant Glass Washer	9
Saunders, William Ernest (32)	Southampton	Saloon Steward	6
Saunders, Frank Joseph (26)	Southampton	Fireman	4
Saunders, Walter Ernest (25)	Southampton	Fireman	4
Saunders, W. (25)	Southampton	Trimmer	4
Savage, Charles James (23)	Southampton	Steward	8
Sawyer, Robert James (31)	Southampton	Window Cleaner	1
Scarrott, Joseph George (33)	Southampton	A.B. Seaman	1
Scavino, Candido (42)	London	Trancheur	9
Scott, Archibald (50)	Belfast	Fireman	4
Scott, Frederick William (28)	Southampton	Greaser	4
Scott, John (21)	Southampton	Cleaning Steward	6
Scovell, Robert (54)	Freemantle	Saloon Steward	7
Sedunary, Sidney Francis (25)	Southampton	Second Third Class Steward	8
Self, Alfred Henry (39)	Southampton	Greaser	3
Self, Albert Charles Edward (24)	Southampton	Fireman	3
Senior, Harry (31)	Clapham	Fireman	3
Sesia, Giacomo (24)	London	Waiter	9
Seward, Wilfred Deable (25)	E.C. London	Chief Pantryman	7
Shaw, Henry (39)	Liverpool	Kitchen Porter	8
Shea, John Joseph (39)	Southampton	Saloon Steward	6
Shea, Thomas (32)	Southampton	Fireman	4

Surname/ Forenames/Age	Abode	Trade/Calling	Section
Sheath, Frederick Robert (20)	Southampton	Trimmer	3
Shepherd, Jonathan (32)	Southampton	Junior Assistant Second Engineer	2
Shiers, Alfred Charles (25)	Southampton	Fireman	3
Shillabeer, Charles Frederick (19)	Southampton	Trimmer	3
Siebert, Sidney Conrad (29)	Southampton	Bedroom Steward	6
Simmons, Andrew (31)	Southampton	Scullion	8
Simmons, Frederick Charles (32)	Southampton	Saloon Steward	6
Simmons, William John T. (34)	Southampton	Passenger Cook	8
Simpson, Dr. John Edward (37)	Belfast	Assistant Surgeon	1
Sivier, William (23)	Paddington	Steward	8
Skeates, William Frederick (26)	Southampton	Trimmer	3
Skinner, Edward (40)	Southampton	Saloon Steward	6
Slight, Harry John (33)	Southampton	Steward	8
Slight, William Henry John (34)	Southampton	Garde Manger	8
Sloan, Mary (28)	Belfast	Stewardess	6
Sloan, Peter Porter (31)	Southampton	Chief Electrician	2
Slocombe, née Walden, Maud Louise (30)	N.E. London	Turkish Bath Stewardess	6
Small, William (43)	Southampton	Leading Fireman	5
Smillie, John (29)	Southampton	Saloon Steward	6
Smith, Charles (38)	Southampton	Kitchen Porter	8
Smith, Charles Edwin (39)	Woolston	Bedroom Steward	7
Smith, Edward John (62)	Southampton	Master/Captain	1
Smith, Ernest Harry (27)	Southampton	Trimmer	4
Smith, Frederick John (20)	Southampton	Assistant Pantryman	6
Smith, James William (24)	Southampton	Assistant Baker	8
Smith, James Muil (39)	Itchen	Junior Fourth Engineer	2
Smith, John Richard Jago (35)	Trebarveth	Royal Mail Clerk	–
Smith, Kate Elizabeth (42)	Southampton	Stewardess	6
Smith, Reginald George (32)	Southampton	Saloon Steward	6
Smith, William (26)	Southampton	Seaman	1
Smither, Harry James (22)	Southampton	Fireman	3
Snape, née Lennard, Lucy Violett (22)	Sandown	Stewardess	7
Snellgrove, George Charles (40)	Southampton	Fireman	5
Snooks, W. (16)	Southampton	Trimmer	3
Snow, Eustace Philip (21)	Southampton	Trimmer	5

Surname/ Forenames/Age	Abode	Trade/Calling	Section
Sparkman, Henry William (35)	Sholing	Fireman	3
Stagg, John Henry (38)	Southampton	Saloon Steward	6
Stanbrook, Augustus George (30)	Southampton	Fireman	3
Stap, Sarah Agnes (47)	Birkenhead	Senior Stewardess	6
Steel, Robert (30)	Southampton	Trimmer	10
Stebbing's, Sidney Frederick (33)	Southampton	Chief Cleaning Steward	6
Stewart, John (27)	Southampton	Verandah Cafe Steward	6
Stocker, Henry Dorey (20)	Sholing	Trimmer	3
Stone, Edmund (33)	Southampton	Bedroom Steward	6
Stone, Edward Thomas (30)	Southampton	Bedroom Steward	7
Street, Thomas Albert (25)	Shirley	Fireman	4
Stroud, Edward Alfred Orlando (19)	Southampton	Saloon Steward	7
Stroud, Harry John (35)	Southampton	Saloon Steward	6
Strugnell, John Herbert (34)	Southampton	Saloon Steward	6
Stubbings, Harry Robert (31)	Lymington	Second Class Cook	8
Stubbs, James Henry (28)	Southampton	Fireman	5
Swan, William (46)	Liverpool	Bedroom Steward	6
Symonds, John Crane (44)	Southampton	Saloon Steward	6
Symons, George Thomas MacDonald (24)	Weymouth	Lookout	1
Talbot, George Frederick Charles (28)	Southampton	Steward	8
Tamlyn, Frederick (23)	Southampton	Crew Cook/Deck Dept.	1
Taylor, Charles William F. (40)	Southampton	A.B. Seaman	1
Taylor, Cuthbert Bernard (22)	Southampton	Steward	8
Taylor, John Henry (42)	Southampton	Fireman	3
Taylor, James (26)	Southampton	Fireman	5
Taylor, T. (or J.?) (23)	Southampton	Fireman	5
Taylor, Leonard (19)	Blackpool	Turkish Bath Attendant	8
Taylor, Percy Cornelius (31)	London	Musician, Violinist	2nd Cl.
Taylor, William Henry (28)	Southampton	Fireman	5
Taylor, William John (31)	Southampton	Saloon Steward	6
Terrell, Bertram (19)	Southampton	Seaman	1
Terrell, Frank (27)	Southampton	Assistant Saloon Steward	7
Testoni, Ercole (23)	London	Assistant Glass Washer	9
Teuton, Thomas Moore (32)	Sholing	Saloon Steward	7
Thaler, Montague Donald (17)	West Croydon	Steward	8

Surname/ Forenames/Age	Abode	Trade/Calling	Section
Theissinger, Franz Alfred Daniel Maximilian (46)	Southampton	Bedroom Steward	6
Thomas, Albert Charles (23)	Southampton	Saloon Steward	6
Thomas, Benjamin James (30)	Southampton	Saloon Steward	6
Thomas, Joseph Waitfield (26)	Southampton	Fireman	3
Thompson, Herbert Henry (24)	Southampton	Second Storekeeper	6
Thompson, John William (42)	Liverpool	Fireman	5
Thorley, William (39)	Southampton	Assistant Cook	8
Thorn, Harry (25) (signed on as Johnston, H.)	Southampton	Assistant Ship's Cook	8
Threlfall, Thomas (44)	Southampton	Leading Fireman	5
Thresher, George Terrill (25)	Southampton	Fireman	5
Tietz, Carlo/Karl (27)	Southampton	Kitchen Porter	9
Tizard, Ernest Arthur (32)	Southampton	Fireman	3
Toms, Fred (29)	Bitterne Park	Saloon Steward	6
Topp, Thomas (27)	Farnborough	Second Butcher	8
Toshack, James Addison (31)	Southampton	Night Watchman	6
Tozer, James (32)	Southampton	Greaser	5
Triggs, Robert William (40)	Southampton	Fireman	3
Turley, Richard (35)	Belfast	Fireman	4
Turner, George Frederick (42) (Relief Fund as Taylor)	Bitterne Park	Stenographer	6
Turner, Leopold Olorenshaw (28)	Southampton	Saloon Steward	6
Turvey, Charles Thomas (16)	London	Page Boy	9
Urbini, Roberto (20)	London	Waiter	9
Valvassori, Ettore Luigi (35)	London	Waiter	9
van der Brugge, Wessel Adrianus (42)	Southampton	Fireman	3
Veal, Arthur (35)	Southampton	Greaser	3
Veal, Thomas Henry Edom (37)	Southampton	Saloon Steward	6
Vear, Henry Harry (32)	Southampton	Fireman	5
Vear, William (33)	Southampton	Fireman	5
Vicat, Alphonse Jean Eugène (21)	London	Poissonnier	9
Vigott, Philip Francis (32)	Southampton	A.B. Seaman	1
Villvarlange, Pierre Léon Gabriel (19)	London	Assistant Potager	9
Vine, Herbert Thomas G. (18)	London	Assistant Controller	9
Vioni, Roberto (25)	London	Waiter	9
Vögelin-Dubach, Johannes (35)	London	Coffee Man	9

Surname/ Forenames/Age	Abode	Trade/Calling	Section
Wake, Percy (37)	Southampton	Assistant Baker	8
Wallis, née Moore, Catherine Jane (36)	Southampton	Matron	7
Walpole, James (48)	Southampton	Chief Pantryman	6
Walsh, Catherine (32)	Southampton	Stewardess	6
Ward, Arthur (24)	Romsey	Junior Assistant Fourth Engineer	2
Ward, Edward (34)	Southampton	Bedroom Steward	6
Ward, James William (27)	Southampton	Leading Fireman	4
Ward, Percy Thomas (40)	Southampton	Bedroom Steward	6
Ward, William (36)	Southampton	Saloon Steward	6
Wardner, Fred Albert (39)	Southampton	Fireman	5
Wareham, Robert Arthur (37)	Southampton	Bedroom Steward	6
Warwick, Tom (35)	Totton	Saloon Steward	6
Wateridge, Edward Lewis (25)	Southampton	Fireman	3
Watson, William (27)	Southampton	Fireman	3
Watson, William Albert (14)	Southampton	Bell Boy Steward	6
Weatherston, Thomas Herbert (25)	Southampton	Saloon Steward	6
Webb, Brook Holding (50)	Southampton	Smoke Room Steward	6
Webb, S. (28)	Southampton	Trimmer	3
Webber, Francis Albert (31)	Southampton	Leading Fireman	5
Weikman, Augustus Henry (51) (signed on surname Whiteman)	Southampton	Barber	8
Welch, William Harold (22)	Bitterne Park	Assistant Cook	8
Weller, William Clifford (30)	Southampton	A.B. Seaman	1
Wheat, Joseph Thomas (29)	Southampton	Assistant Second Steward	6
Wheelton, Edneser Edward (27)	Shirley	Saloon Steward	6
White, Alfred Albert (32)	Southampton	Greaser	3
White, Arthur (37)	Portsmouth	Assistant Barber	8
White, Frank Leonard (27)	Southampton	Trimmer	4
White, Edward Joseph (27)	Southampton	Glory Hole Steward	8
White, Leonard Lisle Oliver (32)	Southampton	Saloon Steward	6
White, William George (23)	Northam	Trimmer	5
Whiteley, Thomas Arthur (18)	London	Saloon Steward	6
Whitford, Alfred Henry (39)	Southampton	Saloon Steward	7
Widgery, Isaac George (37)	Bristol	Bath Steward	7
Wilde, Henry Tingle (39)	Liverpool	Chief Officer	1
Williams, Arthur John (41)	Liverpool	Storekeeper	6

Surname/ Forenames/Age	Abode	Trade/Calling	Section
Williams, Samuel Solomon (27) (signed on as Williams, Edward)	Southampton	Fireman	4
Williams, Walter John (28)	Southampton	Assistant Saloon Steward	7
Williamson, James Bertram (35)	Dublin	Royal Mail Clerk	–
Willis, W. (46)	Southampton	Steward	8
Willsher, William Aubrey (33)	Southampton	Assistant Butcher	8
Wilson, Bertie (27)	Shirley	Senior Assistant Second Engineer	2
Wilton, William (57)	Southampton	Trimmer	4
Windebank, Alfred Edgar (38)	Shirley	Saucier	10 (8)
Winser, Rowland (35) (signed on as Evans, George)	Southampton	Steward	8
Witcher, Albert Ernest (39)	Southampton	Fireman	5
Witt, Henry Dennis (37)	Southampton	Fireman	10
Witter, James William Cheetham (31)	Woolston	Smoke Room Steward	7
Wittman, Heinrich (39)	Southampton	Bedroom Steward	6
Witts, William Francis (34)	Southampton	Trimmer	3
Wood, Henry (30)	Southampton	Trimmer	3
Wood, James Thomas (49)	London	Assistant Saloon Steward	7
Woodford, Frederick Ernest (40)	Southampton	Greaser	3
Woodward, John Wesley (32)	Oxford	Musician, Cellist	2nd Cl.
Woody, Oscar Scott (40)	Clifton Springs, USA	US Post Office Clerk	–
Wormald, Henry Frederick C. (44)	Southampton	Saloon Steward	6
Worthman, William Henry (39) (signed on surname Jarvis)	Southampton	Fireman	3
Wrapson, Frederick Bernard (18)	Southampton	Assistant Pantryman	6
Wright, Frederick (24)	London	Racquet Steward	6
Wright, William (47)	Southampton	Glory Hole Steward	8
Wyeth, James Robert (25)	Southampton	Fireman	3
Wynn, William (41) (signed on forename W. for Walter)	Shirley	Quartermaster	1
Yearsley, Harry (41)	Southampton	Saloon Steward	6
Young, Francis James (32)	Southampton	Fireman	3
Zanetti, Mario (20)	London	Assistant Waiter	9
Zarracchi, Luigi (26)	Southampton	Sommelier	9

DISCHARGED CREW

The following list names twenty-four persons who were to have sailed on *Titanic* but were not aboard for various reasons, according to historical records. Of special interest are John Coffey, who left the ship at Queenstown, and Lazar Sartori, who appears in the list 'Seamen who have failed to join or otherwise left the ship', but according to various accounts from White Star Line from August 1915 was actually on the *Titanic* and died in the disaster. Missing on the list is David Blair, who made the delivery voyage from Belfast to Southampton as second officer and left *Titanic* on 9 April 1912. The later Chief Officer Henry Tingle Wilde had mentioned in a letter at the end of March 1912 that there was possibly to be a change among the senior officers. As this had been known for some time, that would be the reason why Blair is not shown on this list:

Blake C.	Trimmer	failed to join
Bowman F.J.	Assistant Cook	failed to join
Brewer B.	Trimmer	deserted
Burrows W.	Fireman	left by consent
Carter F.	Trimmer	failed to join
Coffey John	Fireman	deserted at Queenstown
Dawes W.W.	First Class Saloon Steward	discharged
Dawkins P.	Assistant Cook	failed to join
Di Napoli E.	Assistant Waiter, Restaurant	failed to join
Ettlinger, Peter	Second Class Saloon Steward	discharged
Fish B.	First Class Saloon Steward	failed to join
Fisher R.	Second Class Plate Washer	failed to join
Haveling A.	Junior Assistant Fourth Engineer	transferred
Holden, Frank	Fireman	deserted
Kilford P.	First Class Saloon Steward	left ship sick
Manley A.	Third Class Steward	failed to join
Mew W.J.	Sauce Cook/Saucier	failed to join
Penney A.	Trimmer	deserted

Sartori Lazar	Assistant Glass Washer, Restaurant	failed to join
Shaw J.	Fireman	deserted
Sims W.	Fireman	left by consent
Slade, Alfred	Fireman	deserted
Slade, Bertram	Fireman	deserted
Slade Thomas	Fireman	deserted

BIBLIOGRAPHY

Beaumont, J.C.H., *Ships – and People* (London: Geoffrey Bles, *c*.1923).

Beesley, Lawrence, *The Loss of the SS Titanic* (Boston & New York: Houghton Mifflin Co, 1912).

Behe, George M., *On Board RMS Titanic: Memories of the Maiden Voyage* (Lulu.com, 2011).

Beveridge, Bruce, *Titanic: The Ship Magnificent*, Vols 1 & 2 (Stroud: The History Press, 2008).

Bisset, Sir James, *Tramps & Ladies* (New York: Criterion Books, 1959).

Bullen, Frank T., *The Men of the Merchant Service* (London: Smith, Elder & Co, 1900).

Chirnside, Mark, *RMS Olympic: Titanic's Sister* (Stroud: The History Press, 2015).

Crosby, Alasdair, *Titanic: The Channel Island Connections* (St John: Channel Island Publishing, 2011).

Elder, A. Vavasour, *The Ship Surgeon's Handbook: Surgeon White Star Line* (London: Baillière, Tindall and Cox, 1911).

Emergency Relief by the American Red Cross after the Wreck of the S.S. Titanic (New York: Red Cross Emergency Relief Committee of the Charity Organization Society of the City of New York, 1913).

Fletcher, R.A., *Travelling Palaces: Luxury in Passenger Steamers* (London: Sir Isaac Pitman & Sons, 1913).

'Formal Investigation into the Loss of the S.S. "Titanic"' (PRO, Kew, 1998).

'HMS Hawke vs. Olympic: In the High Court of Justice, Minutes' (London: 1911).

Helbig, Karl, *Seefahrt vor den Feuern, Erinnerungen eines Schiffsheizers* (Hamburg: Hans-Georg Prager Verlag, 1987).

Herkner, Anna, *Reports of* the Immigration Commission of the United States Senate (Washington: Government Printing Office, 1911).

Holman, H., *A Handy Book for Shipowners & Masters* (Bishopsgate: W.H. Maisey, 1913).

Hopkins, Albert A., *The Scientific American Handbook of Travel* (New York: Munn & Co. Inc., 1911).

Howell, Walter J., *Report on the Sight Tests used in the Mercantile Marine for the Year Ended December 31st 1911* (London: HMSO, 1912).

Hyslop, Donald; Forsyth, Alastair; Jemima, Sheila, *Titanic Voices: Memories from the Fateful Voyage* (Stroud: Sutton Publishing Ltd, 1997).

'List of First Class Passengers, S.S. "Titanic", April 10, 1912'. (White Star Line, 1912).

Marine Engineer and Naval Architect, May and June 1912 (London, 1912).

'Megantic, Laurentic, Olympic Crew Lists, several voyages, 1911–1914' (PRO, Kew).

New York Times, various issues.

Modern Sanitation, December 1911 and January 1912 (Pittsburgh, 1911 & 1912)

O'Donnell, E.E., *Father Browne's Titanic Album: A Passenger's Photographs and Personal Memoir* (Dublin: Messenger Publications, 2011).

'RMS 'Olympic' Restaurant, Tariff and General Information'; White Star Line 1911.

Practical Hints to Young Officers in the Mercantile Marine (Glasgow: James Brown & Son, 1907).

Report of the Merchant Shipping Advisory Committee, Appendix 2, Report of the Sub-Committee on Wireless Telegraphy (London: HMSO, 1912).

'Return of the Expenses Incurred by the Board of Trade and other Government Departments in Connection with the Inquiry into the Loss of S.S. *Titanic*' (London: HMSO, 1913).

Söldner, Hermann, *RMS Titanic: Passenger and Crew List* (Rüti: ä wie Ärger Verlag, 2000).

Spedding, Charles T., *Reminiscences of Transatlantic Travellers* (London: T. Fisher Unwind Ltd, 1926).

'Staff Salary Book, 1906–1912, MS Marconi 2040' (Bodleian Library, Oxford).

Stokers' Manual, 1912 (London: HMSO, 1912).

Störmer, Susanne, *William McMaster Murdoch: A Career at Sea* (Elmshorn: Stormbreakers Verlag, 2002).

The Titanic Collection: Mementos of the Maiden Voyage (San Francisco: Chronicle Books, 1998).

The 'Titanic' Relief Fund (Holborn: Electric Law Press Ltd, Deed & General Law Printers, 1913).

Titanic: The True Story, CD-ROM (PRO, Kew, 1999).

'Titanic' Disaster. Hearing before a United States Senate Commerce Sub-Committee (Washington: Government Printing Office, 1912).

What to Know about Ocean Travel (New York: International Mercantile Marine, c. 1924).

White Star Line First Class Passage Rates (New York: White Star Line, 1912).

White Star Magazine, various issues.

Websites

www.encyclopedia-titanica.org

www.facebook.com (Titanic Passengers and Crew Research Group)

www.titanicpiano.blogspot.ca

www.1911census.co.uk (as well as other censuses in Britain, Ireland and the United States)

www2.hsp.org/exhibits/Balch%20resources/destinationusa/html/body_1steerage.html

You may also be interested in …

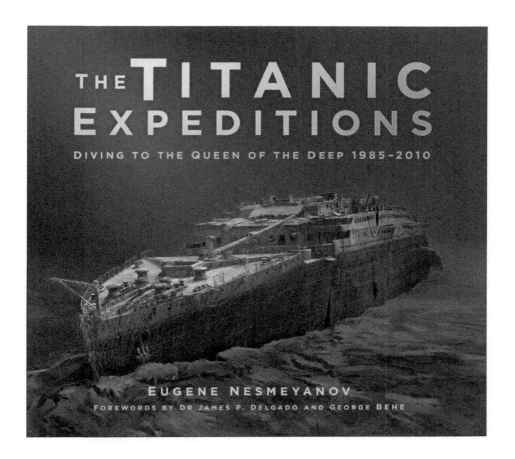

тне **TITANIC**
EXPEDITIONS
DIVING TO THE QUEEN OF THE DEEP 1985–2010

EUGENE NESMEYANOV
FOREWORDS BY DR JAMES P. DELGADO AND GEORGE BEHE

9780750985482

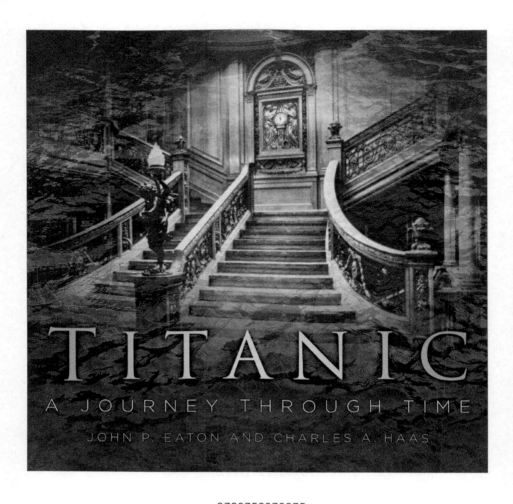

TITANIC
A JOURNEY THROUGH TIME
JOHN P. EATON AND CHARLES A. HAAS

9780750970075